Modern Language Association of America

Options for Teaching

Joseph Gibaldi, Series

1. *Options for the Teaching of English: The Undergraduate Curriculum*. Edited by Elizabeth Wooten Cowan. 1975.

2. *Options for the Teaching of English: Freshman Composition*. Edited by Jasper P. Neel. 1978.

3. *Options for Undergraduate Foreign Language Programs: Four-Year and Two-Year Colleges*. By Renate A. Schulz. 1979.

4. *The Teaching Apprentice Program in Language and Literature*. Edited by Joseph Gibaldi and James V. Mirollo. 1981.

5. *Film Study in the Undergraduate Curriculum*. Edited by Barry Keith Grant. 1983.

6. *Part-Time Academic Employment in the Humanities: A Sourcebook for Just Policy*. Edited by M. Elizabeth Wallace. 1984.

Part-Time Academic Employment in the Humanities

Edited by

M. Elizabeth Wallace

DISCARD

The Modern Language Association of America
New York   1984

Library of Congress Cataloging in Publication Data

Main entry under title:

Part-time academic employment in the humanities.

(Options for teaching ; 6)
Bibliography: p.
1. College teachers, Part-time—United States—Addresses, essays, lectures.
2. Education, Humanistic—United States—Addresses, essays, lectures.
I. Wallace, Elizabeth, 1948–   . II. Series.
LB2331.72.P37   1984   331.7'6137812   84-1124
ISBN 0-87352-306-7
ISBN 0-87352-307-5 (pbk.)

Published by The Modern Language Association
62 Fifth Avenue, New York, New York 10011

Contents

Acknowledgments

I'll start by thanking four people I've never met—Howard Tuckman, David Leslie, Shu-O Wu Yang, and Michele Wender Zak—and all the people who worked with them: it will be apparent throughout how dependent I am on their careful studies of part-time faculty. I also owe a debt to all the administrators who shared their part-time policies with me and most particularly to the good people who wrote the essays in this volume. None of them had time to spare for this project; they created time.

Thanks also to Phyllis Franklin of the Association of Departments of English and Richard Brod of the Association of Departments of Foreign Languages, who gathered additional information from department chairs and passed it along to me; to Gettysburg College and particularly Dean David Potts for institutional support for my research; to Barbara Herman and Patricia Callahan for turning my chaotic data sheets into professional-looking documents; to Joanne Altieri and Ben McClelland for painstaking readings of the manuscript and innumerable apt suggestions for improvement and condensation; to Joseph Gibaldi for encouragement, guidance, and patience and for teaching me a great deal about writing and editing; to friends and family—Elizabeth and Charles Hambrick-Stowe, Helen Rex Shroyer, Miriam and Charles Wallace, Sr., Margaret and George A. Sargent—for understanding, support, and extra child care. A special thanks to Larry Piper and Paul Cross of Basically Computers, Inc., for making my transition from the language and literature business to the word-processing business so easy and affirming and for their good-natured granting of various leaves for me to attend conferences, complete research, and write the manuscript.

Carol Sapora has a unique place in the history of this document; when she and I taught together as part-timers in the Western Maryland College English department, back in the seventies, she wrote to the Association of American University Professors and asked for information on innovative part-time policies. I first heard of Sheila Tobias' "sunlighters" from Carol, and thus this project had its beginnings. Six years later, Carol found herself called on to read and criticize the final manuscript, and her suggestions have proved invaluable. I know now firsthand how lucky the students in her classes are to have her.

I hesitate to thank my daughters, Hannah and Molly, since they both decided to get the chicken pox two weeks before my deadline—but then *they* had to put up with an impatient nurse, whose attention was always wandering off to the word-processing keyboard. Surely they know how their good cheer and tolerance sustained me.

I couldn't have undertaken, let alone completed, this book without the steady support of my husband, Charles Isaac Wallace, Jr. His commitment to sharing work and home responsibilities has made my professional life, such as it is, possible. He has balanced three part-time teaching jobs, an irritable wife, and two beautiful but demanding daughters with a skill, kindness, and grace that I seem able only to admire, never to emulate. This book is dedicated, with love, to him.

M. Elizabeth Wallace
Westminster, Md.
September 1983

For Charlie

Introduction

Some part-time faculty are thoroughly content. Nobody worries much about them. The senior systems analyst from IBM who teaches an upper-level course on computer programming at a nearby university, the distinguished visiting scholar teaching one course a semester while on leave from his or her home institution, or the CPA who occasionally teaches accounting at the local community college—these faculty might need help finding parking spaces, grade sheets, and the copying machine, but they don't care much about getting higher salaries or fringe benefits for their part-time teaching. The dignity of a desk, coat rack, and departmental stationery; a current and complete part-time faculty handbook; a good orientation program on teaching skills for those who lack experience in the classroom; and friendly, respectful recognition from full-time faculty and staff—these are all they really need.

This book is not about them. Many books, articles, and research studies have been devoted to such moonlighting part-timers already. They constitute, after all, the largest single group of part-time faculty in the United States; according to the Association of American University Professors' 1978 study on part-time faculty, roughly one third of all part-timers are moonlighting from another job. In fact, this large group of part-timers tends to dominate the findings of such national studies as Howard Tuckman's research for AAUP (funded by the Ford Foundation) and David Leslie's 1982 work, started at the University of Virginia's Center for the Study of Higher Education and funded by the Exxon Education Foundation. (In Leslie's sample, 50% of the part-timers had full-time work elsewhere.) Numerous dissertations, primarily on part-time faculty in the community colleges of a particular state, and articles on faculty development in community colleges focus on the needs of these part-timers.[1] Community colleges have good reason to concentrate attention on part-time faculty issues since "community colleges employ nearly as many part-timers as all other types of institutions combined" (Leslie 19). National conferences aimed at community college administrators emphasize moonlighting part-timers, as their titles clearly suggest—"Part-Time Faculty: Maximizing Resources."[2]

But these studies, publications, and conferences, valuable as they are, don't tell us much about part-time faculty in English and foreign language departments. Although Leslie's findings parallel those of an excellent 1981 study of part-time faculty in Ohio by Shu-O Wu Yang amd Michele Wender Zak, showing that most part-timers are employed in business and the humanities, Leslie fails to explore important differences between these two groups of part-timers.

The differences are extreme. Part-timers in business are usually employed full-time elsewhere; part-timers in the humanities seldom are, although they may be seeking full-time academic positions and teaching part-time at several institutions. Part-timers in business thus pay little attention to teaching salaries or fringe benefits; part-timers in the humanities are often struggling to survive on their part-time incomes without any fringe-benefit coverage whatsoever. Most business part-timers are men; most humanities part-timers are women, particularly in English. Part-timers in business spend little time outside class on preparations and grading; they often feel that they know their subject thoroughly from work experience, and, in fact, it is their practical expertise and their current involvement in a field that make them attractive to students and administrators. Part-timers in the humanities, however, are more academically oriented; they spend much more time outside class preparing lectures, reading, researching, and, particularly if they teach composition, grading essays and holding conferences with individual students. Part-timers in business want no obligations to committee work or faculty governance; they are too busy in their full-time jobs. Part-timers in the humanities frequently long for precisely such involvement in the affairs of the department and the institution: they are committed to a college teaching career in their chosen field.[3]

For an institution to treat two such different groups of part-time faculty exactly the same amounts to discrimination. In fact, a recurring conclusion of recent research on part-timers is that different part-timers should be treated differently (Tuckman, Vogler, and Caldwell; Leslie; Leslie and Head; Yang and Zak). This book will take that conclusion as a starting place.

How This Book Got Started

In the spring of 1977, as a part-time faculty member of the English Department at Western Maryland College in Westminster, Maryland, I completed a survey on part-time faculty policies at eleven nearby colleges. The faculty affairs committee wanted information on policies at schools similar to Western Maryland while they deliberated changes in part-time faculty policy. Eventually, Western Maryland changed its policy from paying a flat per-course rate (based on final degree earned and years of teaching experience elsewhere) to adding an increment after seven years of service at Western Maryland College (or twenty courses, whichever came first) in each per-course stipend.

In the fall of 1980, I began teaching full-time in the English Department at Gettysburg College in Pennsylvania. The academic dean, David Potts, was interested in part-time faculty issues and gave me institutional support for mailing a questionnaire on part-time faculty policies to approximately fifty colleges and universities. Some of these institutions were listed with AAUP as having developed innovative policies on part-time faculty; others I heard about through chance meetings with colleagues at national conferences or through local contacts; still others I remembered from my previous survey and wrote again to see if their policies had changed. (In 1977, several had mentioned that they were in the process of changing the status of part-timers.)

The results of that research were presented in a special session on part-time faculty issues (organized by Joel Fineman) at the Modern Language Association convention in New York, December 1981, a session that led to the seventh item on the MLA ballot the following spring. The item asked that

> the Executive Director express the MLA's concern about the exploitation of part-time faculty by appointing a committee to formulate guidelines to ensure that part-time academic employees receive compensation prorated in proportion to that of corresponding full-time faculty and equitable treatment in regard to fringe benefits, promotion, and security of employment. (*MLA Newsletter*, Spring 1982, 1)

The data I presented at that MLA special session were published in the *ADE Bulletin*.

In the spring of 1982, I decided to extend my research on innovative part-time faculty policies, particularly seeking out community colleges and state universities, which had been underrepresented in my sample. At that point, I used Maryse Eymonerie's study *The Availability of Fringe Benefits in Colleges and Universities* to guide me. I wrote to fifty institutions that, judging from her report, seemed to give some benefits to part-time faculty who taught at least half-time.

Simultaneously, I began soliciting essays for this book from administrators, department chairs in English and foreign languages, and writing program directors at the colleges and universities that had been good enough to send me information about their policies. Their replies discouraged me in one respect: it became apparent that hardly any of the "regular" part-time positions described in their excellent policies belonged to people teaching basic courses in writing or foreign languages. Also discouraging was the fact that department chairs and writing program directors are overburdened and have no professional incentive to write essays about part-time policy. Buried as they are under administrative obligations, they feel acutely the lack of time for their own research. I mention this to make especially clear my gratitude to those deans, provosts, department chairs, and directors of writing programs who did make the time to write some of the essays that follow.

At no time was I undertaking a statistical survey of the number of colleges and universities that have such innovative policies. There are doubtless many I have missed. There are also many who did not respond to my requests and just as many who sent information that turned out to be of no use or that was presented in an inaccessible form. Those who took the time to fill out the data sheet I sent made my task easier. (These data sheets appear as table 6 at the end of ch. 4.)

My goal throughout has been to highlight interesting and unusual policies that try to eliminate the deep frustrations part-timers in the humanities feel from exclusion, lack of recognition, lack of voice and vote, low salaries, and inadequate fringe benefits. Different kinds of institutions find different policies possible: a small liberal arts college might be able to give prorated salaries and benefits to its regular part-timers, while a state or a community college feels it is doing well to fund a shared office for part-timers and released time for a full-time faculty member to respond to their needs. My attitude has been that all these attempts to treat part-time faculty more professionally are important. I hope that administrators will be able to find here policy suggestions not only useful but possible for them to implement under their own special budgetary and institutional constraints.

The Goals of This Study

Throughout I will focus on three issues: the needs of part-time faculty in the humanities who see themselves as professional teachers in their chosen fields; the innovative and just policies that certain institutions have developed to deal more fairly with these part-timers; and the implications that the part-time faculty situation has for the status of the modern language profession, particularly as it affects programs in basic language instruction and the teaching of writing.

Each of the twenty-three essays in this volume reveals crucial considerations about one or more of these issues, and I refer to the essays repeatedly. I hope that by doing so, and by placing them in a broader context, I can provide some guidance as to which essays might prove most useful to readers with particular needs, interests, and institutions. This volume serves primarily as a reference tool and, if read straight through, will necessarily expose the reader to a certain amount of repetition.

The great joy of working on this book has been reading the essays as they came in from all parts of the country. They give me hope that full-time faculty and administrators care about the plight of part-time faculty in the humanities. They also show highly qualified part-time faculty struggling with dignity to hang on to the profession they love and some part-time faculty treated as fully equal professionals in the educational enterprise. To contrast the essays written by Janet Gemmill, G. James Jason, and Elizabeth Miller with the essays written by Rae Goodell, Julie Klassen, and Anne Ulmer is to know unforgettably what a difference professional treatment makes and how obligated all of us in the profession are to supply it. If this book helps make the force of that obligation felt, it will serve its purpose.

Conclusions: The Varieties of Part-Time Policy

The Absence of Part-Time Faculty or Part-Time Policy

Various institutions have made various choices about how to deal with what is called "the part-time problem." For a few, the decision has been to hire no part-timers, thus renewing a commitment to full-time, resident faculty. For most, the dependence on part-time faculty is too great. As Leslie points out, this dependence is rarely only financial; rather, the indirect costs of hiring part-timers—increased administrative needs, advising and committee work overloads on full-timers, problems in quality control, and perhaps even lawsuits from dissatisfied students (a possibility suggested in Miriam Dow and Cara Chell's essay)—may well outweigh any short-term savings. Other considerations may figure more significantly in the administrative decision to hire part-time faculty. Part-timers often supply expertise the school could never afford full-time (computer scientists are becoming a case in point). Not only do they forge important links with the community, especially for community colleges, but they also provide flexibility in scheduling to meet student demands and shifts in enrollment.

Institutions that find themselves committed to using part-timers for these reasons handle part-time faculty policy in a variety of ways. A distressingly high number have no clear policies at all. In the Ohio study, interviewed administrators often contradicted each other about policy and seemed to be confused about what the policy actually was (Yang and Zak 51). Frequently, administrators believed certain fringe benefits or support services were available to part-timers, while the part-timers themselves had a distinctly different impression (Yang and Zak 42–46; see their data tables reproduced on pp. 16, 18–19).

Cautious Policies: Only Moonlighters or Idealists Need Apply

In places where clearer policies exist and where administrators are cautious about part-time discontent and possible legal problems (probably an unfounded worry, as David Figuli's essay makes clear), institutions may consciously protect themselves by hiring only those part-timers who have full-time jobs elsewhere. In some cases, the reason may be purely economic; the institution avoids liability for unemployment compensation if the part-timer is not rehired during a particular semester. In other cases, the reasons have been stated thus: "Part-timers who aren't employed full-time elsewhere begin to get a sense of entitlement after three or four semesters; they get dependent on the institution and think it owes them a job." What seems like injustice may depend on where one stands. Aren't full-time faculty dependent on their institutions? Don't full-timers feel that the schools they have served faithfully for years owe them a job? But it is precisely the clear distinction between full-time and part-time faculty that such policies try to enforce, because employment commitments to full-timers are expensive and may even be dangerous in the coming decade. It is probably a kind of rough justice to keep part-timers desiring full-time teaching out of such institutions if there is, in reality, no hope of full-time, continuing employment in them.

The implication for such policy on program quality may be great, however, since the institution might reject the best candidate available simply because he or she was not employed full-time elsewhere. A similar bias exists against individuals trying to support themselves by part-time teaching while searching for full-time teaching positions. Such a bias reveals itself in suggestions that only those applicants wishing to teach for primarily idealistic reasons, that is, for love of teaching and personal fulfillment rather than for the money, should be hired (Albert 170; Leslie 73). Again, one wonders if a survey of full-time faculty were taken, how easily full-timers could distinguish between the high motives that once led them into teaching and the low salary they now depend upon from it. I make comparisons to full-time faculty because these are the comparisons that many part-time faculty in the humanities continually make in their own minds. Many of them see themselves as the equals of their full-time counterparts, having missed out on a career in teaching only by the chance of having been born a decade or so too late.

Cautious Policies: Treating All Part-Time Faculty Alike

Other institutions hire all sorts of part-time faculty and then conscientiously treat them exactly alike, even to the extent of paying an English teacher with a doctorate and several years of full-time teaching experience the same per-course fee as someone with a B.A. in English and no teaching experience. Local business executives who whiz in for one evening class a week, who are rarely available to students, and who seldom assign any work requiring time-consuming reading and evaluating, are paid the same as freshman composition teachers with advanced degrees who may spend ten or more hours a week per class conferring with students and grading essays. Such institutions may have the mistaken impression that they are legally on safer ground if they treat their part-timers identically. Research, however, is beginning to suggest otherwise, that the law may look closely at individual cases and individual duties and that the closer a particular part-timer's work is to that of a full-time faculty member, the more legitimate is that part-timer's claim for different treatment (Leslie and Head 65–66; Leslie 53–54).

Realistic Policies: Recognizing Varieties of Part-Time Faculty

Finally, some institutions, for a variety of reasons, have decided to treat different part-timers differently. Tuckman (*Part-Time Faculty Series*) distinguishes seven classes of part-timers, probably too many to be administratively useful: moonlighters, hopeful full-timers, homeworkers (at least Tuckman avoids Leslie's frequent, unintentionally condescending references to housewives), students, part-mooners (those with one or more part-time jobs elsewhere), semi-retireds, and part-unknowners (those whose motives for teaching part-time are not clear). The problem with these categories is that they omit several important kinds of part-timers (e.g., visiting distinguished scholars and full-time faculty on loads reduced temporarily to let them write books, have children, do research), and they also overlap (homeworkers and part-mooners might want full-time jobs eventually; students might be employed part- or full-time elsewhere or might also be homeworkers).

Leslie points out this tendency of Tuckman's categories to overlap and tries to sort part-timers by motivations: personal satisfaction, professional reasons (i.e., to enhance their standing in their nonteaching profession), careerist goals (i.e., they want to be college teachers), and economic reasons (Leslie 41–46). But even these categories impinge inconveniently on each other; the last item, in particular, seems the least useful because it has the least distinguishing power—that is, how can one determine why full-timers do what they do? Since they make their livings at it, whatever it is, are we to assume they chose their work for economic reasons or for personal satisfaction?

More useful, and the first categories to emerge in studies of part-time faculty, are Sheila Tobias' three divisions of part-timers, developed while she was provost at Wesleyan University in Connecticut. Tobias distinguished between moonlighters (those with full-time commitment to other careers), sunlighters (those with career commitment to college teaching but at a reduced teaching load), and twilighters (those whose primary employment is college teaching but who for one reason or another are not eligible for full-faculty status as the sunlighters are). These categories, probably because they were developed at a specific institution to formulate policy, are administratively useful for distinguishing fairly among different kinds of part-timers on the basis of their preparation for, and commitment to, college teaching. William Kerr, current provost at Wesleyan, describes this policy in detail in chapter 8. In effect since 1974, it's one of the few faculty policies at Wesleyan, according to Kerr, that has met with no criticism since its implementation.

Although I prefer Leslie's term "careerist" or the more widely used "regular" part-timer to Tobias' "sunlighter"—even though Leslie gives an oddly negative tinge to his portraits of careerists in his book (44–45)—Tobias' categories are the basis for my own conclusions about part-time faculty policy. This study will conclude that there are three legitimate uses of part-time faculty:

1. Moonlighters from another field who bring to an institution a special expertise that it couldn't afford otherwise.
2. Regular part-timers who have prepared for and planned lifelong careers in college teaching in their chosen fields (corresponds to Tobias' sunlighters).
3. Paraprofessionals who have prepared themselves by a combination of education and teaching experience for a lifelong career in teaching crucial language arts skills to undergraduates (corresponds to Tobias' twilighters).

The Debate over "Paraprofessors"

It is with our paraprofessionals that the teaching of English and foreign language compares so miserably to other professions like medicine and law. The concept is a recent one but has taken hold firmly: there are many tasks a lawyer or doctor performs that someone else with less training could do just as well (and sometimes, perhaps, even better). It is inefficient for society to put large numbers of people through costly and time-consuming training if a more specific kind of training could prepare many of them to deal successfully with numerous important medical and legal problems.

The situation in English and foreign language departments is remarkably similar. Doctorates in Chaucer or Stendhal don't necessarily make good writing teachers; and while teaching writing certainly requires love of and familiarity with literature (see Maimon, Shaughnessy) and a sensitivity to the limits of language, good writing teachers are frequently not published literary critics. Richard Marius argues in chapter 8 that it's a scandal to have nonwriters teaching writing, but the writers he employs are not necessarily authors of literary studies. Rather, they are published authors of poems, stories, newspaper articles, sports columns, novels, and nonfiction works of all sorts.

The essays by Alan Clayton at Tufts and by Howard Erlich at Ithaca document the struggles in a foreign language department and a writing program, respectively, to create alternative full-time positions for their part-time instructors in basic literacy. Both institutions were responding to the needs and wishes of their part-time faculty, many of whom wanted full-time, continuing employment in the teaching of writing or in introductory language courses.

The objections to such alternative career tracks are intense from all sides. The Ohio study on part-time faculty reports one administrator vehemently rejecting a new job definition called "instructional aids associate" (a professional category without suggestion of tenure), because it created second-class citizens in a department (Yang and Zak 59). The problem with such a reaction is that second-class citizens already exist, and they are precisely the ones requesting an alternative career track that would at least give them full-time salaries, fringe benefits, and continuing employment (like paramedical and paralegal personnel).

A more problematic difficulty is the devotion to AAUP tenure rules and the fear that someone employed beyond a certain length of time may automatically become eligible for tenure; the very rules meant to protect the academic freedom of college teachers are now being used to keep teachers in peripheral positions. In some community colleges where everyone serves on one-year contracts, the part-timers feel relatively secure compared to their full-time colleagues. But where most faculty are tenured-in, part-timers and full-timers on terminal contracts of one to five years feel their insecurity keenly. Many would eagerly choose indefinitely renewable one-year contracts if the administration and full-time faculty would let them, but adherence to AAUP principles too often stands in the way. Union College in New York is one institution that has experimented successfully with an alternative to tenure. There young scholars go through the usual strenuous tenure review; if they are recommended for tenure and their department is already tenured-in, they are declared "tenurable" and given five-year renewable contracts until a tenured position becomes available.[4]

Erlich states that Ithaca's legal counsel felt there was enough legal precedent to allow Ithaca to create full-time, non-tenure-track appointments in good faith without danger of de facto tenure lawsuits. And Clayton reports that fidelity to AAUP principles at Tufts may lead to the establishment of an alternative tenure-track for paraprofessionals, that is, excellent teachers who will be judged on their teaching records instead of on their scholarship. However, he finds resistance to the idea of tenure for nonscholars.

Even stronger and more legitimate resistance to the idea of paraprofessional positions may come from teachers of writing themselves, particularly those who have earned Ph.D.'s in rhetoric and who publish regularly in scholarly journals on rhetoric. Are teachers of writing, even with Ph.D.'s and publications, going to be treated like second-class citizens and non-scholars and allowed access only to alternative career tracks? Will the teaching of writing and first-year instruction in foreign languages always be seen as second-rate occupations by the academic community? In their essays, Howard Erlich and Miriam Brody describe sensitively their effort to build a top-notch writing program, respected across the campus and staffed with Ph.D.'s in rhetoric, while yet affirming and building on the work of many excellent part-time instructors who had taught faithfully at Ithaca for many years.

The complex issues raised here deserve a section of their own (which I am going to give them) on part-time faculty and the teaching of literacy. But I think that, carefully defined, the legitimate role of paraprofessionals in college teaching can be affirmed.

In the chapters that follow I will (1) present the existing data on part-time faculty and on the conditions under which they work; (2) discuss the implications of those data for the professional lives of women in academia; (3) examine the interdependence of staffing and curricular issues, particularly as they affect the teaching of writing and of foreign languages; and (4) present my own data on innovative policies for regular part-time faculty at colleges and universities around the country. I hope that my own confusion over which to value most—the profession of teaching language arts or the teachers who profess it—remains clear throughout.

Notes

[1] A partial bibliography of recent dissertations on part-time faculty follows:

Albert, L. S. *Part-Time Faculty Policies, Practices, and Incentives in Maryland's Community Colleges.* Diss. Univ. of Maryland 1982.

Cooke, H. L. *Characteristics of Part-Time Instructors in Comprehensive Community Colleges of North Carolina.* Diss. Duke Univ. 1973.

Fent, James E. *Professional Development for Adjunct Faculty in Michigan Community Colleges.* Diss. Walden Univ. 1979.

Hoffman, C., Jr. *A Study of the Evaluation Practices and Procedures for Part-Time Faculty in the California Community Colleges.* Diss. Oregon State Univ. 1980.

Hoffman, J. *Present and Preferred Personnel Practices involving Part-Time Instructors at South-western Community-Junior Colleges.* Diss. East Texas State Univ. 1978.

Hunt, E. S. *The Distribution, Characteristics, and Employment Benefits of Part-Time Faculty in the Southern United States.* Diss. Univ. of Virginia 1979.

Ikenberry, D. J. *A Description Study of Contract Provisions Affecting Part-Time Faculty Included in the Bargaining Unit at Post-Secondary Institutions.* Diss. Univ. of Virginia 1978.

Kandzer, J. W. *A Comparison of Student Ratings of Teaching Effectiveness for Full-Time vs. Part-Time Faculty in Selected Florida Community Colleges.* Diss. Michigan State Univ. 1977.

Ramsdale, R. L. *Academic and Professional Participation of Part-Time Faculty in New Jersey Public Community Colleges as Perceived by Part-Time Faculty, Full-Time Faculty, and Department Chairpersons.* Diss. Fordham Univ. 1976.

Russell, W. H. *Characteristics and Educational Needs of the Part-Time Faculties at Selected Florida Community/Junior Colleges.* Diss. Univ. of Florida 1979.

Sewell, D. H. *An Investigative Study of Part-Time Instructors in California Community Colleges.*

Diss. Univ. of Southern California 1976. This study led to *Report on a Statewide Survey about Part-Time Faculty in California Community Colleges.* Sacramento: California Community and Junior College Association, 1976. ERIC ED 118 195.

Van Hemert, R. E. *Orientation Programs for Part-Time College Faculty in Selected Michigan Community Colleges.* Diss. Univ. of Michigan 1977.

Other studies involving state or national surveys of part-time faculty are:

Claxton, Evelyn. *Survey of Part-Time Pay Scales for Illinois Community Colleges.* Rend Lake Coll., Ina, Ill., Spring 1981 (unpublished; available through Evelyn Claxton, Chair, Arts/Communication Department).

Friedlander, Jack. *Instructional Practices of Part-Time Faculty in Community Colleges.* San Diego: Annual Forum of the Association for Institutional Research, 1979. ERIC ED 169 971.

Lhota, Robert L. *Multidimensional Model: Adjunct Staff Development* (involves a survey of part-time faculty development programs in Kansas community colleges). Council of North Central Community and Junior Colleges, 1976. ERIC ED 180 510.

Persinger, Garnet R. *Professional Development for Part-Time Faculty. Research and Demonstration Project* (based on a national survey). Council for North Central Community and Junior Colleges, 1977. ERIC ED 168 664.

[2] A conference organized by Donald Greive, Cuyahoga Community Coll., Ohio, sponsored by Resource Control Systems, Inc., and held in Louisville, Ky., 12–14 Apr. 1982. Greive had previously organized two conferences on part-time faculty: in Cleveland, in conjunction with the American Association of University Administrators, and in Orlando.

[3] Barbara H. Tuckman and Howard P. Tuckman explore some of these differences in "Part-Timers, Sex Discrimination, and Career Choice at Two-Year Institutions." They focus on wage differences and to some extent field differences between male and female part-timers.

[4] William W. Thomas, "Folding Chair Appointments vs. Workable Alternatives to Tenure." See also "Union College Tenure Plan, June 15, 1973."

PART ONE:

Part-Time Academic Employment
in the Humanities

1. Who Are These Part-Time Faculty Anyway?

Instructor, transient, migrant worker, freeway flyer, academic third world, freeway warrior, teaching associate, lecturer, part-timer, sunlighter, surrogate faculty member, collateral faculty member, limited service faculty member, instructional aids associate, adjunct, short-termer, twilighter, temporary, field hand, boat people, circuit rider, gypsy scholar, T.A.: these are a few of the terms that refer to part-time faculty members in the literature written about them. It's no wonder full-time faculty get confused about who these people are and what they want. Furthermore, full-time faculty are so hard-pressed themselves, particularly in the humanities, that a legitimate question becomes "Why worry about part-timers when my own tenured job doesn't seem all that secure any longer?" There are some department chairs who rarely teach courses in their specialty, who teach each semester three or four sections of freshman comp or introduction to literature, and who don't have departmental funds available to attend national conferences. It's unrealistic to expect that they should spend their limited free time and surplus energy bettering the lot of part-time faculty. Even if they did, it's not at all clear what they could accomplish.

Nevertheless, there are good reasons why the problems of part-time faculty should be taken seriously by full-timers. First, the quality of education must suffer if any faculty are diminished and embittered by poor treatment, lack of support services, and isolation from colleagues and sources of faculty development. Second, if full-time faculty abandon part-timers, particularly part-timers in the humanities, the status of the profession will suffer dramatically. We cannot convince others to value our work if we do not appreciate the work of our colleagues and dignify it with just rewards.

Studies on Part-Time Faculty

Part-time faculty must be one of the most studied phenomena in higher education. Three grants were given in the late seventies for studies on part-time faculty: the Ford Foundation funded Tuckman's AAUP study, Exxon funded Leslie's work, and the Carnegie Foundation made a smaller grant to the University of Maryland. Recently, the Fund for the Improvement of Postsecondary Education (FIPSE) awarded a grant to the Institute for Research in History to study the role of part-timers in the humanities in the New York metropolitan area. The institute mailed its first questionnaires in February 1983. Numerous doctoral dissertations have been written on part-time faculty in state community college systems. Yang and Zak's *Part-Time Faculty Employment in Ohio: A Statewide Study*, funded by the Cleveland Foundation and the Columbus Foundation, was published in 1981 at Kent State University. Twenty-two colleges, universities, and community colleges in Ohio participated in the study, which is admirably clear, complete, and detailed. Particularly useful are the statistics on part-time faculty by discipline.

Another important contribution to our understanding of part-time faculty in the humanities is the preliminary survey conducted by Ben W. McClelland. His work underscores the difficulty of getting data on part-time faculty; the return rate was 39% (Tuckman's was 38%; in the Ohio study, the response rate was 38% for part-time faculty and 51% for administrators). Part-time faculty can be hard to track down, and, as Leslie points out, many administrators fail to keep detailed and accurate records on their part-time faculty and thus cannot answer questionnaires about them. More discouraging, however, is that McClelland mailed his four hundred questionnaires only to the membership of the Council of Writing Program Administrators; one might have anticipated a higher response rate from directors of writing programs, who depend so frequently on large numbers of part-time teachers.

McClelland's results suggest that part-timers constitute nearly half of the faculty teaching composition, that they average four years' teaching experience, and that 59% of the reporting institutions require part-time English teachers to hold an M.A. or higher degree. (His survey collected no data about how many part-timers actually held M.A.'s or Ph.D.'s.) Only 24% receive some fringe benefits; 25% of the reporting institutions have academic ranks for part-timers (13–15). Unfortunately, the WPA survey supplies no information on numbers of men versus numbers of women teaching composition part-time.

Three quarters of the reporting institutions paid less than $400 per semester hour; if a full-time faculty member were paid at that rate for teaching four three-credit courses per semester, his or her salary would be $9,600 for the academic year. While most of the institutions in McClelland's survey restricted part-timers to teaching loads of three courses a semester or less, 20% allowed them to teach more than nine credit hours per term. Thus, some part-timers could be struggling to survive on that maximum of $9,600 a year—without health insurance, paid vacation, or pension plan (15–17).

In all these studies, certain concerns are key. The abysmal state of record keeping on part-time faculty is deplored. Leslie urges that approval of part-time contracts should be centralized in an academic dean's office where information should be kept straight on part-time employees (143).

Leslie, Yang, and Zak all call for clearer formulations of policy; written policies should establish clear systems of classification for part-timers, and different kinds of part-time faculty should be treated differently. (Leslie 143; Yang and Zak 64–65). Tuckman is especially disturbing on the lack of rewards for part-time teaching; part-timers are not encouraged by merit raises or promotions to improve their skills, earn further degrees, or publish. All the studies emphasize this point: part-timers are unhappy about their invisibility, the lack of respect from full-time colleagues, and the failure of their institutions to reward them financially or otherwise for length of service or for excellence in teaching and scholarship.

In his conclusions, Leslie concentrates on the issue of program quality; the evidence shows that part-timers do not lower standards and detract from a program but, in fact, enrich it if they are carefully selected and supported (140; Yang and Zak's conclusions focus directly on the sloppiness of part-time recruiting and hiring procedures). Oddly enough, Leslie discovered that both shortages and surpluses of part-timers in particular fields could lead to heavy use of part-time faculty. The glut of English Ph.D.'s on the market causes increased part-time hiring to staff writing programs, while the difficulty of finding affordable, qualified, full-time computer instructors forces colleges to hire full-time computer specialists to teach a course or two part-time (30, 33).

Leslie also concludes that part-timers are unusually effective in reaching out to nontraditional students, teaching classes in odd places at odd times. Here he is focusing primarily on the moonlighter who prefers to teach on evenings and weekends. Whether part-timers are cost-effective or not, Leslie is unsure; the hidden costs of administrative overhead, reduced coordination and communication, increased tension and turnover, and uncertain course continuity are all real (142). But he is sure that restrained and reasoned use of qualified part-timers for specific tasks strengthens and enriches academic programs (71).

Not only have major studies been done on part-time faculty, but unions and professional organizations have concentrated attention on the issue and made policy statements about it. While sponsoring Tuckman's statistical study, AAUP developed policy recommendations that focused primarily on regular part-timers, those who were committed to a career in college teaching ("The Status of Part-Time Faculty"). The American Federation of Teachers made a stronger (though perhaps less thorough) statement in May 1980; its *Statement on Part-Time Faculty Employment* is recommended reading for any part-timer who feels that nobody out there understands. There's a certain gratefulness in discovering a public statement that recognizes one's years of hard work, low pay, and anonymity with the fervor one feels about these things oneself.

One won't feel quite the same rush of emotion in reading the nevertheless quite useful, recently approved "Modern Language Association Statement on Part-Time Faculty." This statement was developed by a committee of the ADE. As Richard Lloyd-Jones, one of the drafters of the document, explained in "Drafting Policy Statements on Part-Time and Short-Term Academic Employment," the larger and more powerful an organization one wants to stand behind a document, the broader that document has to be, especially if the plan is to keep it down to a page or two. The MLA statement thus focuses on academic quality and may insult some part-time faculty by referring to their "limited commitment" and "low professional standing"; the intention is not to disparage the contributions of part-time faculty but to describe the issues at stake in such a way as to make full-time, tenured faculty see the importance of facing them.

MLA members might also want to study the recommendations in "Report of the Commission on the Future of the Profession" in section 12, "Part-Time Employment." The report not only deplores the treatment of part-timers as second-class citizens but suggests "a systematic review of experienced part-timers for transfer to tenure-track appointments" (954).

Several other professional associations in English have addressed the issue. Particularly worthwhile was the Fall 1981 *Journal of the Council of Writing Program Administrators*, which was entirely devoted to part-time faculty and included essays by Donald McQuade, Geoffrey S. Weinman, and Wayne Booth, as well as Ben McClelland's survey results. A WPA committee—made up of Maxine Hairston, Donald McQuade, and Ben McClelland—has developed a clear and thorough position statement. The National Council of Teachers of English has held meetings on and devoted pages to the subject in *College English* (see particularly Cara Chell's essay in the January 1982 issue and reader responses in December 1982). Finally, the Conference on College Composition and Communication (CCCC) has established a committee, chaired by Timothy Dykstra of Franklin University in Columbus, Ohio, to focus on part-time faculty.

The American Association for Higher Education devoted one of its monographs on Current Issues in Higher Education to part-time faculty (*Part-Time Faculty in Colleges and Universities*); and the American Council on Education, the AAUP, and the Association of Governing Boards of Universities and Colleges have held leadership seminars on the subject under the direction of Thomas A. Emmet and W. Todd Furniss. Further, ACE has a monograph in the works on part-time faculty policy as part of its Fair Practices series.

With all this research and policy formulation going on, one might hope that conditions would improve for part-time faculty. For many, change can't come a moment too soon.

Battle Scars

I have mixed feelings about part-time faculty atrocity stories, especially since discovering myself involved in one. Yang and Zak refer to a *New York Times* article by Gene Maeroff, in which Maeroff used my husband and me, among others, to illustrate the plight of part-time Ph.D.'s:

> Print and electronic media during the past year have featured horror stories about well-qualified Ph.D.'s without regular academic appointments eking out subsistence incomes for themselves and their families teaching part-time at two or three different, sometimes geographically distant, colleges and universities. Tired, poor, and bitter, these part-

time faculty members have complained to interviewers of exploitation. . . . (61)

To discover oneself referred to in print as "tired, poor, and bitter" is dis-
concerting, to say the least. Looking back on that year, I don't remember
it as all *that* bad, though I do remember worrying occasionally about what
would happen if our VW bug broke down. My primary professional concerns were much the same as always: figuring out how to do the best
possible job teaching the students in my classes. How could I get Sarah to
see what it meant to structure her compositions? How could I convince
Tim to recognize and deal with opposing points of view in his argumen-
tative essays? How could I teach Wordsworth successfully to sophomores
who hated poetry? The fact that my students were spread over several
different campuses didn't change the nature or the importance of these
questions, even if occasionally it did make dealing with them more difficult.

A danger in focusing on the plight of the part-timer is that one may
lose sight of students and the part-time faculty member's commitment to
them. Yet the details of particular stories are necessary to make the problems of part-timers immediate to others. For instance, there's the succinct
comment of a community college "temporary" part-timer in the Ohio study:
"For seventeen years I have worked never knowing whether I had a job
or not until the day or so before the classes started. I wish there were a
better way to arrange things" (Yang and Zak 101). Another woman with
a doctorate and eight years of teaching experience on the college level says
she finds teaching composition a job one can do neither for the money nor
for the sake of being part of the academic community, "because the truth
is that the lecturers aren't members of that community. . . . I feel there
must be at least a thousand things I could do that would be better than
this" (Yang and Zak 101–02).

The *New York Times* published another article on part-time and short-
term faculty entitled "A Lost Generation of Young 'Gypsy Scholars' " and
written by Fred M. Hechinger. He describes a Ph.D. in French literature
from Yale (1974) who taught for five years at Brown and, after failing to
find a tenure-track position, took a temporary, one-year appointment at
the University of Minnesota; he then retrained in banking at the Wharton
School of Business. The chair of the English department at Bowdoin, Her-
bert Courson, told Hechinger that for two one-year openings he had over
four hundred applications; for a one-year replacement he hired "a chap in
his mid-30's who is eminently qualified" but who had received no other
job offers. Courson was eloquent: "I'm 50, and what I see is the profession
dying out behind me."

The Fall 1981 issue of *WPA* included an essay by Susan Blank and Beth
Greenberg, "Living at the Bottom," which described the life of part-time
teachers in New York City. At a 1982 ADE Summer Seminar, an English
department chair from a college in New York City rationalized about the
part-time faculty situation there by calling it a kind of exotic graduate
assistantship before Ph.D.'s moved on to their real jobs in a year or two;
he claimed they got a rich variety of teaching experiences that prepared
them for full-time teaching. His analysis of the situation overlooked the

fact that, after five or six years, most of these part-time faculty in New York have discovered that their unstable teaching assignments are as close as they'll ever come to full-time teaching jobs.

The following account of one New York part-timer's experience makes this instability clear.

> Fall semester I worked at two schools. In November, one of those schools told me I was among the lucky ones who would be rehired in the spring. I would teach two three-hour classes. During intersession, I planned the classes, chose texts, and got thoroughly excited about meeting my new students. Four days before the new term began, the other school offered me two four-hour classes. Although the two extra hours would have meant more money, I decided to stick with the first school, where I had really enjoyed the creative atmosphere and the interaction between adjuncts and full-timers. The day before classes began, I received a phone call saying that due to low registration, my six hours had been cancelled. The caller's warmth and words of sympathy helped little. I quickly called the second school, but, of course, the two classes they'd offered me were already covered. (Blank and Greenberg 10)

Blank and Greenberg also describe bizarre situations in which full-time instructorships were eliminated, replaced with several adjunct positions, and staffed with previous instructors who thus replaced themselves as adjuncts.

Joanne Spencer Kantrowitz's twenty-page essay in *Rocking the Boat: Academic Women and Academic Processes* is a remarkable account of one woman's legal battle to have her years of part-time work in the profession acknowledged and legitimated. She argues that her applications for full-time or regular part-time positions at the institution where she taught were never seriously considered because of her part-time status, even though her credentials were equal or superior to those of men hired full-time. "Paying Your Dues, Part-Time" does not have a happy ending; Kantrowitz won neither a full-time nor a regular part-time position. When I wrote her to ask if she would like to contribute to this volume, she wished me well but refused: "The sheer act of filing a complaint and pursuing it was enough to destroy my career. . . . I've spent six years without income from my profession and simply cannot afford to donate any further time to it" (Letter, 10 Apr. 1982). Publishing significant work, even serving as an expert reader for *PMLA*, was not enough to overcome the stigma of having taught part-time. The additional stigma of having fought an institution in court has prevented Kantrowitz from receiving even one offer of an academic job, despite repeated applications at various universities and colleges over the past six years.

Other essays in this volume (Gemmill, Jason, Miller) describe the plight of the part-timer in individual voices, but Tuckman's work and the recent study *Part-Time Faculty Employment in Ohio* help us perceive part-timers in more general terms: approximately 25% of all part-timers hold the doctorate or the highest professional degree in their field (Yang and Zak 16; for Tuckman, 20%). At state universities, this percentage jumped to 32%, at private colleges it was 23%, and at community colleges 12% (Yang and Zak 17). As in McClelland's survey, the average years of part-time teaching experience numbered four; the average years of full-time teaching experience were two (Yang and Zak 17; for Tuckman, 4.6 and 2.5 years). In the Ohio sample of 1,514 part-timers, 112 had published one or two books, 12 had published three to four books, and 13 had published five or more books; about 30% had published one article or more, and 35% had presented one or more papers at professional meetings (for Tuckman, approximately 20% had published one article).

Most part-timers teach in either business or the humanities. English is the field accounting for the largest single group of part-timers (Yang and Zak 12, and app. C 95; see tables 1 and 2); 58% of all part-timers teach lower-level courses (Yang and Zak, 12), a piece of information that should discourage any illusion on the part of administrators that part-timers are only called in to teach upper-level, specialized courses.

The number of part-timers teaching at two or more institutions to patch a career together may not be as high as expected—15.3% of the total, according to the Ohio study (12). One administrator has pointed out to me that such part-timers are exploiting institutions of higher education; some cases have been reported of part-timers teaching eight to ten classes a semester and earning close to $30,000 a year. (If they were teaching composition, others would argue, they were earning every penny!) However, if colleges don't pay part-time faculty enough to entitle the college to set

Table 1: Teaching Fields of Part-Time Faculty—Ohio Study

Fields	Number of Part-Time Faculty	Percent
Mathematics	113	7.2%
Computer Sciences	52	3.3%
Physics and Astronomy	13	0.8%
Chemistry	12	0.6%
Earth, Environmental, and Marine Science	5	0.3%
Engineering	76	4.8%
Biological Sciences	19	1.2%
Agricultural Sciences	4	0.3%
Medical Sciences	132	8.4%
Social Sciences	145	9.2%
Humanities	230	14.6%
Arts	163	10.3%
Education	110	7.0%
Business	299	18.9%
Other Professional	206	13.1%
Total	1579	100%

Source: Yang and Zak 12.

Table 2: Teaching Fields of Part-Time Faculty—Ohio Study

Fields	Number of Part-Time Faculty
Business:	
Accounting	83
Business Administration (general)	72
Finance	16
Marketing	24
Public Administration	4
Management (all fields)	34
Secretarial (shorthand, typing, etc.)	24
Others	42
Total	**299**
Humanities:	
Art, History, and Criticism	10
History	16
Religion, Theology	13
Philosophy	11
Languages, Linguistics	44
English	130
Others	6
Total	**230**
Arts:	
Art, Fine and Applied	41
Music	86
Theater	12
Speech	18
Others	6
Total	**163**

Source: Yang and Zak 95.

restrictions on courseload, if colleges don't know or care about other teaching commitments their part-timers may have, surely they deserve rather less than what they've got, which at worst may be a surprisingly energetic and enterprising instructor, albeit headed for exhaustion.

A more realistic description of such a part-timer's life reveals not horror, not casual commitment to more courses than one can handle, but humdrum, drudgery, and meticulous scheduling. Jeanne Huffman of Philadelphia does what many have done before her: teaches to earn a living while working on her doctoral dissertation. However, Jeanne teaches composition and writing at three different schools; each requires her to use a different text. On Mondays, Wednesdays, and Fridays she teaches half days at Bucks County Community College (two courses), commuting by train from her home in the city. The other half of the day she spends at Moore College of Art, teaching two courses and tutoring. On Tuesdays and Thursdays she drives forty miles to West Chester Community College to teach two more courses, one at 9:30 a.m., the other at 3:30 p.m.

She is able to survive on her part-time salaries only because one institution, Moore College of Art, pays her a prorated salary and supplies prorated fringe benefits. She carries a much heavier load than a full-time faculty member would at any single school, and she is paid much less. Train fare and gasoline eat up considerable amounts of money, and commuting eats up considerable amounts of time, although she is able to read on the train. If she is exploiting the institutions she so conscientiously serves, I suspect she'd be happy to see the error of her ways and settle for a full-time job at any one of them. Perhaps then she could find more time to devote to her dissertation.

Working Conditions of Part-Time Faculty

Recruitment, Hiring, and Contracts

Under what conditions do part-timers work? Usually, they are hired on semester-long contracts under informal interviewing and appointment procedures. In Ohio, 60% of the part-time faculty reported hearing of job openings by word of mouth only (Yang and Zak 23); state universities and private colleges were more likely to leave part-time faculty hiring entirely up to the department chair and perhaps one other faculty member, while community colleges were more apt to use a formal search committee (25). Rarely is research, creativity, or even previous service to the institution considered in part-time faculty appointments (Leslie 72–76).

It is easy to see where the invisibility of the part-time faculty member begins. Only one or two members of the department ever see the part-timer's credentials, and, even then, dossiers are given only a cursory glance for, perhaps, degrees and previous teaching experience. The assumption that the part-time market is only a local market leads departments to hire from personal contacts and recommendations rather than from advertisements in professional journals, the *Chronicle of Higher Education*, or even regional newspapers. Then, because they have not widely advertised the position, full-time faculty often think less highly of a successful candidate because he or she came, after all, only from the local pool of applicants. This circular reasoning will continue until departments make conspicuous efforts to standardize hiring procedures for at least regular part-time faculty. A formal search committee should be established, and positions should be advertised in local and regional newspapers, the *Chronicle*, and professional publications like the MLA *Job Information List*. Particularly in English and in foreign languages, given the present job market, regular part-time positions might well attract applicants from a national pool.

A thorough review of a candidate's credentials is not only common courtesy but also common sense. Departments may discover talents of great value to their programs. In no case should the hiring of part-timers be in the hands of one person alone; a candidate's credentials should be reviewed by the largest possible number of colleagues.

During formal interviews candidates should feel that their dossiers have been read thoughtfully and their qualifications recognized. Last-minute hiring, which prevents dignified recruitment and hiring procedures, should be avoided by careful planning. For instance, as Weinman points out in his *WPA* essay, it is irresponsible to offer an unrealistic number of upper-level courses each semester, assuming that a few of them will be canceled and will therefore release full-timers to cover extra sections of composition (27). On the one hand, if the upper-level courses unexpectedly go, part-timers must be quickly interviewed and hired, sometimes only a few days before term begins, to teach the uncovered sections. It is equally unfair, on the other hand, to hire part-timers and then bump them when full-timers—finding their upper-level sections undersubscribed—need to teach lower-level courses to fill out their loads. Realistic and responsible scheduling should be the norm.

In situations where enrollments for lower-level courses simply are not known until the week before term, as in community colleges with open admissions, part-time teachers can be interviewed throughout the year and told whether or not they meet the college's standards for employment. Then, if the teachers are willing, they can be kept on call for courses that become available. At the least, such a practice would eliminate the indignity of a hasty, inadequate interview at the last minute.

Once a part-timer is hired, some form of contract is called for. The Ohio study found that a surprising 15% of part-timers in community colleges were given no written contract whatsoever but were hired under oral agreements (11). Written contracts for part-timers often are issued after the first few classes have met and the enrollment for the course is ascertained; otherwise, the contract is so conditional that it is virtually worthless. Here is the exact wording from one community college contract in the Southwest:

> The Board of Trustees has elected you to the call staff as a lecturer for the summer semester, 1982. Your employment is contingent upon: 1) the instructional needs of the college; and 2) there being sufficient students registered to justify your class(es) being taught as scheduled this semester. . . . Employment is for one semester only and does not give you tenure, district fringe benefits, academic rank, or imply future employment. The position of lecturer is itself a temporary position of the community college district and may be discontinued after any semester.

Such contracts are written very carefully to discourage lawsuits over job rights, and apparently they do a thorough job of it.

As the Ohio study shows, 41% of part-timers at community colleges are notified of their appointments less than a week before class. As Leslie puts it, "Part-timers often do not know, until the last minute, when they will teach, what they will teach, how many sections they will teach, where they will teach, or if they will teach" (102). Such conditions have an inevitable impact on instructional quality, even if an institution makes a practice of paying a symbolic cut fee for subsequently canceled courses.

It's hard to know what can be done about such last-minute notice, since administrators rely on part-time faculty for flexibility in scheduling and staffing that full-time, tenured faculty simply do not allow. Even union contracts that have managed to include hard-won seniority clauses for part-timers (see, in ch. 5, Virginia Mulrooney's essay on the Los Angeles Community College District contract) still have to allow for full-time bumping of part-timers if a full-timer needs another course to make up a full load. In a marvelous understatement, Leslie makes clear the essential conflict of interests: "What was identified as a long-term flexibility advantage to full-time faculty and to heads of departments was sometimes personally perceived as insecurity by part-timers" (102).

Evaluation, Orientation, and Faculty Development

Once the semester begins and part-timers can at least count on finishing out the semester, the problem of evaluation surfaces. Some part-timers are humiliated by overevaluation that continues long past their first few semesters of teaching. Such scrutiny of part-time faculty is especially irritating if new full-time faculty are noticeably exempt from it (see Miller's essay in ch. 6). The usual situation, however, is that part-timers are under-evaluated. In the Ohio study, roughly 56% of all part-timers were either unaware of any evaluations or else certain that no formal evaluation of their teaching had taken place (19). The danger is, of course, that informal evaluations based on hearsay and stray student comments will carry great weight when hiring decisions are made the following semester.

Perhaps even more disturbing from the administrative point of view is that frequently no one is supervising part-timers or helping them deal with classroom problems. Often, the job of evaluating departmental part-timers falls on a single individual, such as a chairperson or a writing program administrator, and is too heavy a burden to be carried alone. Evaluation of part-time faculty demands time and care. For example, evaluation can be completely separated from hiring decisions and allied instead with faculty development programs (such a division has been successfully tried at Vista College in California; see Bagwell and Elioff 16). In this volume the essays by Richard Marius and Richard Colwell describe healthy evaluation and faculty development programs. Both authors recognize that evaluation can devastate part-timers because of their insecurity and lack of proper grievance procedures. The problem is compounded, as Leslie points out, by the relative scarcity of good evaluation procedures for full-time faculty teaching; it's a rare institution that knows much about the teaching effectiveness of its full-time faculty, let alone of its part-timers. Student ratings, by the way, fail to show any significant difference between full-time and part-time teaching abilities (Leslie 83).

In general, however, part-timers express a desire for evaluation, orientation, and faculty development because they are eager to improve their teaching skills. Both involving part-timers in curricular development and setting up mentor relationships between specific full-time faculty and part-time faculty seem to help (Leslie 85; Albert 177). Supporting part-time faculty financially if they want to attend professional meetings and conferences is a natural form of faculty development (see Albert 177; Leslie found that one third of the institutions in his study contributed something toward part-time faculty attendance at conferences [84]).

Lately, community colleges have been concentrating their efforts on the issue of part-time faculty development and orientation; numerous faculty development handbooks have been written for the national market to give part-timers tips on teaching, making up tests and syllabi, and understanding adult learners.[1] Many community colleges are putting together their own handbooks, describing their goals, services, calendar, and policies. The handbooks are then supplemented with formal orientation sessions, which seem to be most successful if part-time faculty are either paid a stipend to attend (Albert 177) or required to attend as part of their contractual agreement with the college. (A recently instituted required orientation program for part-time faculty is working well at Catonsville Community College in Catonsville, Md.) Such orientation sessions seem to be most useful if they are practical and focus on instructional development, but almost anything seems preferable to the lack of formal orientation for new part-time faculty by 84% of the institutions in Leslie's study (81).

Since community college faculties are approximately 50% part-time and many of those part-timers are not teachers by training or profession, such an emphasis on faculty orientation and development is sensible. For academically trained part-time faculty in the humanities, more frequent and more rigorous faculty development seminars have been suggested. However, their implementation would probably depend on the creation of regular part-time positions with salaries adequate to justify further demands on part-time faculty time and energy. Continuing faculty development sessions like those described in Marius' essay (ch. 8) or in Booth's essay would involve both full-time and part-time colleagues in weekly discussions of problems in the teaching of writing. An important benefit of such faculty development programs, as Booth points out, is that they make the process of evaluation much simpler. Full-time faculty who have shared openly in discussion with their part-time colleagues have a clearer sense of the commitment and talents of their part-time faculty when part-time hiring and promotion decisions have to be made (Booth 39).

Not only are evaluation, orientation, and faculty development important to part-time faculty but so are things as simple and basic as access to copying machines, secretarial services, departmental mailboxes, offices, and audiovisual equipment. Often, these items are available to part-timers, but no one has bothered to tell them so (Yang and Zak 45). Leslie states emphatically the symbolic importance of such amenities.

> Possessed of natural motives to do a job well, part-timers feel blocked by their lack of access to basic resources. . . . Support services need to be released and used, not pinched and hoarded, and part-timers are as desperately in need of them as full-timers. (81)

Fringe Benefits

How many part-time faculty have access to fringe benefits? Both the Ohio study and Tuckman's AAUP research reveal that a surprisingly high

Table 3: Numbers and Percentages of Part-Time Faculty Not Receiving Selected Fringe Benefits from Any Employment Sources—Ohio Study

	Our Study	National AAUP Study
Retirement Plan	418	
	(26.9%)	30.7%
Unemployment Insurance	1053	NA
	(67.8%)	
Health Insurance	717	
	(46.2%)	42.0%
Life Insurance	858	
	(55.2%)	39.8%
Workers' Compensation	991	
	(63.8%)	58.2%
Sick Leave	850	
	(54.7%)	47.2%

Source: Yang and Zak 40.

number of part-timers are not covered by fringe benefits from any source, even though the common assumption is that most have fringe-benefit coverage through their full-time jobs. For example, 27% have no retirement plan, 68% do not receive unemployment insurance, 46% do not get health insurance, 55% lack life insurance, 64% do not receive worker's compensation, and 55% do not earn sick leave—from *any* source (Yang and Zak 40; see table 3). The Tuckmans' findings are similar: "Few part-timers can count on fringe benefit coverage if they do not get this from their academic employer" ("Who Are the Part-Timers?" 5). Particularly discouraging is the realization that half-time staff and secretaries may be eligible for pro-rated benefits and even tuition credit for themselves and their families while part-time faculty are not; Maryse Eymonerie's study *The Availability of Fringe Benefits in Colleges and Universities* makes it clear that such inequities do occur.

A surprisingly small number of part-time faculty have access to other benefits like recreational privileges, tuition credit, sabbaticals, bookstore discounts, and even free parking. The most commonly granted privilege is use of the library but only 67.6% of the part-timers reported having library privileges (Yang and Zak 42). Interestingly, administrators consistently declared that part-timers had more rights and privileges than the part-timers reported; Yang and Zak conclude that "some part-time faculty members might not know that certain services, facilities, or activities are available to them, or administrators may believe in availability that does not in fact exist" (46; see tables 4 and 5). In either case, it's clear that channels of communication are clogged and need more frequent use.

Salary

What do part-timers get paid for their teaching and how many see low salaries as a problem? The situation is complicated by part-timers who

Table 4: Numbers and Percentages of Part-Time Faculty Receiving Selected Benefits from Their Academic Employment, as Reported by Part-Time Faculty—Ohio Study

	State Universities		Private Colls./Univs.		Community Colleges		Total	
	Received from Part-Time Employment	Would Like to Receive	Received from Part-Time Employment	Would Like to Receive	Received from Part-Time Employment	Would Like to Receive	Received from Part-Time Employment	Would Like to Receive
Sabbatical Leave	8 (0.9%)	195 (29.3%)	1 (0.6%)	49 (28.4%)	0	110 (24.0%)	9 (0.6%)	354 (23.0%)
Tuition for Self	156 (17.1%)	269 (29.5%)	25 (14.5%)	46 (26.7%)	11 (2.4%)	181 (39.6%)	192 (12.4%)	496 (32.0%)
Tuition for Spouse and Dependents	48 (5.3%)	302 (33.1%)	18 (10.5%)	52 (30.1%)	6 (1.3%)	179 (39.0%)	72 (4.7%)	533 (34.7%)
University Parking	249 (27.2%)	309 (33.8%)	131 (76.2%)	17 (9.8%)	40 (8.7%)	232 (50.6%)	420 (27.2%)	558 (36.2%)
Recreational Facilities	311 (34.0%)	133 (14.5%)	103 (59.9%)	19 (11.0%)	127 (27.7%)	93 (20.3%)	541 (35.0%)	245 (15.8%)
Bookstore Discount	353 (38.6%)	195 (29.1%)	98 (57.0%)	38 (22.1%)	25 (54.0%)	212 (46.0%)	476 (30.8%)	445 (29.1%)
Library Privileges	647 (70.8%)	56 (6.0%)	141 (82.0%)	13 (7.5%)	256 (55.9%)	46 (10.0%)	1044 (67.6%)	115 (7.4%)
Subsidies for Professional Meetings	72 (7.9%)	237 (25.9%)	13 (7.6%)	52 (30.2%)	9 (2.0%)	140 (30.6%)	94 (6.9%)	429 (27.8%)

Source: Yang and Zak 42.

would teach without salaries if they could and who sometimes beg the institution not to pay them because the small extra paychecks complicate things at income tax time. Even though it wouldn't cure their tax muddles, such part-timers might be encouraged to return their paychecks to the institution as donations, earmarked for a special fund to provide merit raises for part-timers who teach for a living.

However, part-timers eager to teach for the fun of it (or for increased professional exposure and prestige) are relatively scarce. More common are those who agree, for one reason or another, to teach for demeaningly low wages and thus set or continue a pattern for all part-timers (see Walter Borenstein's essay, ch. 6). The range in part-time salaries is extreme. Marius, arguing that salaries have great symbolic importance (because people pay dearly for what they value), insists on a salary of $3,540 per course for the part-time faculty in the expository writing program at Harvard. Meanwhile, the average per course salary for a three-credit-hour class of, say, twenty-five students in freshman composition at a community college in Ohio is estimated at around $600 (Yang and Zak 33). Most four-year colleges fall somewhere in between.

Several factors influence part-timers' attitudes toward their salaries. First, they are aware of how their earnings compare to those of full-timers doing similar work at their own institutions. They feel there ought to be a reasonable relationship between full-time paychecks and their own. Second, part-timers know that full-timers get cost-of-living increases yearly, while part-time salaries usually stay fixed at a flat rate for several years at a stretch. Third, they realize that no matter how well they teach, how much they publish, what further degrees they earn, or how long they serve an institution, no established procedures exist for acknowledging their achievements with merit raises.

Finally, pay schedules for part-timers can be extraordinarily frustrating: some colleges pay for the course only at the end of the semester, after all the grades are in; others pay an installment halfway through the term or once every six weeks (see Chell). At more humane institutions, paychecks come more frequently. Too often, however, the assumption seems to be that such a small check can't be significant, and the insult is not lost on those who make a living by part-time teaching.

The issue of pro rata pay, basing part-time salaries directly on equivalent full-time salaries, is complicated by the clashing interests of faculty unions and college administrators. Unions like the American Federation of Teachers and the National Education Association encourage the concept of strictly pro rata pay for part-time faculty, believing that it would destroy the financial incentive for administrators to turn full-time positions into part-time ones. However, since part-time positions appeal to administrators for reasons besides cost, it is unlikely that simply prorating part-time salaries would significantly decrease part-time hiring.

Laws on equal pay for equal work don't translate into a legal basis for pro rata pay because full-time faculty presumably do more than teach. At research universities they research and publish their findings. At all institutions they participate in department and campuswide committees; such governance responsibilities can be time-consuming and energy-sapping

Table 5: Benefits Provided to Part-Time Faculty, as Reported by Administrators—Ohio Study

	State Universities		Private Colls./Univs.		Community Colleges		Total	
	Yes	No, but Would Like to Grant	Yes	No, but Would Like to Grant	Yes	No, but Would Like to Grant	Yes	No, but Would Like to Grant
Retirement Plan	91 (45%)	39 (19%)	8 (12%)	20 (29%)	21 (58%)	3 (8%)	120 (39%)	62 (20%)
Unemployment	35 (17%)	54 (27%)	15 (22%)	20 (29%)	1 (3%)	11 (31%)	51 (17%)	85 (28%)
Health Insurance	38 (19%)	58 (29%)	8 (12%)	20 (29%)	0	11 (31%)	46 (15%)	89 (29%)
Life Insurance	26 (13%)	64 (32%)	2 (3%)	21 (31%)	0	11 (31%)	28 (9%)	96 (31%)
Workers' Compensation	64 (32%)	38 (19%)	26 (38%)	14 (21%)	3 (8%)	7 (19%)	93 (30%)	59 (19%)
Sick Leave	41 (20%)	49 (24%)	10 (15%)	17 (25%)	1 (3%)	10 (28%)	52 (17%)	76 (25%)

Sabbatical Leave	6 (3%)	62 (31%)	6 (9%)	19 (28%)	0	11 (31%)	12 (4%)	92 (30%)
Tuition for Self	30 (15%)	53 (26%)	24 (35%)	13 (19%)	2 (6%)	12 (33%)	56 (18%)	78 (25%)
Tuition for Spouse and Dependents	26 (13%)	58 (29%)	18 (27%)	14 (21%)	0	11 (31%)	44 (14%)	83 (27%)
University Parking	108 (53%)	23 (11%)	61 (90%)	3 (4%)	2 (6%)	8 (22%)	171 (56%)	34 (11%)
Recreational Facilities	130 (64%)	18 (9%)	53 (78%)	4 (6%)	21 (58%)	3 (8%)	204 (66%)	25 (8%)
Bookstore Discount	120 (59%)	18 (9%)	55 (81%)	2 (3%)	3 (8%)	11 (31%)	178 (58%)	31 (10%)
Library Privileges	176 (87%)	4 (2%)	66 (97%)	1 (2%)	31 (86%)	2 (6%)	273 (89%)	7 (2%)
Subsidies for Professional Meetings	34 (17%)	51 (25%)	17 (25%)	20 (29%)	1 (3%)	9 (25%)	52 (17%)	80 (26%)

Source: Yang and Zak 42–43.

indeed. And full-time faculty are expected to keep office hours, making themselves available to consult with students and to advise them about course registration, career preparation, and graduate school applications.

For these reasons, Leslie leans away from pro rata pay for part-timers in his conclusions. One can agree with him that pro rata pay is probably not justified for those whose full-time career commitments lie elsewhere. But, as the Ohio study shows, most part-timers invest huge amounts of time (70 to 80% of their working hours) in their part-time teaching, both in and out of the classroom. On an average, they spend 34% of their time in class, 22% preparing lectures and grading, 7% keeping up in their fields, and—interestingly—7% on advising and counseling students. This last figure is worth notice since only 15% of the administrators reported that they required part-time faculty to advise students or confer with them outside class (Yang and Zak 22–23). Thus, all part-time faculty in the Ohio study average 7% of their weekly time doing tasks not officially required.

For part-time faculty in the humanities, particularly those committed to a career in college teaching in their chosen fields, doing more than is required or expected can become a dangerous pattern, because it exhausts a part-timer and usually leads nowhere. The overwhelming evidence is that part-time teaching does not lead to full-time teaching, particularly not at the same institution (see Kantrowitz). One part-timer seeking a full-time position at her institution pointed out that she had published, served nobly on faculty committees, and worked with students on independent study projects and given them individual conferences to help them with their work. The institution merely pointed out that she was not required or expected to do such things by the terms of her contract. Thus, even though her achievements benefited the institution, they counted for nothing in terms of salary, job security, or advancement (see Gemmill's essay in ch. 7). Disillusioned part-timers would be justified in performing at minimum levels, saving their time and energy for outside projects such as research and publication. Yet how is one supposed to get a better job without doing one's best at the present job?

Whereas some tenured full-time professors keep student contact and involvement in college governance to a minimum, many part-timers not only consult with freshmen struggling over research papers or rewritten essays but also spend long hours grading themes every evening. Occasionally, the teaching load of the part-time teacher of composition is equal to or greater than the load of senior faculty members. Advice to publish one's way out of such discouraging situations is hard to follow under heavy work loads and financial strain.

If strictly pro rata salaries are out of the question, there are alternatives. First, a clear connection between full- and part-time salaries ought to be stated. At Gettysburg College, for instance, a relatively decent pay scale for part-time faculty is established by roughly pro rata principles. A full-timer teaches seven courses a year; a part-timer is thus paid one ninth of the salary of a beginning full-timer at similar rank (based on highest degree earned), the rationale being that two ninths of a full-timer's time should be devoted to out-of-classroom duties. Left out of this reckoning, however, is the fact that part-timers receive no contributions toward medical coverage, disability plans, or tuition credit for their families, differences that probably more than make up for the two-ninths work load they are not expected to carry. Also overlooked is that part-time salaries are always figured against beginning salaries of full-timers in the lower ranks, although Gettysburg does supply a per-course stipend for each five years of service.

Second, once some kind of reasoned relationship between full-time and part-time salaries is formed, salary schedules for part-timers need to reflect differences in credentials, teaching experience, and service to the institution. Third, cost-of-living increases should be given annually; tying part-time salaries to full-time salaries is the simplest way to achieve this. Fourth, research on job satisfaction suggests that raises, large or small, are important when linked to good performance (Albert 177); part-time, like full-time, faculty need to feel that extraordinary effort is recognized and rewarded. Finally, part-time faculty not on prorated salaries should be expected to give no more than reasonable amounts of service outside the classroom unless they are individually compensated for such services.

Perhaps some part-time faculty find a low per course salary acceptable for a few years if they live in the hope of soon landing a full-time teaching job. What are the chances that a talented part-time faculty member in the humanities can work his or her way up through the part-time ranks, perhaps even into a continuing, full-time position?

Not great. The Ohio study contrasted part-timers' opinions on this subject with those of administrators; 90% of the part-time faculty felt they should be entitled to promotion in rank but only 54% of the reporting administrators shared their view. Some 88% of the part-timers felt they should be given priority at their own institutions when a full-time position in their field opened up; only 45% of the administrators agreed (Yang and Zak 46–47). While it is heartening that nearly half the administrators felt that promotion and full-time jobs ought to be available to part-timers, the discrepancy in expectation and opinion is clear. Further, Yang and Zak did not investigate the attitudes of full-time faculty on these issues, and chances are that many would have strong resistance to the upward movement of part-time faculty in their departments.

The sobering, realistic note cannot be struck too often. Unfair though it may be, little evidence exists to suggest that part-time teaching leads to full-time academic employment (Leslie 44).

Part-Timers' Legal Rights and Administrative Attitudes

It is doubtful that part-time faculty will win job security and equal pay through the courts. If anything, legal battles seem to have made administrators overly wary and unwilling to experiment with part-time faculty policy. Such caution is uncalled for, as Figuli's essay (ch. 9) makes clear; part-timers can claim equal pay for equal work and expectation of continued employment in only a few specific situations. However, much of the current writing on part-time faculty takes the tone of a legal sourcebook for administrators, focusing on what a college must do to protect itself against part-timers' lawsuits. Leslie's impressive volume, *Part-Time Faculty in American Higher Education*, often leans in this direction. He clearly understands his primary audience to be administrators who care about the continuing existence of their institutions in troubled times. Lawsuits are distracting, expensive, and damaging to public reputations. Deans and college presidents are quite sensible in trying to avoid them.

The part-timer's quest for tenure or for some minimal form of job security seems on especially weak grounds, legally speaking, since the entire concept of tenure is now being reexamined. For example, in an essay written for an ACE Leadership Seminar, "Program Reduction and Reorganization: Part-Time Faculty Usage and Concerns," Ray A. Howe writes that a college or university's "prime reason for existence is the provision of educational services and not the provision of assured, perpetual employment to those who provide the services" (3). Further, a good administrator "bears a responsibility to effect every economy possible within reasonable bounds" (8). Howe clearly shares the same standards of academic excellence and academic freedom that most full-time and part-time faculty hold dear, but he finds that some of these concepts have got muddled along the way. Tenure,

> which was generated to provide assurance of academic freedom, has been transmuted into a concept of job security. Protections from intrusion on the integrity of research and presentation of the results of research are now construed by many, perhaps most in academe, as immunity from layoff for even the most legitimate and demonstrable reasons. (3)

Howe is not the only voice lately to call us back to first principles. The *Chronicle of Higher Education* (17 March 1982) reported on the furor caused by attorney David Figuli's contention that universities need not declare financial exigency in order to dismiss tenured faculty. And Stewart Weinberg, general counsel for California Federation of Teachers, reemphasized in his presentation at the 1982 MLA convention ("Recent Developments in the Law as It Affects Part-Time Faculty in California") that tenure is nothing more than a right to due process in case of dismissal. The institution must show that faculty members were dismissed with just cause (like the termination of an entire program or department) and not simply because someone disliked them or disagreed with the results of their academic work.

These are not cheerful reminders. Reports of tenured faculty being laid off or whole departments being disbanded don't make people eager to better the lot of part-time faculty. But complicated questions arise. If tenure is not job security but simply a protection of freedom of speech and the right to follow one's research to its legitimate conclusions, shouldn't everyone in the academic community have it? Should a department chair be allowed to dismiss a part-time faculty member because he or she finds that part-timer's published essay on Marxist criticism un-American? or considers another part-timer's remarks on deconstructionist criticism off the wall? At present, nothing protects most part-timers from precisely such whimsical dismissals. ("Dismissal," of course, is the wrong word; a part-timer gradually realizes that he or she is not going to be offered a course the following term, and frequently no explanation is given unless a part-timer demands one.)

The fact is that no one does understand tenure in these terms, not the full-timer who sighs with relief when he or she gets it, not the administrator who fights tooth and nail against giving tenure to anyone else and particularly against giving it to part-timers. AAUP may be thinking of tenure in the pure sense; otherwise it's hard to figure out AAUP's continuing devotion to the 1940 tenure rules, which now seem to be mangling so many young people in the profession as they move from one terminal appointment to another. Terminal appointments are, like carefully worded part-time contracts, a way of avoiding legal claims to de facto tenure based on the 1940 tenure rules. As a matter of fact, institutions that depart from AAUP guidelines may be on better legal grounds than those that stick by them. If an institution can show that it has developed alternative systems for hiring and retaining faculty and has tried to follow those systems consistently and in good faith, it is much less likely to be legally bound by AAUP criteria in the courts. (See Erlich's and Brody's essays in ch. 7 and Thomas Werge's essay in ch. 8 on the need for imaginative deviation from AAUP guidelines.)

Meanwhile, part-timers may be better off asking for clear grievance procedures, due process, and standardized hiring practices than asking for tenure-track positions. Tenure is a scare word these days.

The fact remains that few part-timers in the humanities have tenure or access to tenure (a few of these unusual cases are described in the essays by Rae Goodell, Julie Klassen and Anne Ulmer, William Kerr, and Harold Kolenbrander in chs. 7 and 8). In California, part-time teachers in grades K through 12 have job security while part-time community college faculty don't. In places where laws have been passed giving rights to part-timers teaching over 60% of a full load, as in California (in the community colleges, at least), administrators are careful to make sure that no part-timers are given over 60% of a full load. The same process is often at work when good policies are passed at private institutions: if a policy suddenly states that "anyone teaching over 50% of a full load will receive benefits," all at once, like magic, no part-timers are teaching over 50% (see Werge's essay).

For a discussion of case law as it affects part-time faculty, see Figuli's essay, "Legal Issues in the Employment of Part-Time and Term-Contract Faculty" (ch. 9). A specific and crucial case for part-time faculty rights, the Peralta decision, is described by Robert Gabriner in "The Legal Battle for Part-Time Faculty Rights in California Community Colleges" (in ch. 5). Also, Leslie's chapter "Legal Aspects of Part-Time Faculty Employment" and Leslie and Head's article "Part-Time Faculty Rights" are particularly comprehensive and clear. These documents, however, suggest that few part-timers will win tenure, job security, or prorated pay through legal battles. Part-time faculty rights will come, if they come, not through the courts but through colleagues—through the serious interest of the profession to strengthen and affirm itself. Leslie and Head raise the issue in stronger language.

In legal terms, part-time faculty members are indeed the marginal persons of academic employment policy. Their rights have been carefully circumscribed in ways that seem to preserve administrative prerogative and the vested interests of full-time faculty. Only by passing through screens and over hurdles can the part-timer gain rights that bear some resemblance to those long enjoyed by the more entrenched denizens of the academic lair. Evidence suggests that only a small, persistent minority ever succeed. It is possible, of course, that few need or want the prerogatives of full professional partnership. But as a matter of conscience, the academic world might well ask itself how many part-timers are discouraged by the legal and administrative boobytraps that tangle and crush the legitimate aspirations of persons who make a genuine contribution to the intellectual enterprise. (66)

Collegiality, Governance, and Academic Unions

In one department of twelve part-timers and four full-timers at California State University, Los Angeles, the part-timers control hiring in the department since they all have the vote. According to a recent outside evaluation of the department, "the part-time faculty have a vested interest in not recruiting new permanent faculty since that would reduce the need for part-time instructors." The part-timers are paid an unusually high per-course salary of up to $3,200.

In 1982 these part-time faculty denied tenure to a full-timer who then successfully appealed the decision to a higher university committee. Six days later the newly tenured professor's car exploded. The chair of the department, on the evening before a meeting called to consider the dismissal of one of the part-timers, found his garage in flames. The fire melted his car and destroyed ten years of research, stored in boxes. When the department itself was set on fire a few months later, the chairperson began to attribute both fires (and the high incidence of broken windows in his home) to tensions between part-timers and full-timers at work. "The only phase of my life where there is conflict is at work. . . . Otherwise, my life is pretty dull. I don't have any vengeful ex-lovers or mad neighbors. My life is so dull that some people suspect I may be a Jesuit priest." Another full-timer, commenting on the rash of fires, brake-cable sabotage, slashed tires, and confrontations that have plagued the department, said, "I don't know what will happen next. . . . I didn't know being a professor was such a high-risk occupation" (Spiegel).

So you thought things were tense in your department?

Clearly, the situation described above is not the norm; it tends to point up, by contrast, the powerlessness of most part-timers in most departments. However, it also helps focus attention on a rarely discussed nightmare of full-time faculty and administrators: the nightmare of mistreated part-timers suddenly enfranchised and in the majority. Real concern exists about the shifts of power that would be occasioned by giving part-timers a faculty vote: not only could part-timers control departmental decisions if they outnumbered full-timers, but the balance of power between departments could be thrown off. A previously inconsequential department, when it came to major decisions in campuswide faculty meetings, could suddenly carry twice its normal weight if the votes of all its part-timers were counted.

Tensions between part-time and full-time faculty seldom are so openly expressed as they are in the example above, but they are nevertheless very real at institutions where part-timers and full-timers are treated differently in significant ways. The recurring complaint from part-timers is that they feel invisible, excluded, unappreciated, and unable to speak out for fear of losing their jobs.

What needs to be admitted from the outset is that full-time faculty are not villains. Instead, they are, these days, likely to be discouraged, overworked, and disillusioned; if they have serious research interests, they must fight to make time for them among other commitments. Collegiality is difficult to create and sustain under any conditions. Full-timers often don't see each other that much. Their getting together depends to a great extent on physical details like location of offices, class schedules, and days on campus. It also depends on more intangible factors like shared interests, ability and time to listen, and, unfortunately, equality.

The unpleasant truth is that many full-timers feel guilty about the treatment part-timers receive; they may not agree with it and may wish they could change it, but unconsciously they feel uncomfortable and guilty about it. It's human nature to want to avoid those who make one feel guilty; and often, the tendency is to relieve oneself of guilt by blaming the victim or by rationalizing that the victim deserves his or her treatment for some reason or another. As Cara Chell put it, it's hard to be a colleague to "someone you are eating alive" (38).

How justified is such a comment? Are full-time faculty eating part-timers alive? Certainly in the humanities there is more justification for such feelings than elsewhere. Part-time faculty realize that their lower-level required courses in composition and language instruction generate most of the enrollment in the department; thus the tuition that funds department programs is based on the teaching part-timers do for low per-course salaries. Meanwhile, senior professors teach upper-level literature courses that many part-timers long to teach; to intensify the injustice, the upper-level classes are often underenrolled, so that intimate groups of eight or nine students concentrate on Chaucer in one classroom while larger classes of twenty to thirty discuss writing problems in another. The student load (and thus the load of papers to read and evaluate) is far lower for the senior professor, who is paid perhaps two to four times as much per course as the part-timer. It's no wonder part-timers feel that they're subsidizing the literature courses in their departments.

On the other hand, full-timers feel they've paid their dues; they remember difficult days of teaching lower-level courses and struggling for tenure. They also feel that their time for research and reading is important. They may look on part-timers as scabs who demean the profession by teaching for low salaries and who thus make it possible for administrators to hire three or four part-timers to replace one full-timer. (Again, there are many hidden costs that are not acknowledged by this line of reasoning.) The evidence, however, is increasingly validating part-timers' claims that part-timers protect and underwrite full-time jobs. As institutions retrench, administrations are not tending to replace full-time with part-time faculty. Instead, part-timers are being let go first, having served as a buffer to protect full-time faculty positions. Although different kinds of institutions will react to hard times differently, on the whole "part-timers are evidently being sacrificed to protect and conserve the jobs of full-time faculty" (Leslie 90, 30).

In such institutional conflicts, department chairs may often find themselves under fire from three directions—part-timers blame them for low salaries and exclusion, full-timers blame them for giving in to the administration and hiring part-timers in the first place, and administrators warn them to cut costs somehow, either by hiring more part-timers or preferably by bringing their full-timers into line and persuading them to teach basic courses in writing and language. Borenstein's essay in chapter 6 describes the unsavory position of department head in this whole business, and Leslie's section on departmental ecology is also illuminating (93–111).

An issue that brings all these tensions to the surface is that of granting part-time faculty, or at least some of them, a faculty vote. AAUP recommends "erring on the side of inclusion rather than exclusion," but in some cases, as in the explosive department described above, the numbers of part-timers involved may make inclusion dangerous for the health (usually, it is to be hoped, only the political health) of full-time faculty. Even when few part-timers are involved, full-time faculty hesitate to enfranchise part-timers they assume to be transient and uncommitted.

A conversation with a colleague on this issue convinced me that part-timers, in asking for a voice in faculty affairs, are up against a vicious circle similar to the one that operates in matters of recruitment and hiring. "We can't give part-timers the vote," my friend said. "They aren't held accountable the way we are. They don't serve on committees, they don't have to come to faculty meetings, and they don't go through yearly evaluations."

"That's just the point," I argued. "They *should* do all those things."

He looked at me incredulously. "For the pittance we pay them?" he asked.

Thus the chance to speak out and improve working conditions, salaries, and fringe benefits is denied. And to further complicate matters, nonparticipation in governance is frequently cited as one reason part-timers are paid so much less than full-timers. The essays by Miller and Gemmill in chapters 6 and 7 show how exclusion from democratic processes hurts the part-timer committed to a career in college teaching. The vote has two great advantages as a first step in changing part-time faculty policy: it is both free and precious. While costing the institution little or nothing, it can make clear to part-time faculty that they are valued and trusted as colleagues.

Of course, it is not necessary to inflict faculty governance responsibilities on part-timers who don't want them. The Ohio study shows that, while only 19% of part-time faculty have a faculty vote, only 30% say they would like to have it; thus only 49% of the part-timers studied either have or want the vote (44). If categories of part-timers have been established, such categories can be used to determine who should be expected to attend faculty meetings and vote and who should not. Or part-timers can be allowed to make the choice themselves, depending on whether or not they want to commit some time to committee work and faculty governance. The vote can and should be tied to governance responsibility.

Many essays in this volume describe tensions between full-time and part-time faculty and their causes: Trimmer, Sherfick, and Miller movingly depict the slow growth of inequities and bitterness and the equally slow movement toward change. In contrast, Colwell recounts a situation where supportive relationships between full-timers and part-timers have been the norm. Clayton argues, as Colwell does, that the support of tenured faculty is essential to bring about changes in the treatment and integration of part-time faculty. Remarkably little tension between full-time and part-time faculty is reported in institutions where regular part-timers are paid pro-rated salaries and treated as equal colleagues. (See the essays by Goodell, Klassen and Ulmer, Kolenbrander, Kerr, Turner, and Marius.)

Issues of collegiality become even more pressing in the presence of academic unions. Gabriner's essay points out the mixed feelings part-timers have toward full-timers and toward belonging to the full-time faculty bargaining unit. Part-timers might have no voice at all if they were excluded from the union, yet within the union they often find their voices drowned out by louder, full-time ones. Over two thirds of the bargaining units in this country exclude part-time faculty; yet where bargaining units exist, part-timers are more likely to receive pro rata pay (30%, compared to 20% nationally—see Leslie 78). On the other hand, part-timers often see the bargaining unit as blocking progress toward part-time faculty rights (see Miller). Mulrooney's essay stresses the need for part-timers and full-timers to hang together yet acknowledges sources of conflict between them; for instance, some full-timers want to teach (as overloads) courses the part-timers feel they have a right to. Los Angeles Community College District has negotiated a contract that acknowledges seniority rights for part-timers and prevents indiscriminate full-time faculty bumping of part-timers.

Only thirty-one states allow collective bargaining units for faculty, and in twenty-five of those states, community of interest has to be determined to see if part-time faculty should belong to the union or not. Although the principle is essentially sound (i.e., workers without shared interests will run into impossible squabbles at contract negotiation time), the four bases of comparison that have been considered standard since the New York University case in 1973 often seem like self-fulfilling prophecies.

> No mutuality of interest exists between part-time and full-time faculty at NYU because of differences with respect to (1) compensation, (2) participation in University governance, (3) eligibility for tenure, and (4) working conditions. (Andes 11)

It doesn't take an overly bright administrator to figure out that, by these standards, paying part-timers poorly, denying them the vote, keeping them out of tenure-track positions, and generally supplying inequitable working conditions will probably prevent them from joining the union.

Leslie concludes that part-time faculty will probably turn increasingly to separate bargaining units; in his study, he mentions three: Rutgers, C. W. Post Center of Long Island University, and Nassau Community College, all near New York City. Another exists at York University in Toronto, where part-timers have been organized since 1975 and have won some significant benefits and privileges as a result. (Anyone wishing to study copies of particular bargaining-unit contracts can write to the National Center for the Study of Collective Bargaining in Higher Education at Baruch College, CUNY.)

At any individual institution, Leslie argues, probably some part-timers should be included in the full-time bargaining unit and some should not (65). At Kendall College in Illinois, for instance, the National Labor Relations Board found that part-timers with prorated salaries shared community of interest with full-time faculty, while course-contract part-time faculty did not (Andes 11). An extensive study has been done of English departments at two-year colleges with bargaining units to see what factors seem to determine whether part-timers are included in the bargaining unit or not; the resulting list of characteristics can discriminate with 88% accuracy whether a part-timer will be found to share community of interest with full-time faculty. If part-timers are notified of course assignments during the term preceding the assigned course (i.e., more than two weeks before the beginning of term), if part-timers are by written policy expected to receive preferential treatment when full-time positions come open, and if part-timers and full-timers are treated exactly the same in respect to tuition assistance for graduate work, tuition credit for themselves and their families, textbook selection, curricular development, selection of department chairs, voting in faculty meetings, and formal evaluation, they are much more likely to be included in the bargaining unit than not (Swofford).

However, inclusion in the bargaining unit is no guarantee of equality or fair treatment. And even where excellent contracts have been negotiated, with good provisions for part-time faculty rights, part-timers at the individual colleges covered by the contracts don't necessarily benefit from them. Further, creating faculty unions where none existed before cannot eliminate conflicts of long standing, and the organization of separate part-time and full-time bargaining units can serve to emphasize conflicts and differences. Yet Leslie's study of 258 bargaining-unit contracts led him to conclude that part-timers don't usually do very well in full-time units either, which always tend to protect full-time faculty first of all, to limit part-time faculty work loads, and to exclude part-timers from tenure. Faculty unions seem to be little different from most unions in their resistance to the idea of less-than-full-time work (Leslie 11, 59–66).

The complex problems of collegiality, governance, and union membership do not allow for general solutions. Part-timers vary significantly in their desire for inclusion in faculty affairs; political realities vary from department to department and from institution to institution. One might think that attempts at collegiality on the simplest level would stand the greatest chance of success; yet when one department in which I worked as a full-timer decided to give all part-timers a vote in department affairs and to invite them to the Tuesday afternoon departmental meetings and the informal teas that preceded the meetings, not one part-timer appeared. Several had left soon after their office hours ended, hurrying home to family responsibilities; others taught on Mondays, Wednesdays, and Fridays and weren't even on campus that day. Times that were convenient for full-time faculty weren't at all convenient for part-time faculty, even those who were eager to participate in department affairs.

But the offer still stands—as it should.

Note

[1] Donald E. Greive of Cuyahoga Community Coll., Parma, Ohio, has developed an in-service book, intended for use in part-time faculty orientation or faculty development programs: *Teaching in College: A Resource for Adjunct and Part-Time Faculty* (Cleveland: Info-Tec, 1983). Two other such handbooks are Jim Hammons et al., *Staff Development in the Community College: A Handbook*, Topical Paper no. 66 (Washington: National Inst. of Education, 1978; ERIC ED 154 887), and Phyllis B. Weichenthal et al., *Professional Development Handbook for Community College Part-Time Faculty Members* (Springfield, Ill.: State Office of Education, 1977; ERIC ED 156 288).

2. Women, Part-Time Teaching, and Affirmative Action

When Tuckman began to publish the results of his investigations into part-time faculty in 1978, we learned, contrary to some expectations, that most part-time faculty (61.3%) were male (Tuckman et al. 24). A closer investigation, however, was enlightening. For instance, Tuckman's largest and happiest category of part-time faculty, the "full-mooners" (moonlighters), were only 14.1% female. The next two largest categories—students (21.2% of all part-timers) and hopeful full-timers (16.6%)—were 48.5% and 52.6% female, respectively. Those holding down more than one part-time job (13.6%) were 31.6% female; those whose motives for teaching part-time were unknown (11.8%) were 39.3% female; and, not surprisingly, those choosing part-time teaching because of family responsibilities (6.4%) were overwhelmingly female (96.7%; Tuckman et al. 23–24).

Leslie's findings in the Virginia study pointed to 50% of all part-timers classifiable as moonlighters, with very few in the student category. (Both Tuckman and Leslie excluded teaching assistants; students were primarily those teaching part-time at one institution while finishing up their dissertations at another.) He also found more homeworkers than Tuckman did (10.6%). However, Leslie's sample included only 104 part-timers compared to Tuckman's 3,763 (see Leslie 40–41).

The 1981 Ohio study, based on a sample of 1,590 part-timers from a wide range of state and private four- and two-year institutions in Ohio, supplied information by discipline and by sex that the earlier studies did not. The findings seconded Tuckman's that moonlighters are predominantly male; among part-time faculty, "the majority of females (72%) either hold no other job at all, or hold only another part-time position, as compared to a small portion of male faculty members (22%) in that category" (Yang and Zak 28). When women do hold other jobs, they are more likely to be teachers at another educational institution than men are.

About 24% in the Ohio sample reported that they were currently looking for full-time jobs, but more than twice as many women (35%) as men (17%) were in that category (29). Over half the part-time faculty stated that they believed part-time teaching would improve their credentials and enhance their opportunities for future full-time positions (30); in the light of findings that part-time teaching jobs do not seem to lead to full-time teachings jobs, many of these part-timers seem headed for disillusionment, unless they seek careers outside academia. There, oddly enough, their teaching experience may be highly valued.

The Ohio study's ground-breaking research into job satisfaction took as a premise that "the differences between that segment who choose part-time academic employment and those unwillingly confined to it are immense and far reaching" (48). Yang and Zak isolated factors that proved significant in predicting job satisfaction. They found that a part-timer seeking full-time employment expressed more job dissatisfaction than others; part-timers in the arts and humanities were less satisfied than those in other fields; those for whom part-time teaching was their only job were less satisfied than those employed elsewhere; women teaching part-time were less satisfied than men; and married people teaching part-time were less satisfied than unmarried or separated people. Part-timers tended to be more satisfied with part-time teaching if they had other employment or if they were teaching part-time in business or education (49). Yang and Zak draw the following conclusions about their findings.

> . . . employment elsewhere is an important factor in part-time teaching satisfaction. Part-timers in academe tend to be highly educated and specialized, and employment on the limited basis provided by part-time positions is insufficient for job satisfaction unless the part-time teaching experience is perceived as enhancing opportunity for future full-time employment. (50)

In one of their case studies of a large state-assisted university, Yang and Zak found considerable uneasiness over the extensive hiring of part-time faculty to handle the teaching of writing. One administrator "worried that part-time teachers of writing are regarded as second-class citizens in the department: that his department, like other English departments, maintains 'an adamant attitude about writing being not quite the same sort of important activity as the teaching of literature;' that 'in good years, bad years, it doesn't matter, writing has been cheap labor.' " He also insisted that hiring patterns in English were sexist.

> It's a big sexist thing. They are frequently spouses, or single women who have done other things, sometimes keep doing other things, but piece out a little income with this. Single parents. The majority, the overwhelming majority are women. This is a very important sociological aspect of part-time faculty employment in English. (59)

Leslie's findings were similar in his case study of a four-year public college where large numbers of part-timers were used to teach freshman composition: "These are mostly women who do not hold full-time jobs elsewhere" (Leslie 107). Couple with these case studies the data on part-time employment by field in Ohio, which show that business and the humanities account for the highest numbers of part-timers, with English the single field using the most part-timers (see Yang and Zak, app. C, reproduced as table 2 on p. 10 in this volume). In the humanities, the second highest number of part-timers is concentrated in languages and linguistics (Yang and Zak 95).

In their conclusions, Yang and Zak give a full, separate paragraph to their concerns about part-timers in English:

> English is a field in which supply greatly exceeds demand at this point in time, and a field in which the great majority of part-timers so far are women. . . . What emerges is a field in which dependence on part-time faculty appears likely to continue or to increase; in which there is a probability that women in part-time ranks will continue to outnumber women in full-time positions; and one in which there will likely continue to be many persons qualified for full-time academic positions who are unable to find satisfactory alternative employment and for whom no full-time faculty employment is available. All this suggests that the interests of the profession and the employing institutions would be well served by special efforts to create system and equity in part-time hiring in this field. Solutions that have been suggested range from creation of a special category of permanent faculty—perhaps as instructors—with or without tenure, to priority consideration of continuing part-timers for full-time positions when they open. (63)

All this research serves to confirm what anyone having taught part-time in an English department figured out long ago: that part-time teaching in English (and frequently also in foreign languages) is primarily a women's issue. That impression is certainly sustained by the essays in this volume by Sherfick and Trimmer, Dow and Chell, Erlich, Brody, Gemmill, and Miller. The crucial questions depend, however, on whether women choose to teach part-time or not. What can be done to accommodate the needs of women who prefer part-time teaching while their children are small? What, if anything, can be done to protect the rights of women who desire full-time teaching but can only find part-time positions?

Let's examine the first of those two questions by asking how many women prefer part-time to full-time work. Leslie assumes that a significant number do, at least for certain periods in their professional lives.

> . . . numerous studies . . . emphasize the importance of part-time work to the development of women's academic careers. Women are increasingly entering the academic labor market as full participants, and as professionals committed to a long-term academic career. For many, a cruel price is imposed upon them should they choose to pursue at the same time, anything resembling a normal family life. The availability of part-time work opportunities at certain stages in their lives can be taken presumptively as important to women academics. (13)

Goodell's and Tamm's essays in this volume make an eloquent case for balancing part-time academic careers and a normal family life.

Leslie, however, warns against carrying this line of thinking too far: "It is probably dangerous to assume that women in academe prefer part-time positions to a full-time, thoroughly committed pursuit of a professional career. In fact, it may be that women would prefer to have some options for flexible work scheduling, but that to assume part-time positions would be an adequate outlet for women probably does not do justice to the serious aspirations many have" (13). Thus, options currently in force for professional women at universities like Wesleyan (see Kerr's essay in ch. 8) and Yale would seem ideal, allowing for full-faculty status at a reduced teaching load while leaving open the option of a transition to full-time teaching. And it's no accident that the policies at Yale and Wesleyan were framed by professional women or that, according to my data on innovative policies for regular part-time faculty (see ch. 4), women's colleges—like Bryn Mawr, Smith, Wellesley, Mt. Holyoke, and Hood—have some of the best part-time-faculty policies around.

Yang and Zak found that only 15% of the women part-timers in their sample listed family responsibilities as their primary reason for teaching part-time; however, that amounts to fifteen times as many women as men choosing part-time teaching as a way of balancing career and home. Noting women's dissatisfaction with part-time teaching, Yang and Zak challenged the assumption that women preferred part-time to full-time work (50). The evidence, however, also suggests that because part-time teaching is usually their only job, women feel their second-class status much more keenly than moonlighting faculty do; many might still prefer part-time teaching if it were fully professional. (The essays by Goodell, Klassen and Ulmer, and Tamm support such a conclusion.)

In fact, the interest of both men and women in part-time professional careers is increasing. A study of undergraduates at Barnard, Brown, Dartmouth, Princeton, SUNY at Stony Brook, and Wellesley (*Men and Women Learning Together: A Study of College Students in the Late 70's* 102, 276–77) reveals that while 96% of Brown women plan to work, 86% of them (and 96% of Brown men!) feel women should not work at all or should work only part-time while their children are under age two; for children ages two to five, the percentages shifted only slightly (74% women and 83% men). In academia, at least, either dropping out of the profession for a few years or teaching part-time could have damaging effects on these women's careers. Joanne Kantrowitz puts the matter trenchantly:

> The system can allow for any number of variations, such as military service, research leave, "community service," alcoholism, divorce, sexual promiscuity, serious physical or mental illness, but never marriage or motherhood: no maternity leave, no schedules adjusted to child-rearing needs, and so on. The "solution" for such "female trouble" is part-time, temporary status. (17)

Outside of academia, the picture for part-time careers may not be so bleak. The Association of Part-Time Professionals actively supports government workers, lawyers, doctors, writers, and teachers in their attempts to find or create professional part-time positions. They develop bibliographical tools for employers and employees experimenting with flexible work patterns (see Levin, and Cook and Rothberg). Their findings are that almost one fourth of all working women prefer part-time work as compared to only 7% of working men (APTP, "Competition"); in a membership survey of the Washington chapter of APTP (80% of whose members are women), parental responsibilities were listed as the single most important factor in the preference for part-time work.

Changing work roles in American society have led to developments like the Federal Employees Part-Time Career Employment Act of 1978, which called for agencies to set aside part-time positions that could become career civil-service jobs. The act recognized the great increase in chosen part-time employment and in numbers of working women since World War II (Leslie 9). The record of the 1977 hearings before the Subcommittee on Employee Ethics and Utilization, *Part-Time Employment and Flexible Work Hours*, documents the considerations that led to passage of the act.

Business and industry have also been experimenting with flexible career patterns and work schedules, discovering that such changes can lead to reduced absenteeism and improved morale and productivity. The authority in this area is Stanley D. Nollen of Georgetown University, School of Business Administration: his recent book, *New Work Schedules in Practice: Managing Time in a Changing Society*, builds on his 1977 study with Eddy and Martin, *Permanent Part-Time Employment: The Manager's Perspective*. Also worth attention in this area are recent publications by the Work in America Institute, particularly *New Work Schedules for a Changing Society* (Rosow).

Thus considerable evidence suggests that men and women are increasingly interested in part-time careers; women in particular find part-time work attractive as a way of balancing work and family obligations, at least during certain periods in their lives. There is nothing unprofessional about preferring part-time work; there is also nothing to suggest that those who choose such work enjoy or deserve being relegated to second-class status and insecurity as a result.

Allowing, then, that women in academia may prefer part-time teaching at certain stages in their careers (Goodell's proposed study on flexible work patterns at MIT should shed further light on this subject), we must go on to ask the second question mentioned above: how can we protect the rights of professional women who want full-time careers in college teaching and instead are being limited to part-time or insecure jobs? The evidence suggests that not only does a tendency exist "to appoint women more frequently to marginal, 'soft-line,' irregular, nonladder, part-time, exceptional, temporary, or fringe positions" (Robinson 2) but women suffer from salary discrimination when they serve in such positions (Tuckman and Tuckman).

In fact, the one legal loophole for female part-time faculty may be through affirmative action lawsuits; it is illegal for an institution to channel women into part-time, low-status positions. If it can be proved that women are systematically appointed at part-time and lower ranks at a particular institution, especially if their credentials and their duties are similar to those of full-time men in the same field, and if it can be proved that their part-time status prevents their earning equitable wages, fringe benefits, and job security, then a strong legal case may exist. In addition, in cases of sex discrimination, equal protection standards can be used to evaluate individual cases, comparing, for instance, the work load, credentials, and salary of a full-time man to those of a part-time woman. As Leslie suggests,

"It would be a difficult problem if John Doe were a new instructor, with a master's degree, who had only teaching duties, and if Jane Smith were an ABD, with 17 years' service and a substantial record of committee service, student advising, and publication" (Leslie et al. 54; see also 55–56). In fact, several sex discrimination cases have ruled in favor of part-time women faculty claiming back pay and regular, tenure-track appointments (*Lamphere v. Brown University* and *Rajender v. University of Minnesota*—see Yang and Zak 61).

In the light of such affirmative action cases, Coffinberger and Matthews' suggestion that institutions use part-time positions as a way of adding women and minorities to their faculties seems remarkably naive. Overrepresentation of women and minorities in part-time positions and underrepresentation of them in full-time positions, particularly if part-timers are underpaid and their work closely resembles the work of full-time colleagues, could lead directly to lawsuits.

And yet, what are the alternatives? Coffinberger and Matthews seem genuinely to want more women and blacks represented on college faculties and recognize that chances for full-time appointments are decreasing almost monthly in this decade. The only legally safe option for bringing large numbers of women and minorities into college teaching through part-time careers would seem to be the creation of part-time positions with full faculty status, pro rata pay, and fringe benefits, like those described in the essays by Goodell, Kerr, Kolenbrander, Turner, and Klassen and Ulmer. (Other institutions with such regular part-time positions are mentioned in ch. 4.) Only if part-time faculty have duties and obligations clearly different from those of full-time faculty, an unlikely situation in English or foreign language departments, is an institution on safe ground hiring lots of women and minorities in low-paying, insecure part-time positions.

The alternative is, of course, to hire women and minorities only into full-time, tenure-track positions, or to create alternative paraprofessional career positions for them. Not only does the current state of affairs in higher education make a proliferation of full-time, tenure-track positions unlikely, but the fact remains that some women, at least, prefer part-time teaching—with full-faculty status.

One final issue that should be considered is the impact of geographical factors on women in the academic job market. I discussed earlier the damaging effect that careless recruitment and hiring procedures can have on part-timers hired into a particular department; the assumption that someone hired from a local pool is automatically inferior to someone hired from a national pool is hard to break. Leslie makes this assumption repeatedly (53, 73), as does at least one administrator included in this volume.

Yet what are talented men and women to do about this assumption when they follow their spouses to new locations and begin to look for work? Traditionally, such disruption of one's work life has been a woman's problem, although more and more men may be facing it if they follow their wives' careers. In the Ohio study, however, none of the male part-timers mentioned geographical restrictions as the chief factor in their taking a part-time job; 4.6% of the women part-timers did (Yang and Zak 27). Women academics may find themselves forced to leave tenured, full-time positions behind if they follow their husbands to new locations; Miller's essay (ch. 6) is particularly good on the strains of moving from full-time to part-time teaching and on the damaging assumption that one is less talented simply because one teaches part-time or is limited to a particular geographical area in one's search for work. Gemmill's essay (ch. 7) is also a moving description of a part-timer's restriction, because of husband and children, to a limited geographical area over a long period of time.

A source of both joy and discouragement to another such long-term half-timer, tied to one section of the country for many years and thus to one institution, is seeing students once inspired by her teaching return, after years in graduate school, to take up full-time, tenure-track positions at their alma mater at starting salaries more than twice her own present income. One can't help wondering why, after fifteen to twenty years of loyal, even inspired service, a ripe Ph.D. can't be valued at least equally to a green one fresh from far away.

And why should the Rhodes scholar down the street never be as attractive as the new Ph.D. from Berkeley, who flies cross-country for an interview? Such assumptions can affect both men and women, as is clear in Suzanne and Joseph Juhasz' essay in *Careers and Couples: An Academic Question*. Meeting and marrying as equals, as many graduate students do, Suzanne and Joseph soon discovered that his full-time position in psychology at Bucknell left her stranded and denigrated as a "faculty wife." Unable, after several years of trying, to find suitable work in a limited geographical area, Suzanne finally applied for and took a full-time position in English in Boulder, Colorado. Joseph left his thriving career behind and even turned down a job offer from Berkeley in order to follow his wife, confident that someone with his qualifications, experience, and publications could find good work anywhere. The reality of casual interviews, lack of interest, and prejudice against a man in his position startled him.

> My own reaction toward myself was increased confusion, resentment toward Suzanne, and inability to work. Despite my paper qualifications, I had become a pariah—people could not even articulate their own derision at my unmasculine "role change." They knew that there had to be something wrong with an accomplished professional searching for a job in a limited area, with a man who would compromise his career for his wife's, but they did not have a ready word for his condition. . . . My personal contacts with Suzanne's colleagues were very disturbing. Used to being the center of intellectual attention, I found it inexplicable and disturbing that people paid little attention to what I said. (20–21)

Clearly, Joseph Juhasz's case is not the norm for men. But it is for women, and such discrimination against those caught in a local market can destroy careers.

In conclusion, part-time academic employment in the humanities and particularly in English is clearly a women's issue. While women ought not to be channeled only into part-time careers, "part-time work (with full rights and obligations) is often the only route to an academic career for those whose aspirations are thwarted by tight markets and family obligations" (Leslie 60). Such family obligations and the geographical restrictions that often accompany them have for too long been quickly equated with unprofessionalism; as more academics acknowledge the obligation of married men to share equal responsibilities for the care of their children— and equal displacement when their wives find jobs in other geographical locations—these assumptions will surely change. Meanwhile, though, another vicious circle will remain for many. The professor's wife first has to *find* a full-time job so that her husband can follow her to it.

3. Part-Time Faculty and the Teaching of Writing—Full-Time Faculty and the Commitment to Fundamental Literacy

Among the three general fields using the most part-timers—business, the humanities, and the arts—"English, particularly the teaching of writing, represents the greatest number of part-timers," according to Yang and Zak. "Accounting and music, the fields with the next greatest number of part-timers, each represents about a third fewer part-time faculty than English" (63). What implications does this finding have for the status of the profession?

Lest we think that such figures hold only in Ohio, we should note that Leslie's findings confirm that part-time faculty are used most in business, the arts, and the humanities. And in terms of undergraduate credit hours, when we talk about the humanities, we are primarily talking about English. (See fig. 1.)

Leslie's case studies of individual institutions also illustrate this tendency to use part-timers heavily in English departments for the teaching of writing, except that large, private universities seemed to use teaching assistants instead of part-timers (19–20, 104, 107, 114–15, 119).

Although Leslie comments on the heavy use of part-timers in English departments, his primary focus remains the moonlighting part-timer, as is clear from his repeated assumption that part-time faculty usually have no responsibilities beyond the classroom. This leads one to conjecture that Leslie has never taught freshman composition! Significantly, in a 145-page book on part-time faculty, he doesn't use the word "English" until page 95 and never explores the crucial differences between part-timers teaching business and those teaching English, French, German, and Spanish—or history, philosophy, and religion. To repeat the dichotomy set forward in my introduction, part-time business faculty are usually men moonlighting from another career; humanities part-timers are usually without full-time jobs elsewhere (unless they are teachers in nearby high schools or colleges), are more committed to a career in college teaching, and—in English departments, at least—are usually women.

The previous chapter dealt with implications of such findings for affirmative action; many essays in this volume also deal with the implications for English and foreign languages as disciplines. We might assume from the evidence that many full-time faculty in English and foreign languages don't believe in the importance of fundamental language study; at least, they don't feel it's important enough to commit time to it themselves.

The refusal of many full-time faculty to involve themselves in problems of freshman literacy seems to be more extreme in English than in foreign languages, although, as Borenstein's essay (ch. 6) makes clear, a problem in valuing basic language acquisition exists in modern language departments as well. Borenstein's sobering reflections point out how the gradual devaluation of part-timers teaching lower-level courses spreads to the devaluation of foreign language instruction at all levels. Where he once had the chance to hire part-timers to replace full-timers on sabbatical, now no replacements are offered. Where he once staffed exotic languages with part-time staff, now the administration suggests that one can do just as well without Russian, Japanese, Chinese, or Italian. He links the part-time-faculty problem closely to the failure of our culture to value language facility in its citizens.

Alan Clayton, describing plans to strengthen the program in language instruction at Tufts, feels that senior faculty in modern languages are more appreciative of the work done by part-time faculty in foreign languages than English faculty are of the work done by their teachers of composition, because senior faculty in French or German simply cannot teach upper-level courses in literature if the fundamental language training has not been done well. Part-timers in modern languages, therefore, must be integrated into the majors' program and understand its purposes, or the whole enterprise falls apart.

Figure 1: Undergraduate Student Credit Hours in Four Humanities Fields by Level of Instruction and Field of Study

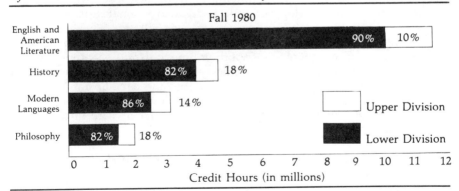

Source: Atelsek and Anderson, *Undergraduate Student Credit Hours* 10. Reprinted by permission of the Higher Education Panel, ACE, Washington.

In many English departments, however, the teaching of fundamental literacy and the teaching of literature are segregated activities. Indeed, one major attitude of English full-timers is that teachers of composition are the garbage men and women of higher education. Geoffrey Weinman quotes a full-timer from a 1976 *College English* article:

> Freshman composition is an elementary course, one readily taught by teaching "interns" . . . ; it is dubious that the best interests of the department are served by . . . requiring . . . highly experienced members to expend their energies in this manner. (Weinman 25; taken from "Who's Minding Freshman English at U.T. Austin?" *College English* 38 [Oct. 1976]: 127)

One could hope that such attitudes had changed by now, but Yang and Zak, interviewing English department chairs and full-timers in Ohio, discovered otherwise. They found the opinion that tenured faculty should teach some writing courses, but not too many "lest the important humanistic charge of the discipline be lost," causing "destructive change in the humanities orientation of the department, in the study and teaching of literature" (55, 58). There was "an adamant attitude about writing being not quite the same sort of important activity as the teaching of literature"; one reason for not setting up a permanent relationship between the institution and teachers of comp was that "composition instructors 'burn out' after a period of teaching all, or nearly all, composition courses" (59, 55). While agreeing that such a situation involved inequities, one administrator reflected, "the world is full of inequities, and I think that this is one more case of the thing. I don't think that you can change it" (56).

One obvious way of eliminating inequities is to create full-time positions in the teaching of writing, but that idea met with resistance from senior English faculty: "should full-time positions in regular faculty ranks be created in this department for an instructional component that is not within what members of the profession consider the mainstream of the profession?" (58). Yet the idea of creating full-time positions outside the regular faculty ranks led an administrator to protest, "we will not have second-class citizens in departments; if an instructional area is basic to English, it has to be taught by English faculty" (59).

In other words, comp is not central to the discipline of English, because full-time faculty don't devote most of their time to it, and part-timers won't be given full-time positions because they teach something that is not central to the discipline of English. Sherfick describes the circular nature of this dilemma in chapter 6: the teaching of writing is devalued as schoolmarmish because primarily women teach it, and women faculty are undervalued because they teach writing.

Another aspect of the problem is that many part-timers long to teach literature and thus seem to devalue their own work. Yet they were trained in literature and feel increasingly swamped by freshman themes. Especially abrupt is the drop from being the cherished, talented graduate student, showing so much promise (and, besides that, filling up the dwindling graduate courses that senior faculty most love to teach), to being the invisible case of burnout whose speciality is never needed or acknowledged. Dow and Chell (ch. 8) show how the frustrated aspirations of the Ph.D. in literature figure into the part-time problem, while emphasizing that the teaching of writing needs to be made an attractive career if it's going to be done well by talented people.

Of course, as Wendell Harris points out in chapter 6, society has never been willing to pay for careful writing instruction; or, as Maxine Hairston puts it, the public isn't upset if English teachers are poorly paid; in fact, the present situation not only saves administrators money, it satisfies the public's desire to have writing taught cheaply so that salaries for expensive computer instructors can be squeezed into the budget. Even the vested interests of full-time English faculty are well served (even if only in the short-term), since part-timers doing the dirty work allow full-timers the luxury of teaching specialized literature courses. All in all, the teaching-assistant and part-time-faculty system works better than anyone has a right to expect, depending as it does on the talents of energetic and devoted young scholars before they leave the profession or the talents of more experienced ones who have decided to stick with it.

The opinion is strong among some, however, that part-timers themselves are responsible for lowering the status of the teaching of writing, perhaps precisely because they do stick with it and accept such demeaning conditions. Marius, for instance, has no patience for the whining tone of writing teachers who feel they are undervalued by literature professors; Hairston, too, counsels that people who act like professionals doing important work get treated like professionals. Both suggest that publication is the way to earn respect and admiration from full-time colleagues and to legitimate one's work; publication might also be a means of escape into a full-time, tenure-track, and thus validated, position.

Happily, the attitude that teaching composition is grub work may be on the way out. Talented and energetic professors of rhetoric, publishing their research on the teaching of writing, are discovering that much can be learned about successful and not so successful methods of teaching composition and that, as Booth puts it, "nothing in the world is more interesting than the question of how to transform those confused and semi-literate freshman souls into alert, curious, and effective writers" (38).

In the midst of such important and necessary attempts to upgrade the field of rhetoric—or, perhaps, return it to its rightful place—part-time faculty may again find themselves on the periphery. Their years of experience in the classroom, instead of being recognized as a source for writing pedagogy, may instead be ignored in favor of new Ph.D.'s earned in rhetoric and technical writing. Ideas to create positions for full-time paraprofessionals may anger those who rightly want nothing less than full citizenship in English departments for their research, publication, and teaching in the field of rhetoric. Long-term part-time teachers of composition who want to keep their jobs dare not ignore the recommendations of the report of the MLA Commission on the Future of the Profession—that "promotion and tenure committees give scholarship in composition theory and pedagogy as much respect as they do literary scholarship" and "that faculty explore the research methods and theories involved in the teaching of writing, participate in regional institutes and seminars, and familiarize themselves with recent developments in composition theory, research, and practice" (951).

Important questions must be asked about the real qualifications for teaching writing and about developing first-rate writing programs, able to win the respect of academic colleagues.

One definite trend seems to be toward separate writing departments or programs with distinct structures apart from English departments. Some of these programs have emphasized writing across the curriculum: a full-time writing program staff train colleagues from other departments to teach rhetoric. Surely, English departments have no exclusive right to writing skills, and all departments have a vested interest in training undergraduates to think and write clearly and persuasively.

Among the essays in this volume that describe separate writing programs, one—by historian Richard Marius at Harvard—focuses on practice as the primary credential for teachers of writing, that is, teachers of writing should write and publish. By enforcing this one requirement, Marius has succeeded in winning respect from Harvard colleagues for the professional writers he hires part-time into his program.

Two other essays describing separate writing programs—by Trimmer and Sherfick and by Erlich and Brody—emphasize and value teaching experience as a credential in teaching composition, but not teaching alone. Dennis Szilak points out that "the teaching of composition has become a highly refined skill . . . that is learned almost entirely by diagnostic practice rather than advanced study. . . . The Ph.D. is usually not required nor encouraged among teachers of writing" (26).

Szilak wrote that, however, in 1977. As the essays about Ball State and Ithaca College show, winning respect for a writing program and for the teaching of writing as an academic discipline has depended to a large extent on either the professional development of existing teachers (at Ball State, many of the women part-timers went on to earn their doctorates, to deliver papers at professional meetings, and to publish, after years of teaching) or on the hiring of highly qualified Ph.D.'s in rhetoric. (At Ithaca, national job searches were conducted to staff the writing program, but the job description was carefully worded not only to attract Ph.D.'s in rhetoric but to show that long experience in teaching composition would also be valued; thus several long-term part-timers at Ithaca were hired for some of the newly defined full-time positions.)

Both institutions have found that giving a writing program the status it deserves within an institution can depend on issues in staffing and that, important as years of classroom experience are in the teaching of composition, full-time colleagues tend to lack respect for a writing program until its personnel have credentials and/or publications equal or superior to their own. Erlich's realism on this score is instructive: he warns that part-time faculty ignore the realities of the marketplace at their peril; that if they don't develop professionally, they may lose their jobs; and that the standards of rhetoric instruction are on the rise—and it is important that this be so. Both Ball State and Ithaca College, by the way, remind us of the great debt we owe the Council of Writing Program Administrators in their work to improve the teaching of writing in English departments and in separate writing programs across the country.

Two further essays in this volume stress that teaching writing is noble and backbreaking work and that experience in teaching writing should be valued more highly than it is. Werge points out what cannot be said too often: composition teachers are usually part-time in name only, often working harder and longer than full-timers in other fields and working at peak concentration as well. (It is impossible to judge how a whole essay or research paper hangs together, to examine its structure or question its transitions from one section to another, without energetic and focused attention.) Colwell records the successful efforts of his English department to adjust the loads of those teaching writing because of their extraordinary levels of paper processing. (Donald McQuade, in "Integrating Part-Time and Short-Term Faculty into English Departments," reports on a similarly successful effort at Queens College, CUNY, to make composition courses count five teaching hours.) Such a move has the double advantage of ensuring that part-time faculty will be paid more for teaching writing courses and of attracting senior faculty to teach them (since they would then be able to adjust their total course load).

All these efforts to strengthen writing programs and to make clear that we value the long experience, dedication, and skill of those who teach writing are more than laudatory; they are essential to the future of the profession and the preservation of cultural literacy. In the long run, only such insistence on excellence in writing programs and in the training of those who staff them will make a permanent change in the status of the full-timers and the part-timers who teach composition. In the short run, there may be some very real suffering. The long-term part-time teacher of composition may find less and less job security as more Ph.D.'s in rhetoric and/or technical writing (from programs like those at Rensselaer Polytechnic Institute, Carnegie-Mellon University, and Indiana University of Pennsylvania) move into the market looking for teaching jobs. There may not be much of a threat at the moment since such Ph.D.'s are in demand now in business and industry; in fact, a spokesperson for IBM at a 1982 ADE summer seminar at RPI said that the ideal future employee will combine backgrounds in English and computer science. Business, trying to educate the public about computers, has discovered that it is easier to teach a writer how to program than it is to teach a programmer how to write. (Is this news to any teacher of composition?)

If any humanities graduate program seems healthy in this decade, it is the M.A. and Ph.D. program in technical writing. Full-time, tenure-track job opportunities actually exist for Ph.D.'s in rhetoric and technical writing; institutions advertising for such openings find that few adequately qualified candidates apply. It's probably no accident that the only tenure-track, full-faculty-status, regular part-time teacher of writing represented in this volume is Rae Goodell, who teaches science writing. Further, graduate programs in technical writing are discovering that there is financial support for what they are doing: possibilities for cooperative programs with business and industry are many, and graduate students are flocking to such programs.

However, if such degree programs in technical writing evolve out of and/or maintain their contacts with traditional English departments, tensions will develop over the question "How far have the humanities sold their soul in buying into this new venture?" The attitude that writing ought not to be taught separately from literature, that the best writing is taught by those who also love and teach literature, and that the best literature courses are taught by those who love and teach writing has lost none of its appeal. It describes, for most of us I think, the best of all possible worlds.

Wayne Booth, in "A Cheap, Efficient, Challenging, Sure-Fire and Obvious Device for Combatting the Major Scandal in Higher Education Today" (the major scandal being the "intellectual, economic, and social abuse of part-time faculty," 35), describes a weekly seminar in which he participated during his first year of teaching—part-time—at the University of Chicago College. In that seminar, beginning teachers of comp shared problems and classroom techniques with senior literature scholars; discussions about grading essays led to discussions about ethics or philosophies of teaching: "What we were being offered," Booth says, was "a superior kind of liberal education: a sustained and intense conversation about the arts of reading and thinking and writing, and about how to teach those arts" (37). Booth believes that freshman teaching is "the single most important task any of us faces" and that "in the teaching of how to write, there can be as much intellectual challenge and excitement as in the most recondite subject we know" (39, 38). He further asserts that

> you can tell whether a college is serious about teaching its students at any level simply by looking closely at how many freshmen are taught by part-time faculty members who have had no training and who have no stake in the future of the institution and its programs, no sense of how their work relates to anything else the college is doing, no long-range prospect of full-time or permanent appointment, and thus little reason to think that what they do matters to anyone. (36)

Thus, the belief that writing is at the heart of the curriculum, that therefore the situation of part-time faculty in English affects the entire institution, and that "any college that takes seriously the problem of how to teach writing will become intellectually alive, and any college that is intellectually alive will automatically train and integrate its part-time faculty" (Booth 38), all leads to an aversion to separating the teaching of writing totally from its roots in the liberal arts and literature in particular.

One danger in creating separate writing programs is that writing teachers might never have the refreshment of teaching a literature course, and literature faculty might never face the challenge of teaching writing. Establishing separate full-time, even tenure-track, positions for paraprofessionals in the teaching of writing would mean essentially the same thing—full salary and benefits but never the chance to teach even introduction to literature or English literature survey.

Why is it important that teachers of writing also teach literature and that teachers of literature struggle to write and to teach writing? Why should the teaching of technical writing be complicated, in the positive sense, by a study of literature and of current issues in critical theory and interpretation; and why should teachers of literature, from specialists in Anglo-Saxon to deconstructionist critics, have to struggle with the demands for clarity characteristic of teachers of technical writing?

These questions were heatedly debated by English department chairs during the 1982 ADE summer seminar at Rensselaer Polytechnic Institute. Morse Peckham presented the essence of the conflict succinctly: technical writers believe in the straightforward, clean adaptability of words to experience, while our greatest works of literature are a testimony to the difficulty of using language to describe experience at all. Peckham argued that our country's decision makers need to realize the inadequacy of language to meet, describe, and analyze reality and that we are all in danger if they do not. They need to understand how our finest writers have stretched and extended the powers of language; they also need to understand the disruptive power of literature and its ability to increase the flexibility and adaptability of our words. The technical writing assumption that composition is a direct translation of reality into words, a simple equation, needs to be contradicted by the findings of a T. S. Eliot:

> Words strain,
> Crack and sometimes break, under the burden,
> Under the tension, slip, slide, perish,
> Decay with imprecision, will not stay in place,
> Will not stay still.

What Peckham decries (Booth and Hairston do so elsewhere) is that English departments alone have the chance to teach this aspect of the unreality and the fascination of language to a captive audience of all college students, to the future power centers of our society, but they blow it, year after year.

Clearly, the tension that Peckham describes is an important one that needs nurturing and sustaining. We need our literature scholars and critics to be writing, struggling to adapt language to experience with clarity and simplicity, and to be teaching writing; we need our teachers of writing, particularly technical writing, to struggle with great works of literature and to teach literature. We need to keep this tense balancing act going, while insisting on the place of rhetoric at the heart of the curriculum.

Yet this balance will be lost, and no one will ever believe that writing is at the heart of any institution's curriculum if the only people who teach it are insecure, underpaid, part-time faculty who are never allowed near a literature course—unless, perhaps, they want to pay to take it. Failing to maintain such a balance inevitably results in weakening the teaching of both writing and literature.

Another dimension of the composition-literature split should be considered. English departments may feel uncomfortable for many reasons if technical writing programs continue to flourish and if business moves into closer and closer alliances with them to make sure that the kind of training businesses now need is being provided. Such healthy programs may end up underwriting the expense of upper-level literature courses and simultaneously having a major influence on departmental decisions on curriculum and personnel. Literary scholars could find themselves on the periphery, while rhetoric professors—running handsomely funded programs in technical writing for large corporations—control the pursestrings. Not the least of the reasons for discomfort would be the sense of having sold out, of having lost the moral distance English and the humanities in general have always kept from the business world and its practices. One full-time English professor, debating these issues during the ADE seminar at RPI, bemoaned the fact that graduates of degree programs in technical writing would move too easily into the business world without that sense of moral reservation that academia ought to maintain toward business ethics. His comment gave me pause.

The usual working conditions of part-time humanities faculty, as described in this volume, don't allow for stereotypical contrasts between cutthroat business people and ethical humanists. We may have lost whatever moral superiority we thought we had, without even realizing it. It seems to me unlikely that the first instinct of a part-time teacher of composition who decided to leave academia for a career in technical writing with IBM or Xerox or Bell, who was all at once being treated with respect, whose considerable talents and energies were suddenly being valued and rewarded, and who was for the first time in his or her professional life being paid a decent living wage and supplied with reasonable fringe benefits—it seemed unlikely to me that his or her first instinct would be to challenge or criticize the morality of the *business* world.

Figure 2: Percentage of Institutions Reporting Faculty Eligibility for Sabbaticals, by Faculty Classification

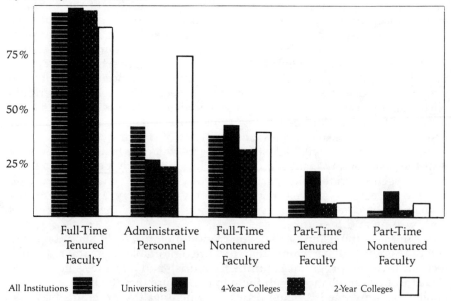

Source: Anderson and Atelsek, *Sabbatical and Research Leaves* 11. Reprinted by permission of the Higher Education Panel, ACE, Washington.

4. Innovative Policies for Regular Part-Time Faculty

There are expensive and inexpensive ways to improve the lot of part-time faculty and simultaneously strengthen the quality of educational programs; both are simple to describe. The inexpensive method is to treat part-time faculty exactly like full-time faculty in every respect, except to pay them a low per-course fee and refuse to contribute any funds toward their fringe-benefit costs. The expensive method is the same as the above with two differences: pay part-timers a strictly prorated salary based on the salary a full-timer with their credentials and experience would be paid and provide full or prorated fringe benefits for them.

During 1981 and 1982, I collected data on colleges and universities that had developed innovative part-time-faculty policies. If a part-timer, a department chair, or an administrator can point to institutions treating part-timers more professionally in terms of salaries, job security, and fringe benefits, he or she can more easily convince others to change existing policies or develop new ones—or, at least, such is my hope.

As I stated in the introduction, I made no attempt to be comprehensive. Thus, I have not found every good part-time-faculty policy in higher education, but I have tried to follow every lead to an unusual policy and have pestered many weary administrators to provide data.

Most innovative policies for regular part-timers seem to come from private colleges and universities. While a few of the respondents were reacting to the part-time-faculty situation by eliminating all part-time faculty positions, most found that such positions (if accompanied by fair pay, fringe benefits, acceptable levels of job security, possibilities for advancement, and full-faculty status) enriched and diversified their faculties and provided flexibility for teachers at various stages in their careers. Experimentation with such flexible career patterns seemed to contribute to the quality of the faculty and to have a positive effect on morale.

Out of eighteen state colleges and universities, only six responded with usable information. Two more deserve mention, although the data I received applied only to one department or program and therefore couldn't be applied to the institution as a whole. First, the University of Maryland uses a good number of part-time faculty in its Junior Composition Program (approximately fifty), and those teaching over 50% of a full load (approximately fifteen) receive all fringe benefits, including full medical coverage. Second, in the Department of Foreign Languages at SUNY, New Paltz, two of the five part-time faculty are paid prorated salaries (see Borenstein's essay on SUNY, New Paltz, ch. 6). Several other state universities sent xeroxed pages from benefit booklets or faculty handbooks instead of filling in the provided data sheets: in some cases, I was able to extract enough concrete information to include that institution on the data sheets (University of Michigan); in other cases, there were simply too many gaps. Some institutions, state or private, sent information only on fringe benefits or, conversely, only on additional academic responsibilities. Instead of ignoring such data, I have tried to use what I could, even if the entries on the data sheets are thus incomplete.

Community Colleges

Out of thirty-six community colleges questioned, only three are presented, although many more responded to my request. The difficulty was that few of them distinguished among types of part-time faculty or provided information on fringe benefits or prorated salaries. Community colleges seem to be laboring under severe financial constraints coupled with commitments to open admissions and therefore last-minute unpredictable registrations. In spite of such pressures, however, admirable and energetic work is being done on faculty development and orientation, on more careful interviewing and hiring (establishing a qualified pool of part-time teachers well before the last minute), and on full-time and part-time faculty interaction.

Perhaps because there is less discrepancy at the community college level between the credentials that define full-timers and part-timers, often less tension exists between full- and part-time faculty. Part-timers may be serving on semester-long contracts, but since many full-timers are serving on yearly contracts, community college part-timers often seem to feel more secure than their four-year-college counterparts. Further, more mobility to full-time positions seems to exist for community college part-timers, and their prior service to the community college is often seen as an advantage when they apply there for a full-time teaching job.

Many community colleges sent me copies of their part-time-faculty handbooks; the best of these gave some teaching tips and guidance on dealing with adult learners. None of them, however, mentioned prorated pay or fringe benefits. Some sent me statements on salary scale—how much part-timers were paid per contact hour. Still others sent letters saying they had no written part-time policies.

When a community college did provide fringe benefits, the usual item mentioned was access to the retirement plan. Solano Community College is fairly typical in this regard. Monroe Community College in Rochester, New York, allows part-time faculty to participate in the retirement plan at their own expense. Evelyn Claxton found that two Illinois community colleges—Black Hawk and Lincoln Trail—allowed part-timers teaching more than half-time to participate in the retirement plan if they chose. Occasionally, leaves of absence (without salary) for child rearing were available for part-timers.

Some community colleges sent copies of union contracts. One of these, "Agreement by and between the Board of Trustees of Whatcom Community College, District No. 21, and Whatcom Community College Federation of Teachers, September 14, 1981–August 31, 1983," provided interesting information. Part-time teachers of composition were paid more per in-class contact hour than other faculty: $27.60 compared to the usual $22.08 for all other courses, if their composition courses enrolled at three quarters or more of the enrollment limit. Teachers were also paid $11.15 per hour for out-of-class duties such as keeping office hours, serving on college committees, working on curriculum or program development, or course coordination (11). Further, part-timers were encouraged to attend department meetings; "a guiding principle is that those affected by a policy or procedure should have a voice in the development of that policy/procedure" (16). However, the grim realities of part-time insecurity were made clear in the section on reduction in force: in case of layoffs, part-time faculty were the first to go (35).

Frequently, the data from community colleges were discouraging. One chair of a language and communications department responded to my request for innovative part-time-faculty policies by painstakingly filling in the data sheet with a "no" in every slot except possible committee work and attendance at faculty meetings. Then, under "hiring/firing/evaluating" in column 18, he added a note: "Evaluations more frequent than full-time. Hiring/firing at discretion of division chair. Firing is really a misnomer; unsatisfactory part-timers simply aren't invited back." What he describes is certainly a reality, but a reality considerably more troubling if it is perceived as innovative policy in certain quarters.

More heartening was information from Monroe Community College in Rochester, New York, that the Department of English passed a resolution in the fall of 1981 allowing the chair to appoint an adjunct as a nonvoting member of the department's advisory committee, the only elected committee in the department. This adjunct committee member, while expected to represent adjunct concerns, is privy to and may discuss any issue that comes before the committee.

Such efforts to improve part-time-faculty involvement in governance and to build channels of clear communication between part-timers and full-time faculty and staff are crucial. Anne Agee in her essay in chapter 5 discusses her own role as liaison between part-time and full-time faculty members; she also emphasizes the difference that small details—like desks, telephones, coatracks, and bookshelves—can make. The essays by Colwell and Mulrooney are also encouraging on what can be done at the community college level. An important collection of essays and studies on part-time faculty in community colleges is *Using Part-Time Faculty Effectively*, edited by Michael Parsons; it concentrates on the community college situation in a way I am unable to do here.

Let me emphasize that the data on the Community College of Denver and on St. Clair County Community College are quite unusual because of the attempt at both institutions to define a category of regular part-timer. At Denver, the regular part-timer is entitled to due process while other part-timers are not. In two years of research, I have found no other community colleges attempting to distinguish categories of more permanent part-timers and to pay those part-timers prorated salaries.

Summary of Research Findings

The data sheets presented in table 6 (see pp. 162–64) are enriched and balanced by the essays in this volume, particularly when an institution is represented in both places. The complexities of the part-time-faculty problem are such that a simple reading of the data sheets can be misleading. Further, data from some institutions reflect current practice rather than written policy; some reported that they were in the process of formulating or changing policy. Others (like the University of Tennessee) submitted drafts of policy: in these cases, the data sheets indicate the provisional nature of the information. Figures and effective policies reported on the data sheets reflect the situation at these institutions in 1981–82.

Leslie's definition of a part-time position is operative here: "any appointment for which there is less than a normal range of assigned duties, and the terms of employment recognize the fractional involvement of the worker" (1). Graduate students or teaching assistants employed at the institution where they were simultaneously working on a degree were not included in this study.

The first three columns in the table allow the institution to define types of part-timers. Column 1 gives the number of part-time faculty of any category; column 2 asks how many of those are paid prorated salaries; and column 3 supplies the minimum, average, or maximum teaching load and often the criteria for benefits. In a few cases, institutions paying no prorated salaries to part-timers were included because they defined a group of part-timers who received fringe benefits or other unusual academic benefits or responsibilities. Data in all subsequent columns refer to only those part-timers eligible for benefits.

Some schools defined regular part-timers by length of service (Tennessee), others by proportion of teaching load (Yale and Carleton, for instance). Occasionally, regular part-timers were defined by their rank or their credentials or by their level of commitment to college teaching (at Central College, full-time employment elsewhere disqualified one as a regular part-timer). At some colleges and universities, a regular part-timer was defined by some combination of these four criteria.

Administrators should note how seldom an institution treats all part-timers exactly alike. To imitate these policies, one would not need to pay all part-timers prorated salaries and prorated fringe-benefit contributions. Institutions have clear needs for moonlighting part-time faculty, those who share a special expertise that the college or university could never afford full-time; a need also exists for occasional temporary part-timers in cases of emergency or as replacements of full-time faculty on leave. Neither moonlighting nor temporary part-time faculty are usually included in the regular part-time category.

My research suggests that part-timers in English and foreign languages are seldom included in regular part-time categories either; of the institutions on my data sheets, only Carleton and Ball State have regular part-timers in the modern languages as far as I know. Three other institutions not on my data sheets sent me information about part-timers in their modern language departments: SUNY at New Paltz, mentioned above; Reed College, which has one part-timer in modern languages who is paid a prorated salary; and Dartmouth, where part-timers in the English department who teach more than half-time receive pension and medical benefits, plus a per-course fee slightly over one fifth of a full salary (the prorated amount) because they don't qualify for certain extras like travel funds to attend conferences.

Columns 4 through 8 reflect the extra responsibilities that accompany prorated pay and prorated fringe benefits. The expected involvement of regular part-time faculty in a full range of faculty duties lightens the administrative burden on full-time faculty and ensures that part-time faculty are more engaged in college activities, curriculum development, and faculty governance. The resulting increased understanding of the institution, its goals, and its needs has an immediate impact on part-time faculty, their courses, and their students. For some institutions, the faculty vote seemed like a logical and inexpensive first step in involving part-time faculty as colleagues; for some other institutions, the faculty vote was the last frontier, a precious prerogative reserved only for the tenured or nearly tenured. In either case, part-timers are more likely to receive the vote if it is tied to responsible involvement in college governance.

Columns 9 through 11 deal with academic benefits for which part-time faculty might qualify, the rarest one being tenure. However, as the data show, there are quite a few institutions where it is possible for a part-timer to have or to earn tenure: American, Bryn Mawr, Carleton, Central, Columbia, Cornell, Dickinson, Grinnell, Harvard, Mt. Holyoke, Notre Dame, Oberlin, Princeton, St. John's, Smith, Stanford, Wellesley, Wesleyan, Wisconsin, and Yale. Goodell's essay in chapter 8 adds MIT to that list, and the AAUP ("The Status of Part-Time Faculty" 33) also mentions Colgate, Rutgers, and UCLA.

In allowing part-timers to advance toward tenure, some schools extend the probationary period proportionately, that is, if one teaches half-time, one waits for a tenure decision twice as long. Other institutions keep to the AAUP guideline of seven years (if an institution did not specify whether the wait for a tenure decision was extended or not, the box was simply marked "yes" if tenure was available to part-timers). Each alternative has advantages and disadvantages; Goodell, part-time on tenure track at MIT, raises the question of how many years the peculiar strain of waiting for a tenure decision should be prolonged.

A significant number of regular part-time positions allow, not for tenure accrual, but instead for renewable contracts of from one to four years. Some professional status is lost when tenure is not a possibility; generally, sabbaticals depend on one's being tenured, although other faculty leaves might not (see fig. 2 on p. 46). For instance, leaves without pay but with guarantees of reemployment ought to be available to regular part-timers as they are to full-time faculty (see Tamm's essay).

However, there are distinct advantages to part-time faculty of staying off the tenure track, particularly if geographical limitations figure in their search for teaching jobs. Smith College has spelled out those advantages with useful clarity. (At Smith, regular part-time appointments are nationally advertised and are tenure-track; emergency or occasional part-time appointments are not.)

> To the teacher, appointments of this kind offer the modest benefit of small, temporary jobs as opposed to no job at all in the Northampton area. More important, perhaps, such appointments enable a competent individual to teach in the Department repeatedly for an unlimited number of years without having to compete with candidates from all over the country and undergoing the stress and uncertainty of coming up for tenure. Persons who come up for and are denied tenure at Smith can never teach there again. In other words, appointments of this kind are attractive to persons who cannot deal with intense professional competition, who will not or cannot leave the Northampton area, and who do not need full-time paid work. (Smith College 2–3)

This document from Smith makes very clear the choices that a temporary part-time faculty member may have to make and prevents misunderstandings and complaints of injustice later on. It also raises an interesting question about the willingness of part-time faculty to undergo tenure decisions; at Wesleyan, where tenure-track part-time positions have been available since 1974, a part-timer has yet to take up the tenure-track option. Particularly where part-timers are limited geographically in their search for jobs they will be unwilling to box themselves into an in-or-out situation, even at the expense of professional status. Yet other part-timers jump at the chance to prove themselves as full colleagues through rigorous tenure review.

A related issue is the debate over full-time terminal appointments versus continuing part-time appointments. An administrator interviewed in one of the Ohio case studies commented that the faculty feel "it is very cruel to bring people into the institution on three-year appointments with no possibility for tenure nor for continuation on any basis beyond that time." He felt, however, that the faculty were mistaken, "for in the long run such an appointment is more equitable for the faculty member and for the students who need the faculty to be around and available" (Yang and Zak 56). But how "around and available" can such a faculty member be when he or she is constantly preparing job applications and traveling to interviews? Having talked with some of these peripatetic academics, a year here, two years there, I tend to agree with Harris that the pressure such teachers work under is too great (see his essay in ch. 6); always lurking in consciousness is the realization that this may be one's last year in the profession. The alternatives may not be perfect—regular part-time or renewable one-year full-time contracts—but they are preferable, and Harris is convincing on the moral imperative to fight for what one can get, even if one can't get everything.

One further word should be said about the data on tenure-track part-time positions; it is impossible to tell from the data how many of these tenure-track part-timers are full-time faculty teaching reduced loads temporarily and how many are actually hired as part-timers on to tenure track. Additionally, just because the possibility of tenure exists for part-time faculty at a particular institution doesn't mean that any part-timers have earned or are earning it. Frequently good written policies are used to keep part-time faculty from getting into certain categories (i.e., if one has to be half-time to earn benefits, one's class schedule might be kept scrupulously below half-time). Thus, studying institutional policies can be tricky, and one should not jump to conclusions based on printed policy alone.

Columns 12 through 17 cover fringe benefits available to part-time faculty; in general, a positive answer here implies some contribution from the institution toward the cost of the benefit. Some institutions have been more specific than others and made clear that their contributions are either full or prorated; except for tuition credit and medical coverage, prorated contributions are probably the norm since most benefits are based on a proportion of one's salary.

The greatest variation existed on answers to tuition credit and medical coverage. Several institutions felt that each employee needed full medical coverage regardless of his or her income and thus paid the full share (Central, Cornell, Dickinson, Oberlin, Wellesley, Wheaton), particularly if the part-timer taught half-time or more; others paid a proportion of the share they paid in for full-timers. Still others allowed part-timers to participate in the group plan, but at their own expense, a practice that nevertheless amounts to a significant savings on medical insurance for the part-timer.

Tuition credit seems to be more acceptable to the institution if it involves no exchange of funds, that is, if it applies to tuition at the home institution only. I suspect that most of the "yes" answers belong in this category. Tuition credit can easily be prorated: for each course taught, a free course can accumulate for the part-timer or anyone in that part-timer's immediate family. For long-term part-timers in particular, this can be a significant benefit; the absence of it can be a cause of bitterness, as in the case of one part-timer who had taught on and off for thirty years at a college to which she could never afford to send even one of her children.

Unemployment compensation has been omitted since it depends to some extent on the laws of a particular state; in some states, colleges are required to cover part-time faculty and in others they are not. Some colleges have found that they risk high unemployment compensation payments if they hire part-timers who don't have full-time jobs elsewhere, and so avoid such part-timers if at all possible.

A final note on fringe benefits—occasionally an insurance company may prohibit part-time faculty from a particular plan. (The disability plan at Yale is an example.) If the company in question cannot be persuaded to include part-timers at a reasonable additional cost, the only alternative is to change companies, an expensive and time-consuming process. However, usually insurance companies don't care if part-timers join a group plan or not; part-timers simply widen the pool of risk (and increase the payments coming in to the insurance company).

The last three columns, 18, 19, and 20, cover job security and advancement possibilities. Often where no tenure is possible for regular part-timers, regularized hiring and evaluating, a clear sense of a possible move to full-time teaching, and renewable yearly contracts (or even two- or three-year contracts) give greater job security than most part-timers experience. Those who replied that hiring, firing, and evaluating were the same as for full-time faculty presumably meant what they said, that hiring was not casual or last minute but done after formal advertisement, search, and interview; that part-timers went through formal evaluations like those of full-timers; and that part-timers had rights to due process and grievance procedures in case of brusque dismissal. The Community College of Denver, in fact, solely distinguished its "regular" part-time faculty from its "limited" part-time faculty by the access of "regular" part-timers to due process in case of dismissal.

Usually, transitions to full-time appointments are easiest where regular part-time faculty are in tenure-track positions; such transitions are often described as "by mutual agreement." In most other cases, mobility to full-time employment is described as "possible"—but then, it is also possible that England will reestablish the empire and perhaps even reclaim its American colonies.

The final column on contracts includes either time limits on service (up to a tenure decision, perhaps, or an arbitrary limit set on years of part-time teaching) or possible length of renewable contracts. Unless a particular limit is stated beyond which a nontenured faculty member cannot teach, it should be assumed that the contracts described are indefinitely renewable. One interesting option was the three-year rolling contract at University of Wisconsin at Madison; after three one-year contracts, lecturers were eligible for continuous contracts. If their contract was not to be renewed, notice had to be given by the end of the first year in a three-year period, thus giving them two years' notice. If notice was not given, the contract was assumed to be extended another year. A lecturer would therefore have a continuous three-year contract with a minimum of two years' notice of dismissal (see Faculty Document 113, 11 Sept. 1972, " Guidelines for Making Appointments of Lecturers").

The research justifies a few general conclusions. First, such innovative policies for part-time faculty seem most likely at large private institutions of national reputation or at smaller private liberal arts colleges. The reasons for this are probably primarily financial, these schools being free of yearly state and local government budget hearings and strong enough economically to support ideas of justice with action (i.e., prorated salaries and benefits). However, in the case of institutions of national standing, one suspects that there is a certain independent stature that permits experimentation. Such colleges and universities define excellence in American higher education; they feel secure in their abilities to recognize, reward, and nurture talent. Also significant is the intimacy of the small residential college, where the injustices of continuing part-time employment are obvious to everyone and thus less tolerable. Anonymity can more easily lock part-timers into peripheral, low-status positions on huge state university campuses.

Second, where part-time faculty closely resemble full-time faculty in terms of degrees, experience, publications, interests, and commitment to the institution, innovative policies are more likely to evolve.

Third, such policies are more probable at schools where full-timers have validated part-time teaching by occasionally going on reduced teaching loads: the policies at Yale and at Wesleyan grew out of proposals for full-timers to experiment with flexible career patterns at certain stages in their lives. At Dartmouth, senior faculty have taken reduced teaching loads in order to write. At Johns Hopkins (as at an increasing number of colleges and universities), reduced teaching loads have been offered as a way of "gradual and graceful withdrawal from full-time work" (Leslie 13). Such part-time positions have always been respectable for senior scholars; by association, they begin to seem respectable for junior scholars as well.

Fourth, the hope seems slim for prorated salaries and benefits for part-timers at state colleges, universities, and community colleges. The financial dependence on the state and the large numbers of part-time faculty, particularly in community colleges, make the necessary financial outlay unlikely. Only if community colleges carefully differentiate between those teaching general education courses (those with academic backgrounds and commitments to careers in college teaching) and those teaching in other fields will they be able to convince administrators that the cost of prorating regular part-time-faculty salaries would be limited rather than astronomical. It seems as if progress in state and locally funded higher education will come on other fronts.

Finally, the innovative part-time policies described in the data are remarkably similar overall. The guiding principle is to treat qualified part-time faculty as much like full-time faculty as possible, seeing such experiments with flexible career patterns as beneficial to the teaching profession as a whole.

Strategies for Change

Administrators, department chairs, full-time faculty, and part-time faculty might find the following guidelines useful as they consider working for changes in part-time-faculty policy.

1. Be realistic about the extreme fiscal pressures under which administrators are laboring in this decade. The numbers of college-age students are dropping yearly, and institutions are scrambling for students. It is not reasonable to expect colleges and universities to find a stray hundred thousand to pay some part-time faculty prorated salaries; it is reasonable to expect that administrators will be sensitive to issues of program quality since such issues could have a direct impact on student enrollment. Emphasize the benefits for students of having more involved and committed part-time faculty in the classroom. Under this guideline can be listed a number of inexpensive possibilities for treating part-time faculty more professionally. Timothy Dykstra, Geoffrey Weinman, and Anne Agee (see her essay in ch. 5) have all made excellent suggestions about what can be done for part-time faculty, even under severe financial constraints.

   a. An important beginning could be made by standardizing part-time-faculty hiring. Advertise part-time positions, conduct formal interviews in which most full- and part-time faculty are involved. Particularly in writing programs, it makes sense for the part-timers teaching the comp courses to help select, train, and evaluate their colleagues (see Weinman 24).

   b. Involve part-time faculty fully in departmental governance; give them a vote in department meetings, and work to enfranchise them in campuswide faculty meetings. The campaign for a part-time-faculty vote is more likely to meet with success if numbers of part-time faculty are small; if part-timers outnumber full-timers, it might be wise to develop categories of part-timers and petition for only regular part-timers to have governance responsibilities.

   c. Ask that clear policies be formulated, written down, and shared with all faculty and staff. Such policies should work to define categories of part-time faculty and their duties and privileges.

   d. Ask for more careful planning of courses and staffing, for a clearer distinction among genuinely temporary, emergency, and more long-term continuing needs. Colleges and universities without access to computer-simulation facilities for long-range planning ought to consider the expenses of last-minute confusion and bad planning and weigh those against costs of installing a computerized data base.

   e. Tenure is a scare word and should be avoided, but issues of basic job security and academic freedom should not. Ask for access to grievance procedures for part-time faculty; suggest longer contracts for part-timers (yearly if they now are contracted semester by semester; two- or three-year renewable contracts if they are now limited to annual ones). Ask that part-timers receive notification of reappointment or nonreappointment earlier in the year. Ask why long-term part-timers who have served the institution for five, ten, even fifteen years should automatically have to bear the brunt of retrenchment and why recently hired full-timers should not? Can regular part-timers be given some seniority rights in case RIFs (reductions in force) are necessary?

   f. If fringe-benefit contributions are out of the question, ask that part-time faculty be allowed access to group plans at their own expense. Such a move will rarely cost the institution a penny but will result in considerable savings for a part-time faculty member over individual policies.

   g. If prorated salaries are an impossibility, work to have particularly difficult courses defined differently, that is, freshman comp can easily be defined as a four- or five-hour course instead of three because of the inordinate amount of paper processing (see McQuade, Colwell, Whatcom Community College Agreement). Insist that out-of-classroom responsibilities, like student conferences or committee work, be paid for fairly if part-timers are paid by the course or especially by the class contact hour. Also urge that part-time faculty be paid a cut fee for new courses they prepared to teach that were canceled at the last minute.

h. Ask that a full-time faculty member in each department using part-time faculty in any quantity be given some released time to serve as coordinator of adjunct faculty. Such a person should be available when part-timers are on campus to give advice, hear their complaints, and help them locate necessary supplies and equipment; this person could also serve as mentor, evaluator, and representative of part-time-faculty concerns if part-timers themselves did not have a faculty vote. Such a person could also organize an advisory committee of part-time faculty and make sure that clear communication lines exist among part-timers, the department, and the administration.

i. Encourage professional development among part-time faculty; if no funds are provided for part-timers to attend conferences, full-timers could forgo a conference or two to enable some part-time faculty to present or hear papers (see Weinman 24). Search out grant opportunities for part-time faculty, especially if college faculty grants are not available to them. For instance, NEH has worked out a way for part-time and short-term faculty to apply for fellowships for independent study and research; if a part-timer designates himself or herself as "unaffiliated," checks in Block E "exempt from nomination," and writes after his or her title "terminating contract," that part-timer will not need the nomination of his or her home institution in order to apply. Establish a distinguished-teaching award for part-time faculty to encourage and recognize excellence in teaching (see the Council of Writing Program Administrators, "Statement about the Use of Part-Time and Temporary Faculty in College and University English Departments").

The remaining guidelines are less involved.

2. Work for opportunities for full-time faculty to teach reduced loads at certain stages in their careers, for personal or professional reasons. Not only is such flexibility good for faculty creativity and morale, but the resulting validation of part-time-teaching benefits part-time-faculty status as well.

3. Encourage the institution to deal with different part-timers differently. The national studies on part-time faculty give ample justification for such a procedure. Part-time-faculty needs and qualifications vary considerably, and to treat all part-timers exactly alike results in severe injustice for some.

4. Educate oneself and one's colleagues about the legal realities and about union resistance to the idea of professional part-time work. Enlist the aid of full-time colleagues in efforts to change part-time-faculty policy; part-timers are too vulnerable to carry the burden alone and will make little headway without the support of full-time, tenured faculty. Don't assume that full-timers understand part-time working conditions or complaints; they may have been too busy to notice.

5. Don't underestimate the power of the printed page. It may be that national publicity can do more for part-time faculty than all the legal battles or bargaining units in the world. Cara Chell, upon publishing her story about part-time teaching in *College English,* expected to lose her job. Instead, the department secretary put xeroxed copies of the article in every full-time faculty member's mailbox, and part-time policies have been improving in that department ever since. The role of accrediting bodies has not been used fully enough yet; not only can comments in college guides bring action (Dow and Chell mention the effect that Fiske's comments on the overuse of part-time faculty may have had on one institution), but professional organizations like MLA or WPA could do more to draw national attention to offending departments or institutions. (See Leslie 68–71, for a fuller discussion of accreditation and part-time faculty employment.)

6. Be on the lookout for data on the use of part-time professionals in government and business and the resulting benefits in terms of efficiency, productivity, morale, and a wider pool of available expertise. Academia can't stand to be stodgier than government or business.

7. Don't spend an undue amount of time and energy trying to organize all part-timers at one institution. Many part-timers with full-time jobs elsewhere have to fit their teaching obligations into very carefully circumscribed times and places; they can't attend meetings, and if they do, they won't want the same things most regular part-timers want or need. Other part-timers may feel that they lack credentials to compete equally with more qualified part-timers; they will resist any attempt to regularize hiring practices if personal contact and familiarity are their chief recommendations. Higher standards will frighten them, although they might be happier with higher pay. More highly qualified part-timers may not see eye to eye on priorities; those who have benefit coverage elsewhere, perhaps through a spouse's full-time employment, will press for higher salaries but not for fringe benefits. Those without benefits or seniority will care more about job security and fringes than will others. Time wasted trying to get all these different part-timers to agree on one thing is probably better spent persuading administrators to do what will most benefit the institution in the long run—increase the quality of the part-time professoriate.

8. Seek support from national organizations such as the Association of Part-Time Professionals or the National Job Sharing Network. There are part-time lawyers, doctors, civil servants, editors, writers—professionals of all sorts—who share information and expertise on creating professional part-time positions.

9. Stress that regular part-timers take on additional responsibilities in return for prorated salaries and benefits, thus lightening the administrative work load on full-time faculty and increasing faculty productivity in terms of committee work and publications.

10. Whenever possible, strive for prorated salaries and fringe benefits for regular part-time faculty. Such equity removes financial incentives to replace full-time positions with several part-time positions. It also increases the commitment of the part-timer to the institution and makes clear to everyone in the academic community that a part-timer's work is highly valued.

11. If tenure-track positions for regular part-timers seem impossible or even undesirable, work for three-year renewable contracts; encourage institutions to reconsider blind adherence to AAUP tenure rules (see Union

College in New York, and Erlich, Werge, and Clayton's stories in this volume) if such rules are standing in the way of continuing employment for talented professionals, part-time or full-time.

12. Realize that altruism does not impress administrators nearly as much as issues of institutional quality do. Focus on student benefits and excellence in teaching and argue that, for a superior academic program, there are only three legitimate uses of part-time faculty on a continuing basis.

a. True adjuncts, moonlighting from another career, who bring to the program unusual expertise that the college could never afford full-time.

b. Regular part-timers, equal to full-time faculty in terms of credentials, experience, preparation, commitment, and expectation, paid prorated salaries, supplied with prorated or full fringe benefits, and given full-faculty status.

c. Paraprofessionals: here we fail miserably compared to other professions like law and medicine. We have paraprofessionals, but we don't train or support them adequately, pay them a decent living wage, or give them reasonable access to fringe benefits. Especially in the modern languages, we give the message to society that not even English and foreign language professors value the teaching of basic literacy; rather, we benefit from our belief in teachers of basic language courses as a cheap commodity. In so doing, we undercut our own work and the profession as a whole.

A Postscript for Part-Time Faculty

Nothing would please me more than to hear that excellent policies for regular part-timers were being developed in one institution after another. But I would be sadly neglecting the demographic realities if I didn't mention one further alternative.

This past summer, after eight years of banging my head against the wall, I left the profession. I took a graduate course in computer programming and a faculty workshop on computers. Then I invested my last few paychecks in a second-hand microcomputer and printer. I learned how to use WordStar well enough to word-process a résumé and landed a job at summer's end as an educational associate for a computer company.

I find that all my experience in academia is valued and necessary. I learn more about computers every day, more than enough to keep me challenged and interested. I set up class schedules, hire instructors, and teach classes (even one at the local community college, which makes me a moonlighting part-timer). However, I no longer stay up all night grading freshman themes; I come home in the evening to read—a balance of books on computers and books by or about George Eliot or D. H. Lawrence. I have more time than I did before for my own writing, and I have good professional and personal reasons to stay in touch with my old friends in the academy. I am continually flabbergasted at how easily I made this transition.

The computer field is only one out of many in which my part-time colleagues could easily outshine the competition. I want them to realize how incredibly bright, capable, and flexible they are and how highly their abilities to write, speak, and teach would be valued in the business world: as my boss said when he interviewed me, a look of astonishment on his face, "I guess you wouldn't be afraid to teach a class to a bunch of teachers, would you?" Programmers say that English and foreign language teachers take to computer languages much more quickly than many scientists do. Businesses need writers to bridge the gap between computer freaks who can't speak English and the hordes of the computer illiterate that do. Technical writing, computer-literacy classes, word-processing classes, innovative composition or language acquisition programs using computers— part-time faculty in the humanities can forge their own positions.

Certainly, summers off are nice. But so are evenings off all year round. So are a decent salary, fringe benefits, job security, and—if you so desire— part-time career opportunities with dignity. If you must have the academic life, consider the severe shortage of computer-literate faculty and the growing need to staff basic computer courses.

There is, of course, a hitch. Sooner or later you'll be teaching your fifth class on a particular word-processing program, and you'll realize you're not picking up anything new in the manual any longer; it's not like rereading *Othello* and trying to teach it for the fifth time. And sooner or later you'll feel the pain of old longings; perhaps you'll stumble into Wayne Booth's presidential address at MLA and weep for a quarter of an hour afterward, because he reminded you why you wanted to teach literature, to spend a lifetime dwelling in it, in the first place. And every time you think about his devotion to bringing freshmen to a critical understanding of a great literary work, a part of you will want to go back to teaching English part-time, no matter how low the status or the pay.

Another part of you will be more matter-of-fact and will agree with the Eastwood coal miner's son who saw no honor in being a pauper: "It is only decent that every man should have enough and a little to spare, and every self-respecting man will see he gets it."

There are clear choices to be made, but the tensions will never fade; if they do, a part of oneself is lost with them. Nothing matters more than the glory of language, its assured preservation, its honor, its beauty, and the excellence with which it is created, studied, understood, taught, and extended. And nothing matters more than the human lives devoted to the service of language, their preservation, their honor, their beauty, and the excellence with which they are trained, understood, supported, and extended.

It may be that in this decade we can't have both. Either choice is honorable: to sacrifice oneself in the service of the profession or to sacrifice the profession to preserve oneself. It may also be true that both the honor of the profession and the honor of its professors will be best served by abandonment: that is, part-time faculty will be paid fairly and treated with respect for the important work they do only when they are in short supply—because so many of them have found other ways in which their love for teaching, reading, and writing and their considerable talents can be fully used, developed, and appreciated. Perhaps then their dignity will dignify their first love—the study of language and literature.

PART TWO:

Case Studies:
A Sourcebook for Just Policy

5. COMMUNITY COLLEGES

Shadow into Sunshine:
Integrating Part-Time Faculty

Anne Scrivener Agee
Anne Arundel Community College

If your community college is like most, it is probably haunted. Mysterious wraiths appear in your classrooms and wander your halls. These phantoms, invisible to your regular faculty, teach about a third of the sections at your college, and, for their labors, they are consigned to a shadowy underworld of low pay, little job security, and nonexistent fringe benefits. The name of these unwearying shades of academe? The part-time faculty.

Suffering from a notable lack of orphic heroes, Anne Arundel Community College, the suburban Maryland institution where I have taught since 1971, has not yet resolved the large questions of economic justice for adjunct faculty members. The pay, a graduated scale based on academic credentials and teaching experience, never goes above $1,000 for a three-credit course. Fringe benefits consist of a faculty parking sticker and a pass for the college swimming pool.

While Anne Arundel's compensation system for adjuncts leaves room for improvement, it is also true that money is not the only reward for teaching or for any other job. Psychic rewards—a feeling of importance, recognition of a job well done, a sense of community—can be just as crucial as salary in determining job satisfaction and are just as frequently denied to adjunct faculty members. In this area of nonfinancial rewards, Anne Arundel's English Division can easily serve as a model for other community colleges.

In 1979–80 Anne Arundel employed 197 full-time faculty and 210 part-time faculty to teach just under 5,000 full-time-equivalent students. Adjuncts, hired on a semester-by-semester basis, staffed 437 sections that year, approximately 22% of the college's offerings in the fall and spring semesters. In semesters since then, the percentage has grown slightly but remains under one third of the total.

The English Division, where I am the coordinator of adjunct faculty, is one of the largest employers of adjuncts, hiring from 15 to 30 a semester. The adjuncts teach from 15 to 50 classes, roughly 20% of the division's offerings in a semester.

The presence of a coordinator of adjunct faculty is probably the most visible sign that the English Division values its adjuncts. The coordinator, who is not the division chair, receives released time from teaching to handle the hiring, scheduling, orientation, and evaluation of adjuncts. The coordinator's continuing and personal contact establishes an important kind of psychic reward for adjuncts, a sense of belonging.

While functioning as a resource person on college and division policies, instructional questions, and the like, the coordinator introduces adjuncts to their colleagues, full-time and part-time, and to appropriate support staff and administrators. Such introductions provide an easy entrée into the network of professional relationships at the college, releasing adjuncts from the nonentity status in which they might otherwise languish.

Providing written support material to adjuncts also facilitates their integration into the department. As part of the divisional orientation process, the coordinator provides such material as

- copies of all texts and instructors' manuals
- sample syllabi, tests, and writing assignments
- copies of division guidelines for courses
- information on instructional resources such as the library, tutoring center, and media center
- information on college academic policies
- copies of the academic calendar and exam schedule

This written material, besides communicating practical information, enables the adjuncts to absorb more quickly the professional standards and expectations of the division. Like knowing the people they work with, knowing what is expected of them increases the adjuncts' sense of being an important part of the work of the college rather than isolated individuals acting on their own.

Moving beyond the written guidelines, the coordinator sets up informal workshops or discussion sessions on various aspects of teaching, such as approaches to fiction or evaluation of student papers. Since there is an almost constant flow of new teachers into the division, these workshops help establish a sense of community among the adjunct faculty. In addition, because many of the adjuncts have been away from academics for some time or have taught only at secondary schools, the workshops provide an opportunity to sharpen or revise teaching strategies for the college level.

Another important way the English Division recognizes adjuncts' needs is by providing office space. As recently as two years ago, adjunct faculty trudged the halls laden with books, papers, coats, coffee mugs, and other impedimentia, waiting for their classrooms to be vacated. They held conferences with students on the stairs of the humanities building or in the cafeteria. In the face of such demeaning conditions, it would take a strong ego indeed to remain convinced of one's inherent worth as a teacher.

The division has now set aside a large office with three desks for the use of adjunct faculty. This space allows them to hold conferences in some degree of privacy and to enjoy the simple pleasures of a telephone, a coatrack, and bookshelves. The coordinator of adjunct faculty has an adjacent office and is thus easily accessible.

One of the reasons that a large, shared office for adjuncts can work is the scheduling policy of the English Division. Adjuncts are not isolated into little "ghettos" in the evening and off-campus sections. Therefore, it is unusual to have more than three adjuncts needing office space at the same time.

But besides being convenient for office-management purposes, the placement of adjuncts throughout the division's schedule means that they have greater opportunity for contact with the full-time faculty and greater access to the instructional and administrative resources of the college. In addition, such scheduling gives the coordinator greater flexibility in honoring the adjuncts' preferences for teaching assignments.

Also, because full-time faculty regularly teach evening and off-campus classes, the college has more incentive to provide support services in the evening and, to a lesser degree, at off-campus centers.

Although these policies benefit the adjunct faculty, the benefits are not the secret to their successful implementation. An abstraction like justice for adjunct faculty members appeals very little to pragmatic college administrators. What moves their souls, and occasionally their checkbooks, is an argument based on benefits for students, an increasingly large number of whom are being taught by adjunct faculty.

What kind of education can students expect from a teacher who has had no guidance from the division as to the objectives of the course? How seriously can a student take a hurried conference on a crowded stairway? If part-timers are the only ones who teach evening sections, why shouldn't students assume that evening classes are strictly second-class education?

Questions like these can move a college administration to action much faster than complaints about unfair treatment of adjuncts. In the administrative view, adjuncts come and go; students are forever. When students no longer believe that a college can serve their needs, the college dies. The key, then, to any improvement in the situation of adjunct faculty members is the right of students to a quality education.

Using this principle of student benefit, Anne Arundel's English Division has successfully dissipated at least some of the shadows of indifference imprisoning the adjunct faculty. And while this may be a long way from the full sunshine of justice, it is progress.

Roadblocks to Research:
One Part-Timer's View

G. James Jason
San Diego State University and Saddleback
Community College

Billie Holiday, a gifted artist, was also a keen observer of the human condition. She observed in a classic ballad:

> Them that's got shall get,
> Them that's not shall lose,
> So the Bible says
> And it still is news.
> Papa may have,
> Mama may have,
> But God bless the child
> that's got his own.

Her point is that the social system often puts people on tracks—the winning track and the losing track—and, once on the lower track, it is virtually impossible to get on the higher one.

I believe that Holiday's law governs the academic world no less than the social system as a whole, specifically, that two tracks have developed in the college world, one holding most full-timers and one holding most part-timers, and that once on the part-time track it is nearly impossible to get off. My personal experience suggests this but of course doesn't necessarily prove it. Nonetheless, my experience may give readers insight into aspects of part-time employment they may have overlooked.

On what basis are people hired for tenure-track positions? My experience, garnered at the four universities I have attended and at the dozen colleges and community colleges where I have taught, is that the primary factor in hiring is the publications list a candidate can present. If such is the case, you may wonder why part-timers don't simply publish as much as full-timers. The answer is that Holiday's law works against them: part-timers face impediments to research that full-timers rarely face, and this makes it a very unfair race.

For example, since part-timers are almost never paid pro rata, they face much lower incomes. (I currently teach four large classes per semester at two colleges but earn only about $1,000 per teaching month.) Consequently, part-timers must either get nonacademic jobs, in addition to teaching, or else must "overload"—teach *six to nine* courses per term, and extra courses during the summer. Either way, they wind up with little time to spare for research of any kind.

Moreover, traveling time from one job to another further limits the time available for writing. (My own case again: I teach at two colleges eighty miles apart and spend eight hours a week commuting.) Needless to say, traveling expenses further reduce income, which reinforces the first impediment.

In addition, part-timers are usually assigned to teach lower-division classes, which have much higher enrollments and therefore require much more work per student. (Lower-division students also tend to require more "intensive care" to develop their skills.) More time for the freshmen, less time for research, hence less chance to join the blessed: Holiday's law again.

Of course, it is obvious that teaching upper-division and graduate-level courses in one's field of specialization will enhance opportunity for publication. But since part-timers teach mainly lower-division courses, few of which touch on their immediate areas of specialization, they are thus further handicapped. Moreover, since their outside work and the inordinate amount of grading they do take up so much time, they don't experience the kind of interaction with well-established colleagues that sparks research.

Failure to produce scholarly articles has another consequence. Grants usually go to academics with publications and a record of past grants. Part-timers—in my experience at least—almost never get research grants. Often those who least need the grants get them, while those who are desperate for just six months' financial support to get some ideas down on paper are denied any opportunity to do so. Again, let me make the point concrete with an example from my own career. Two years ago, I coauthored a paper with a political scientist on the impact of warfare on technology. It was accepted for publication immediately. But we have found it impossible to get even a small grant for follow-up research, because we lack the track record of prior grants. Without such a grant, the data coding (of patent statistics) cannot be done, and a novel approach to an important issue has been stopped dead.

Need I add that part-timers never get sabbaticals? Nor can they take leaves of absence with the assurance that their jobs will still be there when they return.

And is it surprising that they usually lack the wherewithal to attend lectures, seminars, and conferences in their respective fields?

Another impediment to research facing part-timers is lack of secretarial support. At many (though, thank goodness, not at all) colleges, part-timers can have neither scholarly papers nor even *class handouts* typed. Thus, it seems, the rich get richer while the poor get poorer: those with publications get full-time jobs and support for producing more articles; those without publications have impediments put in their path.

A scholar vitally needs to have his or her ideas challenged, clarified, and encouraged. But those on the lower track almost never get to the track on which such fruitful dialogue takes place. This situation leads to a sort of anomie or even alienation among part-timers. They often feel themselves strangers, half in the academic world and half out, uncertain where they belong.

As a philosopher I cannot resist an ethical observation. The Holiday syndrome offends, not merely because it wastes human potential. It offends because it is unjust. It is unjust to deny qualified scholars the opportunity to add their voices and their ideas to the scholarly dialogue. In the long run, scholarship itself is the ultimate loser because of the roadblocks put in the way of part-timers.

Part-Timers:
A Problem That Can Also Become
a Solution in the Community College

Richard J. Colwell
St. Clair County Community College

Just as the County is our campus, since we depend so much on the goodwill of its citizens, the best public relations tool we can ever have is a dedicated, student-oriented instructor in every classroom.

Richard L. Norris, Ph.D., President
St. Clair County Community College
Port Huron, Michigan

The part-time-faculty phenomenon in the community college can be exciting and rewarding if approached in a positive manner. Some community colleges, especially in urban areas, depend so heavily on part-timers that students and full-time faculty and administrators are hard put to keep up. Fortunately, our college has grown into this situation more gradually during the 1960s and 1970s; the English department, for one, has developed a system to ensure that students receive the same or almost the same student-oriented instruction from part-timers that they would get from the full-time English staff members. This system has required the support and encouragement of the administration, but, most of all, it has been made possible by the willingness of the full-time English faculty to help in recruitment, hiring, orientation, and evaluation of part-time instructors.

No system is perfect, and financial stress in the public two-year college, especially here in Michigan, has necessitated constant monitoring and updating of the system. Yet I truly believe that our system makes our use of part-time English faculty not only manageable but in many ways an asset to the department. Much of this success is due to our college's long history as an excellent institution and to the direct participation of both full-time and part-time faculty in the development and operation of the system.

Our college was started in 1923 as a transfer liberal arts institution, part of the Port Huron Area School System. Over the years, many of the professionals in Port Huron's mid-sized area of some 80,000 people and in St. Clair County's 130,000 graduated from what they affectionately call "J.C." When the time came in the early 1960s for a rapid growth in community colleges across Michigan, our college had already begun some vocational programs in fields like nursing and industrial technology and was, therefore, committed to serving the two-year associate-degree-only student as well as continuing our respected transfer program. When I came in 1963, however, the use of part-time English instructors was virtually nonexistent in the English department. Night-school courses and the few college-credit courses offered off-campus were always filled by regular instructors on an overload basis.

Around 1968, an event occurred that changed that situation drastically and perhaps permanently. First, the college became a countywide institution by a vote of its citizens and changed its name to St. Clair County Community College, a name that the students soon shortened to SC$_4$. There were many challenges to be met. The college expanded its vocational offerings greatly until, by the middle 1970s, over half of its student body were two-year terminal students in job-oriented programs such as electronics, agriculture, and auto mechanics. The student body grew to perhaps 2,000 equated students, with as many as 4,500 to 5,000 students enrolling for at least one or two classes at a time. We still took transfer students just out of high school, but the average age of our student body rose to almost twenty-seven.

Another event, perhaps even more significant to our English department in its use of part-time instruction, was the rapid growth of negotiation for faculty contracts. Within a few years, the English faculty was able to have its association negotiate an equated class load on the grounds that the teaching of composition requires an unusual amount of paper processing and much more individual and small-group conference work in the office. For their part, the full-time faculty agreed to give up overload classes completely. This change then necessitated a rapid growth in the use of part-time instructors to supplement the department's ten basic instructors. Some semesters we have used as many as seventeen part-time teachers in day-school, night-school, and off-campus centers as far away as seventy-eight miles.

Fortunately, the contract set a clear guideline for hiring liberal arts faculty. Even though the English department was developing courses in technical English and a basic writing skills program to serve its changing student body, we took the guideline—master's in English or equivalent—literally. Sometimes we have stretched it to include persons close to completion of the master's degree, and we can say proudly that those few unusual cases have all completed their M.A.'s while they have been with us. At present, the dean of instruction has given the hiring function to his division administrators in conjunction with our department-elected department chairpersons. Although some of our part-time individuals have been with us for seven or eight years and four have become permanent faculty, others have moved on. Each summer, the English department chair and the division administrator interview several applicants, and the two have been fortunate in that of perhaps forty or so hired over the years, only three have failed to meet our standards.

When a new person is hired, a full-time faculty member volunteers to serve on his or her classroom evaluation committee along with the division administrator and the English department chair. After three or four semesters, the committee often votes to discontinue regular visits, and the person is then considered a regular part-timer.

New part-time members are oriented by a written document prepared by a committee made up of two part-time instructors and the department chair. It includes a section on general college procedures (such as getting parking permits, office keys, paychecks, and grade sheets) and another section dealing with departmental matters (such as syllabi, sample course outlines from several instructors, where to turn for student models of required papers, and what is expected in paper processing). This orientation includes both the department chair and the full-time faculty member on the evaluation committee; indeed, the new part-time person soon finds that *any* of our ten regular members is helpful. Their commitment is sincere, and they feel a real comradeship, especially toward the person that they were pledged to orient. Our English department has a get-together at a full-time or regular part-time member's home soon after the semester starts, and almost all the part-time members attend and get to know us.

We keep our part-timers because, as one of our regular part-time instructors said, "I like to work here because I really feel that I'm wanted and appreciated. . . ." We have included our part-time members in all social functions, and they have responded in kind by attending department meetings when they can and by serving on department committees such as the one in which we developed, with our learning resources center, an unusual system of freshman library orientation of which we are very proud. A regular part-time member also helped in planning, teaching, and evaluating our basic writing skills program for the less prepared students when we saw that need a few years ago.

Our evaluation of part-time instructors requires our full-time faculty to accompany the division administrator and department chair to night-school classes and to off-campus locations. Since we have already stressed in our orientation program that evaluation is for improvement and help, when we review part-timers' student evaluation forms, sample processed papers, and course outlines, they often respond with questions and ask for help. Full-time faculty members admit that they themselves have become better teachers by observing—and learning from—part-time instructors.

We cannot say enough about the administration's support for our efforts to maintain what we consider the student-oriented excellence of our program. They have given us the autonomy to develop a program that we feel meets our needs well. They have shared complaints about part-time instructors with the department chairperson so that problems can be caught and worked out before they become more serious. Our division administrator has become an important friend in the system. Our system works, I think, because we all—full-time faculty, part-time faculty, and administration—work hard at it. Any changes that we have made in the system have come because we have worked together to improve it.

But whatever successes we have had here at SC_4 can be attributed mostly to our full-time English faculty's commitment to making the system work. Their willingness to help in orientation and evaluation has made success possible. The community college could not operate in the present educational situation in our country without its part-time faculty. Our gradual development into this situation, our gradual growth as an English department, and our ability to change with the times have served us well. We do not succeed in every case with part-timers, but it is not because we do not try hard to do the job. Part-timers are with us and will continue to be. With all its problems, the part-time system—in our English department anyway—has been an exciting and often rewarding experience. English instructors are lucky in that they meet almost every kind of student at the college. They can be lucky, too, if they use their part-time instructors to stimulate new ideas and growth in their departments.

The Role of the Union in Representing Part-Time Faculty: California Community Colleges under Collective Bargaining and Proposition 13

Virginia F. Mulrooney
Los Angeles Valley College

In the past quarter century, the nation's two-year colleges have witnessed three stages of development. In stage one, junior colleges emerged. These colleges were attached to K–12 elementary and secondary school districts and often described as grades 13–14. Their major articulated purpose was to prepare college students for junior year at a four-year institution. Those junior colleges were often divided into day and evening divisions, and their students were often divided into full-time (day) students and part-time (evening) students. Not surprisingly, the faculty was also similarly divided. Day students had a full-time faculty—often promoted from the K–12 teachers in the school district to which the college was attached. Evening students had a part-time faculty—often also K–12 teachers teaching an extra class at night. These evening teachers frequently became full-time day teachers as vacancies on the full-time staff occurred.

In stage two, the faculty of these junior colleges grew tired of their position in the educational world. They fought to separate the colleges from the K–12 districts to which the colleges were attached. Their success resulted in the creation of college districts with separate boards and with separate sections of state education codes. They fought to eliminate the "junior" from their names, arguing the appellation suggested second-class citizenship. (In their second attempt, they were aided by administrators who, for vastly different reasons, wanted to exterminate the junior college.) The joint success of faculty and administration resulted in the creation of community colleges with a wider scope of mission than their junior college predecessors.

Also in stage two, the faculties of the new independent community colleges changed as a result of their new status. A larger number of new faculty came from the colleges and universities rather than the once-joined K–12 district. A larger number of university graduate students taught in both full-time and part-time, day and evening, positions. But although the educational composition of the faculty shifted, the distinction between day and evening, full-time and part-time, faculty and students did not disappear. Most full-time faculty didn't give a thought to most part-time faculty. Most part-time faculty considered their night work only as a source of extra income.

In stage three, two cataclysmic events took place at roughly (but—importantly—not exactly) the same time. Collective bargaining came to the California community colleges (1976–77), and Proposition 13 was adopted (1978). Both events affected the future of community college faculty in ways never dreamed of and not yet fully understood five years later. Let us look at each in turn.

Collective bargaining in California differed from collective bargaining elsewhere. The California state law said that a "unit" of teachers would not be "appropriate" unless it included "all classroom teachers." Most people, reading the law, assumed that "all" meant all and that part-time and full-time faculty must be included in the same unit. Although the Public Employment Relations Board went through years of wandering in the wilderness on this issue, the faculty reading was adopted in most districts; part-time faculty are included in the same unit as full-time faculty in most California community college bargaining units, although I hasten to add that there are exceptions.

Bargaining elections were held. Part-time teachers had full voting rights for the first time. They were a volatile voting force, prey to the suggestion—or distortion—of the moment, and they were decisive. By this time, part-time faculty constituted a majority of the faculty in most California community colleges. Although full-time faculty voted at 99% and part-time faculty at 63%, part-time-teacher votes were significant. Sometimes the full-time faculty voted for one agent and the part-time for another: the resultant tension was oppressive. Sometimes the part-time faculty won the bargaining election but could not bargain effectively. Sometimes full-time faculty won the election and retaliated against the part-timers who had supported the loser. Sometimes everyone voted for the winner, and everyone cooperated afterward.

In the first generation of collective bargaining, bargaining agents fought hard to win rights for the part-time faculty, because they had seen the power of the part-timers at election time and understood that it might be translated into power at contract ratification time. In this atmosphere the Los Angeles College Guild, the American Federation of Teachers affiliate in Los Angeles community colleges, negotiated its first contract. Ratification of that first contract was opposed by part-time faculty organized by our losing National Education Association opponents. Two events took place in connection with that contract. First, fewer than sixty part-time faculty appeared to cast their secret ballot on ratification of the contract (and this in a unit of more than five thousand faculty, half of whom were part-timers). Second, the contract that the unit ratified turned out to be the only community college contract in California to give some modicum of job security—in the form of seniority—to our part-time faculty. The contract specified that hourly-rate teachers (part-timers) had a right to their course assignments and could not be bumped by a full-timer unless that full-timer needed another course to make up a full teaching schedule.

That contract was ratified in January 1978. Six months later, Howard Jarvis and Proposition 13 hit California, and the ton of bricks predicted by its opponents began to fall in earnest in the autumn of 1982.

Proposition 13 and its fiscal fallout have created a series of major dilemmas for our colleges and their bargaining agents as both relate to part-time faculty. Let me list several:

1. Lack of money at the bargaining table has resulted in salary adjustments less than the Consumer Price Index increases of an inflationary era. Even our 10% salary increases—the largest in the state—have not kept pace with inflation and this year we've spent more than twelve months at the bargaining table in an attempt to negotiate a twelve-month salary increase.

2. As a result of insufficient salary increases, full-time faculty members are seeking course overloads and therefore competing for part-time teaching assignments for the first time in years. Where hourly-rate seniority systems do not exist (and full-timers thus find it relatively easy to bump part-timers out of courses the full-timers wish to teach in order to earn supplementary income), tension between full- and part-time faculty has increased dramatically. Where such systems do exist, as in Los Angeles, bargaining agents are being asked by some full-timers to eliminate them at the table.

3. The fiscal crunch originally resulted in the firing of large numbers of part-timers—who lack tenure rights—as a money-saving measure in 1978 and 1979. However, as full-time faculty retire, and also as a money-saving device, full-time positions are being turned into part-time positions. Between 1979 and 1982, the number of students increased, the number and percentage of part-time faculty increased (as they had for years), but, most significantly, the number of full-timers began to decrease for the first time ever.

4. As the fiscal crunch worsens, bargaining agents are able to negotiate retirement incentives ($7,500 if you retired in 1982–83 in the Los Angeles Community College District), because colleges either will not replace expensive maximum salary teachers or will replace them with hourly-rate, nontenurable, part-time faculty. One's chances of getting a part-time job in a California community college increase, at least in certain areas, every day. However, one's chances of parlaying that part-time job into a full-time job diminish with each dawn—and maybe with each hour of the day.

Sensitive bargaining agents find themselves increasingly trapped among full-time faculty who want extra money, part-time faculty who want job security, administrators who want cheap teachers, and students who want tuition-free education.

And what of stage four, the stage yet to come? Will it be a repeat of stage one, or two, or three, or will it be something else? I don't know what it will be, but I can tell you that it won't be good if part-time and full-time faculty do not unite to advance the interests of both, each a bit at a time. (For that reason, the AFT has urged all part-time and full-time faculty to belong to the same organization and bargain either in the same unit or in coordinated bargaining if the same bargaining unit is illegal.) It won't be good if faculty do not unite with students for their common interest—which means faculty opposition to tuition (California community colleges are tuition-free) and student support for decent salaries and working conditions for faculty. And it won't be good if we cannot approach the general population and convince them that what we do is both worth doing and worth paying for. One of every ten Californians has attended a California community college, and most have found the experience worthwhile. If we can get to them, we can persuade them to provide the support, once provided to them, to the next generation of community college students.

Recently I paid two yearly bills, one for automobile insurance of the sort required in California, the other for property taxes. My automobile insurance, which covers my one car, cost $1,000. My property tax, which pays for myriad local services, public servants, and public education, was only $800. It seems to me there is something wrong in a society that so clearly values automobiles over public education.

We cannot get to the public—or to the legislature—without money. Faculty members who earned 10% more last year than they earned the year before ought to be willing to tithe 10% of that 10%—or 1% of their income—to political, legal, and public action. (That's a maximum of $360 for a full-timer where I come from.) If they are not willing, we cannot tell our tale and deliver our message to those who need to hear it and who determine our future.

If we don't do these things, there may be more part-time teaching opportunities—for persons being poorly paid, to teach larger and larger numbers of students, at institutions without a core of committed faculty, run by administrators concerned only about enrollment and attendance and the courses that bring them in, attended by students shortchanged because they can't find the faculty member, who's out looking for a better job somewhere else.

The Legal Battle for Part-Time-Faculty Rights in California Community Colleges

Robert Gabriner
Peralta Federation of Teachers

During the 1970s, a group of part-time faculty from the Peralta Community College District in Oakland, California, initiated a campaign to gain equal pay and tenure for part-time instructors in the California community college system. The centerpiece of this effort was a lawsuit, known as the Peralta suit, filed in Alameda Superior Court in 1974. This statewide organizing drive for equal pay and tenure was perhaps one of the most significant efforts in this country to mobilize part-time instructors around their own interests. It raised some important questions about the chances of successfully organizing part-time faculty, about faculty unions, and about the relationship between part-time and full-time faculty.

California has the largest two-year community college system in the nation. It was also tuition free until September 1984. There are 70 districts with 106 colleges currently employing 31,400 part-time instructors and 14,200 full-time faculty. Part-time instructors teach about 35% of the current work load for community colleges in the state.

The growth of this system was concentrated in the 1960s and early 1970s when the state was at the peak of its prosperity. In that period, community college budgets depended on local property taxes for a large share of revenue, and over the years these taxes were gradually increased to pay for local city and county programs as well as community college programs. But in the mid-1970s, student enrollment began to level off and then decrease; and since enrollment was a key determinant of how much revenue any district would receive, the growth of community colleges began to slow down. In 1978, when the taxpayers revolted and passed Proposition 13, the initiative that drastically slashed property taxes, community college revenues dried up. And while the state of California picked up the revenue responsibilities, the community college system was put on notice that the era of retrenchment and tight budgets was at hand.

During the growth period from 1964 to 1972, large numbers of faculty were hired into tenure-track positions; many of these instructors previously had taught part-time in the community college districts. But as student enrollments leveled off, most districts stopped hiring full-time faculty, thus shutting off any opportunity of moving up the job ladder.

The Peralta suit and the campaign for tenure and equal pay grew out of a collision between the expectations of thousands of bright, highly motivated, liberal arts part-time instructors who sought tenure-track positions and the decision of administrators to establish a hiring freeze on all such jobs.

This was the situation in the Peralta Community College District located in the San Francisco Bay area. Peralta had grown rapidly into a five-college district during the late 1960s with over 450 full-time tenured instructors and approximately 550 part-time "temporary" faculty. Like other districts in the state, Peralta had part-time instructors teaching the same classes as full-timers but at one third to one half the salary. There were neither fringe benefits nor compensation for holding office hours or advising students. The tenured teachers were the "core" of the instructional program, and the part-timers were the "periphery" who could be hired and fired at will since part-time instructors had no tenure or seniority.

Many part-time instructors perceived their status as the community college equivalent of "purgatory" before one ascended to tenure-track "heaven" with all the attendant rights of full-time instructors. When it became clear that tenure-track jobs were drying up, part-time instructors realized that "purgatory" led only to hell: no job security with no prospect of relief in the future.

So it was not surprising that over fifty angry part-timers showed up at a meeting in the fall of 1973 called by the Peralta Federation of Teachers (PFT), the local affiliate of the American Federation of Teachers in the Peralta district. The meeting turned into a wide-ranging discussion about the plight of the Peralta part-time instructor. More meetings were called, and more part-time instructors showed up. The Peralta discussions were to set off a series of events that would have statewide significance for the community college system and its faculties.

Three of the main leaders who emerged from these early meetings were Jeff Kerwin, an English instructor, and LeRoy Votto and Mark Greenside, both history instructors. Kerwin had had no background in political organizing; Votto and Greenside considered themselves "activists" nurtured in the antiwar and civil rights movements of the 1960s.

"All of us realized that we were being treated like 'stoop labor,' " noted Kerwin. "We were paid less than full timers; we had no job security, no fringe benefits. . . . It was a case of clear cut exploitation."

According to Votto, the group decided to take the issues of equal pay, tenure, fringe benefits, and compensation for office hours directly to the Peralta Board of Trustees, the locally elected governing body. Throughout the spring of 1974, the trustees heard presentations from part-time instructors and eventually responded by establishing a committee to study the status of part-time instructors. The committee consisted of the chancellor of the district plus administrators, tenured faculty, and one part-time instructor. Surveys were taken, reports were written, and after six months the committee recommended additional monies be allocated for more administration to keep better track of the part-time faculty. There were no recommendations to improve their economic status or to remedy the lack of job security.

The part-timers' group was furious; another strategy had to be tried, and the legal route was becoming more attractive.

In 1974, the California Supreme Court ruled in the *Balen* decision that a Peralta part-time instructor, H. Pat Balen (now a Peralta trustee), must be granted tenure-track status because he had been employed for more than two consecutive years. The court decided in favor of Balen because the state's education code did not provide any classification for part-time temporary instructors who taught more than two consecutive years. Since there were no categories for Balen, the court concluded that he must have tenure status.

The *Balen* decision gave a strong legal basis for a lawsuit by the Peralta part-time instructors, and the Peralta Federation of Teachers indicated a willingness to sponsor such a suit. The part-timers' group felt the suit could at least be used as a bargaining chip in negotiations with the district about tenure and equal pay.

As Jeff Kerwin put it, "if we had any career at all it would come from the deus ex machina of the courts which could rescue us and give us justice." It was this perception that propelled many part-time instructors around the state to throw their energies into prosecuting the suit.

While most of the group had joined the Peralta Federation of Teachers, there was a strong feeling that an independent organization of part-time instructors was also necessary to promote the interests of the part-time faculty. The Peralta Part-Time Teachers Association (PPTA) was established in 1974; membership dues were two dollars per month. In less than a year, over half the Peralta part-time faculty joined. Soon after the formation of PPTA, similar organizations were formed in other districts. Later the same year the California Association of Part-Time Instructors (CAPI) was formed with much of the leadership coming from Peralta.

The establishment of a separate part-timers' organization emanated from a "go it alone" mentality that arose from very real divisions between the full- and part-time faculty.

When the Peralta Federation of Teachers called its first meeting with part-time faculty in 1973, there were many part-time instructors who were as angry with the union as with the district. The PFT was viewed by some as exclusively representing the interests of full-time faculty. Further, there were some who felt that full-time faculty would not support the demands for equal pay and tenure because it would hurt their status. "We subsidize the full-timers," noted one part-time faculty member, "because we are paid two-thirds and that enables the District to pay full-time faculty more."

Many full-time instructors would not support the part-timers' program because they saw a fixed pot of money, and if some of it went to remedy the part-timers' problems, then there would be that much less for cost-of-living adjustments, fringe benefits, and sabbaticals. They looked down on part-timers as less serious instructors who taught for extra money they didn't need. Few understood what it took to make a living by stringing together two, three, or four part-time jobs in different districts (today these part-timers are known as "freeway flyers").

The relations between full- and part-time faculty were good throughout 1973 and 1974, especially when the PFT and its state and national affiliates, the CFT and AFT, decided to support the Peralta lawsuit. But things got rocky in 1975 when part-time faculty who were PFT members felt they were being sold out by the full-timers in the union. The dispute centered on the use of the Peralta suit as a bargaining chip with the board of trustees. The part-timers perceived the PFT leadership were willing to drop the suit for a monetary settlement. The part-timers felt that job security and equal pay were the bottom line.

The episode ended when the trustees decided not to offer anything. But some of the ill feelings and mistrust continued and prompted the PPTA to demand that it become a coplaintiff to guarantee that the PFT leadership could not drop the suit in the future if an offer was made by the district. PPTA did become a coplaintiff and subsequently spent most of its time raising its share of the legal costs.

According to Mark Greenside, the PFT was the "best we had . . . but you always hoped for something better. . . . All of us wanted to believe in the union, but by creating a separate organization, we could threaten, we could keep them honest." The threat was the possibility of withdrawing the support of the part-time faculty from the union and thereby injuring PFT chances of winning the collective-bargaining election.

LeRoy Votto was a founder of the PPTA and later became the executive secretary of the PFT: "Without the PFT, the part-time faculty would have been nowhere. We needed the PFT as much as the union needed us." But Votto adds that the divisions within the faculty were very serious: "I remember attending meetings of the Merritt College history department where Mark (Greenside) and I had worked for years. These meetings were about the part-time issue, and full-time faculty who had been our friends for years ended up screaming at their colleagues who were also long-term friends. The issue drove a wedge within the full-time faculty as well as between the full-time and part-time faculty. The arguments were extremely heated and antagonistic."

The part-time issue became so heated, in fact, that the Peralta District Teachers Association (PDTA) was established in reaction to what some faculty perceived as part-timer-dominated PFT. PDTA and PFT strenuously competed to become the collective-bargaining agent in 1978 and 1979. PFT won by a two-to-one margin with the help of part-time faculty and became the collective bargaining agent in May 1979.

In the same month the State Supreme Court ruled that *Balen* did not apply to the Peralta petitioners, because most of them were hired after November 1967. The court established this date because the legislature had passed a provision in the education code establishing a new category of temporary part-time instructors. Those part-timers hired before November 1967 were lawfully entitled to tenure and retroactive compensation based on the salary schedules of the tenured instructors. Twenty-six Peralta instructors benefited from this decision; statewide perhaps a few hundred received tenure status and retroactive compensation, but the thousands who hoped for some legal relief were left out in the cold because they were hired after November 1967.

The court's decision reflected the times: Proposition 13 had passed the previous year; the court had already come under fire for being too liberal; and the Peralta case could potentially cost the state over $200 million. Some faculty felt that the court "sub silento" was unwilling to face the economic consequences of generalizing the *Balen* decision to all part-time instructors in the state's community college system.

Despite the court's response, a few small victories resulted from the part-timers' efforts.

After the Rodda Act was passed in 1976, providing collective bargaining rights to community college faculty, many little Peralta suits were filed by unions and faculty organizations in order to win part-time faculty to their membership rosters. The net effect was unsettling for many district administrations because of the prospect of a protracted legal battle that might end in tenure for hundreds of teachers. In one district, the Los Angeles Community College District (the largest in the nation), the specter of the Peralta suit was sufficient to push the administration to sign an agreement with AFT College Guild establishing a seniority system for part-time faculty. While other districts did not follow L.A.'s lead, there were efforts to upgrade the salaries of part-time faculty.

In 1976 and 1977, the PPTA leaders led the fight before the California Public Employment Relations Board (PERB) to include part-time faculty in the same bargaining units as full-time faculty. The PERB ruled that each faculty member, part- and full-time, would have one vote in the collective bargaining elections, thus enabling part-timers to play important roles within faculty unions. The result is that now part-timers can influence the development of contract proposals as well as negotiations regarding part-time issues.

Today there is a rebirth of part-time-faculty activity, most of it focused inside the unions. Subcommittees are being established in some locals; the California Federation of Teachers recently formed a northern and southern committee on part-time-faculty issues.

Furthermore, the tight revenue picture has pushed faculty negotiating teams to emphasize noneconomic issues, and some locals are making headway at the bargaining table on job security and seniority provisions for part-timers.

Faculty organizations are also developing legislative proposals to restrict the hiring of part-time faculty or at least to discourage reliance on part-time instruction. This approach seeks to consolidate many part-time positions into fewer tenure positions.

What can be learned from this bit of history? Is there any hope part-time faculty can successfully organize to win equal status with their full-time counterparts?

Votto, Greenside, and Kerwin agree that errors were made during the 1970s, but the nature of those mistakes is still being debated. "Our biggest error was putting our eggs in one basket, in the hands of the six justices," noted Kerwin recently. Such a criticism suggests more should have been done in the legislative, political-action, and collective bargaining arenas.

But his colleague Mark Greenside sees it differently: "Legal action was our only remedy. We lacked political clout, and we were fighting a rear-guard action against full-time faculty and frontline action against the administration. Furthermore, we did not have enough resources or support for a strike. What could we do but take legal action?"

All three agree, however, that there is still hope that part-timers' status can be changed. Looking back over the last ten years, Greenside concluded: "We gave it our best shot. We shook up a lot of people. At every step of the way, we talked out what we were doing, we knew what we were doing. It was amazing that so few people could organize such a large presence in the state. It can be done again. Certainly there are others who potentially could shake up the system as we did."

6. STATE COLLEGES AND UNIVERSITIES

Demotion and Displacement: Career Paths for Women in Academe

Elizabeth W. Miller
Bloomsburg University of Pennsylvania

It is that time of year again when part-time faculty must reapply and compete for their own jobs. An annual evaluation and search for each part-time position already filled by existing faculty members are demoralizing. They imply, among other things, that the part-time faculty member has inadequately performed.

Those of us "rehired" usually find ourselves subsequently exploited by being assigned to teach the least respected and least rewarded courses: introductory, lower-level courses that many full-time faculty choose not to teach.

In my department, each faculty member must teach at least one lower-level course each semester; many upper-level courses are being canceled because of low student enrollment. At the same time, the administration faces retrenchment as well as natural attrition through retirement or resignation. The result is that there are fewer full-time people to handle the required lower-level courses. The choice is clear: either overloaded lower-level classes or part-time faculty to handle the overload. English departments, especially, have this problem since English literature requirements for the humanities have been drastically cut, while writing requirements have increased. Thus often fifty percent of the department is made up of part-time people.

This, unfortunately, frequently develops into a situation where half the department is hostile to the other half. To full-timers, the part-time faculty are the "they" and full-time faculty the "we." Many discussions develop along these lines: "they" do not advise students, thus "our" loads are too heavy; "they" do not serve on committees, thus "we" are overwhelmed in this area; "they" must be observed and evaluated each semester, and "we" must do all the time-consuming observing and evaluating; "they" are not totally committed to the college (that is, not at their desks daily or involved in college activities), therefore "we" must take up the slack. The "they–we" list goes on and on, and the friction increases. Moreover, "they" are kept firmly in their place. "They" are not assigned to student advisees; "they" are not selected to serve on committees ("they" are not allowed to vote even if "they" served); "they" do not develop curriculum, since "they" would never be allowed to teach courses "they" might be able to develop; "they" also get tired of being observed and evaluated by the same people each semester, sometimes three times a semester; "they" are being paid only a low salary per course, so why should "they" be required to spend full-time at their desks or at other college activities? Finally, when policies are being developed concerning "them," "they" are never present or consulted.

Occasionally, some of "them" do have an impact and get grudging recognition from department heads or deans for specific contributions to their disciplines or to the school in general. I and many of my peers have made and continue to make contributions to our fields. We attend conferences, give papers, serve on panels, serve as resource people for graduate students, and write and publish articles, books, and poetry. In my experience, the accomplishments of part-time faculty compare very well with those of full-time faculty. In fact, I believe that administrators and colleagues are beginning, at long last, to realize the contributions we make and are beginning to take action to retain their part-timers and, at the least, to humanize the job of the part-time faculty.

Some of this change in attitude has recently been translated into positive action at Bloomsburg University of Pennsylvania. The year 1982 saw a change from no benefits to limited benefits. "Rehired" part-time faculty are now offered 50% medical coverage with Blue Cross–Blue Shield. The employee pays 50% of the premium, and the employer pays 50%. Each part-time faculty member has life insurance coverage according to percentage of salary. There is a retirement plan option as well as a sick-leave and personal-leave policy. However, the pension and medical coverage lapse from May to September and the vision, dental, and supplemental health care program offered by the Association of Pennsylvania State College and University Faculties to full-time faculty is not offered to part-time faculty.

In the past, the collective bargaining unit has been hostile to part-time faculty. Whatever the reasons, the roadblocks to improvement of the part-timer's lot have come from the bargaining unit. The recommendation for dealing with part-time faculty came from the administration, which proposed that individual departments determine what should be included in the contract of a first-year, tenure-track faculty member. Thus the administration put this responsibility where it belongs: in the individual departments. Consequently, the departments would determine promotion, leaves, evaluation procedures, service on committees, and vote procedure and policy related to attendance at departmental meetings for part-time faculty.

Previous to this proposal, attendance by part-time faculty at departmental and APSCUF meetings was not encouraged; it was merely tolerated. We were not invited to offer any input related to such crucial matters as curriculum development in our areas of expertise, nor were we invited to make contributions to the discussions about the "problem of part-timers." We *could* unofficially complain or give our ideas to full-time faculty to present to the department for perusal and eventual vote. In other words, the democratic processes of the college, the bargaining unit, and the department were denied to a substantial number of the college community.

It is not only in my own institution that I have observed these attitudes and policies. They are also present in other colleges and universities, for I have discussed with other part-time faculty even more repressive policies and dismal attitudes. One publishing, teaching Ph.D. was told that because her husband was a member of the faculty, she could not teach on that same faculty. She subsequently was forced to take a part-time position elsewhere. Like myself and many other married women our age, she had dutifully pulled up stakes to follow her husband from job to job in order to keep the family together and to ensure the husband's advancement. This situation has been repeated hundreds of times in the business and industrial communities as well as in the academic community and has unfortunately resulted in the displacement of women. (I have never met a man who periodically gave up full-time, tenured positions to accompany his spouse to a better position in another community.) Such women then must accept what they can find in the new area. A whole new exploitable class has been created through this practice. We have all heard the infuriating responses to these situations, ad nauseam. I suspect that the "part-time problem" inevitably tangles with what is called the "woman problem."

But even as a woman I had never before suffered the indignity experienced at a recent English conference. As a member of a group amicably discussing student writing, my comments were cordially received. In the course of the conversation, however, my part-time status was revealed. In effect, the group moved away from me, and, for the rest of the conference, they not only ignored me but would not even establish eye contact.

I dislike the subtle and not-so-subtle demoralization of part-time faculty taking place in a supposedly enlightened community. Perhaps it has its source in the all-too-common assumption that there is something deficient about an unemployed or part-time person. Yet even in a time when institutions of higher education are paddling frantically to stay afloat, we should not direct blame and hostility toward people who cannot be welcomed aboard the sinking ship. Sometimes a temporary life jacket is a means of survival for those of us who for various reasons find ourselves struggling in the icy, numbing waters of unemployment. These are new and dangerous waters for most of us.

So the time-consuming yearly application for one's own job continues: a formal application to be submitted (notarized) in triplicate, with all typing, notarizing, and xeroxing to be done at each part-timer's expense.

In Praise of Part-Time Employment

Merike Tamm

University of South Carolina at Spartanburg

At 6 a.m. I nurse my ten-month-old son and return him to sleep. At 8 a.m. I am riding from South Carolina to Atlanta in a university van with my colleagues to attend the annual convention of the South Atlantic Modern Language Association. We discuss the papers we are going to present, new research directions in our specialties, and university politics. At 1 p.m., while I am presenting my paper on sexist language and enjoying the intellectual stimulation of questions from the audience, my husband and son are driving to the convention. By the time the afternoon sessions are over and our family is reunited in a hotel room, my breasts are painfully full, because of several missed feedings. The next day I listen to and discuss several papers; between sessions I play with and nurse my son. After the convention closes, as we drive home, I feel a peaceful joy. Why am I fortunate enough, I ask myself, to know the contentment that comes from feeling that two of the major forces of my life—my work and my family—are in balance? One important reason is that I work only part-time.

As a graduate student in a demanding Ph.D. program at the University of Wisconsin, I did not expect to become an enthusiastic advocate of part-time employment. After my husband and I completed our degrees in 1976, I accepted a full-time, term-by-term appointment as assistant professor in English at a state university in Minnesota, while my husband accepted a tenure-track job in political science at a small liberal arts college in South Carolina. We would both evaluate our jobs, our institutions, and our towns, to see which of us should relocate. It was a happy, productive year for both, despite the distance between us. When it became apparent that my job would not continue the following year, I had to decide whether to seek a tenure-track job, regardless of location, or to move to South Carolina, where my husband was satisfied with his job and new hometown. I got to the interview stage for several appealing jobs when I finally decided that getting a tenure-track job in a state far from South Carolina would only complicate the future of our family. I was thirty-one and ready to settle down and have a baby.

Spartanburg has three four-year colleges, a two-year college, and a technical college. My initial round of interviews brought no job prospects. Some months later, however, women faculty members at the University of South Carolina at Spartanburg, whom I had met through the National Organization for Women, told me that part-time faculty were being hired in English. Thus I got my first part-time, one-semester contract at USCS.

I found I liked part-time teaching. I had more energy and enthusiasm for each class. I had time to write—scholarly articles, free-lance nonfiction, and gropings toward a novel—and time to prepare for life with a new baby. I stayed at home for eight months after my son was born, then returned to teach one course per semester, in the evening, so my husband could care for our child. For three years this has been a perfect arrangement for us.

As a feminist who had grown up on literature denigrating women's traditional roles, extolling professional achievement, and proclaiming women's and men's equal capacities in child care, I was totally surprised and overwhelmed by my feelings after giving birth. I discovered that I loved being at home with my child, that breastfeeding involved a nurturing capacity belonging only to women, and that the daily wonder of a child's developmental changes and the growth of love easily equaled the professional rewards of status, intellectual stimulation, and a paycheck. For the greatest emotional satisfaction and optimum physiological functioning, nursing mothers must avoid prolonged separations from their babies, and hence they have a particular need to limit outside employment. If the opportunity for part-time work had not existed, I would have chosen not to work at all rather than to work full-time.

This is the reason many women, I suspect, are willing to accept the exploitative conditions of part-time academic work: contemplating the probable consequences of withdrawing totally from the profession for years is even more depressing. The loss of skills and professional contacts, at a time of numerous unemployed Ph.D.'s and fewer college-age students, would almost certainly mean that these women would never be able to return to the academic world.

Mothers who prefer part-time work do not receive much emotional support from traditional mothers, who believe in restricting women's role to the home, or from traditional feminists, who believe in women's full commitment to the world of work. We are charting new patterns of work and family life, living out the "second stage" of feminism discussed by Betty Friedan.

In these new patterns of family life, the husband's role will be extremely important in enabling a woman to combine career and motherhood. In my own case, I would not have wanted to return to work if I had had to leave my eight-month-old child with anyone other than his father. My husband feels that an important advantage of my working is the close relationship he has developed with his son. He knows he would not otherwise schedule so much time alone with him.

Graduate departments in the modern languages are producing male and female Ph.D.'s in approximately equal numbers. But if the academic profession does not wish to exclude women with children from the next generation of scholars and teachers and if it wants to encourage the highest potential achievement of all its members, we may need more rather than fewer part-time positions. The push by some dissatisfied part-timers to make all academic jobs full-time jobs would harm the profession as well as many individuals.

I have been grateful that the University of South Carolina at Spartanburg continues to use part-time faculty to teach many of their courses. In recent years, about twenty classes per semester in the Division of Fine Arts, Languages, and Literature have been taught by part-timers, more than in any other division in the School of Humanities and Sciences. There are no universitywide policies regarding part-time employment; each division sets its own. With few exceptions, the salary is $1,000 a course, with no fringe benefits, no committee assignments or advisement responsibilities, and no vote in the faculty senate.

I naturally resent receiving a salary so disproportionate in comparison with full-timers with comparable credentials but otherwise have no complaints about working conditions. A deliberate effort is made to include part-timers in course-planning meetings and social events and to provide secretarial and other support services (like photocopying) for part-timers as conveniently as for full-timers.

I have had no unpleasant personal experiences with full-time faculty. This may be because I feel and act like a professional: I have a Ph.D., I have published, I present papers at conferences, and I attend professional meetings. Another contributing factor to the cordial relations between our full-time and part-time faculty may be the newness of the institution. Since USCS opened in 1967 and has been a four-year institution less than ten years, there is no large body of older, full-time faculty who identify deeply with the institution and would therefore find it difficult to accept part-timers as colleagues.

Perhaps in the future, when children take up less of my time, I would be interested in the opportunity to serve on committees, advise students, and have a voice in faculty governance. But at present, my major desire (apart from a better salary) is for job security. Although I have been teaching at USCS five years, I never know if I will be rehired next semester. Whenever I hear that there will be a new division chairperson (who is in charge of part-time hiring), I get nervous.

As I write this, I am four months pregnant and planning to stay home for a year after the baby arrives. This time I am eager. For a short period in my life, while my children are small, I want my primary identity to be as a mother rather than as a teacher or scholar. But I would feel even better if I knew that my part-time job would be there when I was ready to return to work.

Part-Time Instruction of Foreign Languages in a State University College

Walter Borenstein
SUNY, College at New Paltz

Part-time faculty members at the State University College at New Paltz fall into three categories: those appointed for a semester or a year to replace permanent full-time staff on leave; those appointed on an irregular basis, often semester by semester, to fill the changing needs of the larger language areas (French, German, Spanish); and those kept on as members of the department, also on an irregular basis, to teach in language areas that do not attract large numbers of students (Arabic, Chinese, Japanese, Hebrew). Since most languages are taught in combined departments rather than in separate departments of individual languages, appointments to the less taught language areas can be made under the auspices of a larger department and its chair rather than by a dean or other college administrator.

Because almost all graduate students in the state colleges are part-time, often enrolling in only one or two courses per semester, and because there is little funding of graduate assistantships in any area and none in foreign languages, the part-time lecturer or adjunct instructor takes the place of the graduate assistant found in most larger universities. Also, because of the budgetary restrictions of the past few years, leaves of absence without pay and year sabbaticals in foreign language departments are rarely replaced by full-time persons, thus allowing the institutions, hard-pressed for needed funds, to make other use of the $15,000 to $25,000 or even more that has come into their hands. Of the $15,000 a full professor may leave when on a year's sabbatical, an institution may return only $2,500 to a department.

At the state university college where I teach, twenty-nine part-time teachers were appointed between 1969 and 1982 in the departments of foreign languages. For nine of those years I served as head of the total department and of one of the language areas that was part of it. I was directly involved with the appointment of most of these part-time faculty.

French, German, and Spanish accounted for thirteen of these appointments, and the remaining part-timers taught Arabic, Chinese, Hebrew, Hindi, Italian, Japanese, Russian, and Swahili. All seven part-timers in Spanish and one in Russian replaced department members on leave. All the others taught the less frequently taught languages. Nineteen of the part-timers were women, and ten were men. The appointments were either for one semester or for one year, and none was on a track leading to a permanent full-time position. One of the part-timers worked on this basis for nine years and another for five, but the majority taught for less than two years.

During the greater part of these years the foreign languages found themselves in a difficult situation: they were not enrolling enough students to justify the number of faculty members teaching. This ratio is referred to at this institution as a Faculty Teaching Equivalent (FTE). Under such circumstances, as department head, I would find myself in a very disadvantageous position each year, struggling to defend the numbers of staff members in languages in my discussions with the administration. I defended the replacement of faculty on leave in French, German, or Spanish and the need for continued part-time staffing in the other languages.

With the elimination of the language requirement in 1971, what had been a gradual decline turned into a veritable disaster. Only during the past few years has the present Department of Foreign Languages begun to recover from this decline and it has done so without a restoration of the language requirement. But the price has been shattering to morale and to future expectations; almost half the original twenty-seven faculty members have been eliminated by attrition: retirement, nonrenewal, and retrenchment. The attitudes of three different administrations since 1971 have reflected a philosophy of survival in the face of diminishing resources; the part-time sabbatical replacement in foreign languages or part-time instructor in less frequently taught languages has always been one part of that plan for survival.

Appointments generally fall into two broad categories: those made with funds taken from the salary lines of faculty members on leave and those for which funding must be found from outside the department. In the lesser taught languages—Arabic, Hebrew, Hindi, Japanese, and Swahili—a well-established tradition provides low remuneration through a program of self-instruction in neglected languages. Under this program, for a period of about ten years, individuals had been hired without an official contract to serve as tutors in a highly structured special arrangement making considerable use of tapes in the language laboratory. Such tutors, generally native speakers of the language, were paid up to ten dollars per hour for about four hours of contact per week for each course or level taught. These persons were not allowed to give a final grade, and an outside reviewer would be invited to evaluate the students at the end of the semester. Student pressures in a number of the languages taught in this manner led us to convert the neglected language courses (which were not official courses in the catalog) to regular courses with an arrangement for a contract with the instructor. Individuals already accustomed to the low hourly wage were often only too willing to accept a low remuneration for a semester's work. Then the part-time instructors who accepted these low salaries established a pattern for all part-timers teaching less frequently taught languages. A means was sought to offer class instruction in these languages at the lowest possible cost, sometimes by increasing the number of contact hours at the same salary.

It would not be fair to say that part-time instruction in foreign languages is done at a lower pay scale than in other departments. But one could say that, during the past ten years, there has been a tendency in foreign languages to use part-timers excessively; perhaps this was the only way that neglected languages could be taught. It could also be argued that foreign language part-timers spent more hours teaching than faculty in other departments, for the same remuneration. Now, however, other departments are increasingly in the same position as the foreign language department. Faculty on leave or sabbaticals are not replaced with temporary full-timers in most departments, and, if it is absolutely essential to replace a vital staff member, part-timers are used.

Meanwhile, the situation in the Department of Foreign Languages has deteriorated further, reaching a point where not even part-timers are offered for some areas. The extraordinary cutbacks of the past five years have led to a situation where it is easier to eliminate a lesser taught language than to staff it with a part-timer. If someone can be found in the college community to fill the limited needs of one course, the course may be offered; but the high qualifications once expected of all faculty are not always taken into consideration.

Now, there is only one "regular" part-time assistant professor in the department, and this person was transferred to foreign languages only last year. Such a regular part-time position is rare in the college and should not mislead anyone into thinking that there may be many others. All other regular part-time faculty members in foreign languages are in reality full-time and have split appointments with other areas. At present, only three persons are teaching as true part-timers. One is a department head from a nearby college who teaches a single course here. The other two are visiting scholars, teaching two courses under a special arrangement. This may very well imply that the days of part-timers have come to an end, even for the foreign languages, because of the ever deeper cuts in funding. The part-time instructor was the first step toward elimination of certain courses entirely.

Through the years it has been the difficult task of the head of the department to struggle to maintain the dignity, the standards, and the equitable compensation of part-time instructors against a background of steadily worsening conditions. The typical part-timer has been a woman, holding a master's degree, often the wife of a faculty member, almost always unwilling, unable, or afraid to reject inadequate remuneration for her work. As head of the department, one could dispute the salary offered, only to be told that the alternative would be nothing at all. Even the strength of a union contract has been unable to deal with this thorny issue because of numerous problems that have taken precedence in such troubled times. Where the part-timer was once considered an unhappy compromise, departments now feel fortunate to be offered the use of a low-salaried substitute for one semester. They willingly sacrifice the $15,000 of a leave line and accept $1,300 for a one-semester replacement. For the administration, part-timers offer endless opportunities to save funds and avoid encumbering a tenure-heavy college with new pretenders to tenure.

The Modern Language Association and the American Association of University Professors have sponsored numerous studies and published articles on the plight of part-time faculty members. The statistics published annually, the awareness that extension centers staffed by part-timers have spread out across many states, and the realization that administrators, legislators, and accreditation agencies accept the part-timer as the ideal solution to a financial dilemma pose serious questions for all persons involved with the educational establishment. This awareness comes, unfortunately, at a time of deep financial retrenchment, fear, and disenchantment among many academics striving to become professors. The foreign languages have been precursors in this unhappy arrangement where part-timers are carrying the burden of instruction in so many areas with the same intensity and dedication as full-time faculty—for only a fraction of full-timers' salaries.

In many state colleges, foreign language departments, struggling to increase productivity without the benefit of a language requirement and unable to convince unfriendly administrations that classes of fifty are unsuitable for quality instruction find they must accept endless compromises. Other departments now take higher priority for college administrations. The part-timer has become the ideal response to a shrinking budget. Unless there is a major reversal of priorities and unless the importance of language facility for all citizens is taken as seriously here as it is in so many other nations, the part-timer may be only the first step in a reduction of standards, and even newer "solutions" may reduce the educational ideal to some form of misguided bureaucratic mediocrity.

Fixed-Term Lecturers in English at Pennsylvania State University

Wendell V. Harris
Pennsylvania State University

Given the structure of university budgets, the first thing to recognize about the widespread dependence on non-tenure-track and part-time faculty members for the teaching of composition and other lower-level English courses is that most departments face not so much a problem they can hope to solve as a situation they must attempt to palliate. Over the last dozen years in most institutions the demand for composition and other basic writing courses has increased, often as a result of the movement back toward stricter institution-wide requirements, while the number of graduate students available to teach basic writing courses has decreased. At the same time funds have become a great deal tighter, so that the conversion of vacant full-time positions into much less well-paid part-time ones has become a standard strategy. In its partly generous, partly selfish, certainly shortsighted rush to increase the number of doctoral programs and at the same time to meet demand for more writing courses, the discipline of English has made itself peculiarly vulnerable to budgetary exigencies.

Perhaps most important, however, our society has never cared to pay the cost of careful, conscientious instruction in writing at any level. We ought not to forget that even in more prosperous times, departments of English staffed their composition courses in ways other departments would have regarded as unethical. For instance, when I entered the profession at the beginning of the 1960s, many a state university supplemented its corps of graduate assistants by appointing new Ph.D.'s as instructors or lecturers for a maximum period of three to five years.

It may be that my concern to underline the root difficulties of being responsible and humane in employing non-tenure-track faculty results from my own frustrating lack of success in finding a happy solution. But the very pervasiveness of the problem—coupled with the different budgets, employment policies, and assignments of nontenured faculty at different institutions—suggests that the best most of us can do is whittle away however we can at the inequities incident on the employment of non-tenure-track faculty within our own institutional settings. Even that effort requires some difficult initial decisions.

For instance, there is the possibility of returning to that earlier practice of advertising for ABDs and/or Ph.D.'s to fill non-tenure-track instructor-ships renewable for a fixed number of years. This approach is perhaps necessary for institutions located in geographical areas that do not afford a sufficient pool of qualified persons to fill non-tenure-track positions, and it can be of real service to the new Ph.D. wishing three or so such years to establish scholarly credentials. However, we have decided against such an approach at Penn State because, first, the department cannot find the funds to pay what we regard as a minimal instructor's salary; second, the relationship with an instructor facing the end of a contract that may be his or her last in the profession can easily, despite good intentions on both sides, be unhealthily stressful; and third, asking a person to go through the expense and turmoil of moving here under such circumstances is not something we are comfortable doing.

Therefore we have attempted to take advantage of a distinction that exists at Penn State between two types of fixed-term contracts for lecturers. The first type allows only term-to-term appointments and carries no in-surance benefits; the second allows for annual appointments with those benefits. The humane direction to pursue is, of course, to convert as many as possible of the first type of contracts into the second. Certainly non-tenured faculty members who conscientiously serve the department de-serve to be able to plan a year at a time and also deserve health insurance coverage—to be without the latter today is to be exposed to the winds of fortune indeed. At the same time, an advantage for the department has been that, in place of the committee and other assignments that tenure-track faculty members carry, those on annual lecturer appointments assume such necessary duties as supervising new graduate students and part-time lecturers.

An annual struggle to find the funds for salary increases for part-time and/or non-tenure-track faculty occurs on our campus as on many others. The solution toward which we keep working is an obvious one: the salaries of non-tenure-track lecturers ought to be indexed either to faculty salaries or to graduate assistant stipends. Ad hoc adjustment each year is a weary process for both department chairs and their deans, and the frequently disappointing results of such tinkering on the fringes of the budget is not likely to encourage faculty not on standing appointments to believe that the department thinks their contribution important.

Such local strategies are, as I have suggested, merely palliatives, but working in whatever way one can to improve the conditions of those to whom we are able to offer only positions outside the tenure track is better than fully acquiescing in the inevitable pressure to have the necessary courses taught as cheaply as possible.

Part-Time Faculty Employment at Ball State University

Kathleen Sherfick and Joseph F. Trimmer
Ball State University

University administrators currently enjoy the same credibility as our country's economic advisers. All agree that the difficulties of part-time faculty (like the rates of inflation, deficit spending, and unemployment) are serious problems that must be solved if the university is to survive. Each year, they try to search for a solution in the midst of:

- constant need for writing courses
- declining enrollment in undergraduate and graduate literature courses
- deepening inflexibility of tenured literature faculty
- an expanding pool of young teachers seeking employment
- consistent demand for cost efficiency
- increasing concern about what students learn in the classroom

Administrators despair of finding a solution that everybody will consider responsible and fair. Instead of solving "the personnel problem" this year, they are forced, once again, to patch it—defending their decisions by citing economic adversity or university policy or promising to revise their decisions once they sense economic prosperity or the possibility of policy reform. New part-timers find these public statements confusing, painful, and unjust. More seasoned part-timers register the same emotions but usually resign themselves to a cynicism reminiscent of Louis Rukeyser (the genial host of *Wall Street Week*), who sees the promises and prophecies of all economic advisers as predictably absurd.

Like all American institutions of higher learning, Ball State University has participated in the absurdity of the part-time scandal. This report will document some of our abuses in this area, but its ultimate purpose will be to demonstrate that we are slowly developing a new spirit of cooperation on our campus that is making the status of part-timers more acceptable and amenable.

The history of part-time employment at Ball State University begins in benign indifference, changes to bitter disagreement, and moves toward a collegial compromise. Twenty years ago, the university's attitude toward part-timers was simple, insensitive, and ignorant. Part-time teachers were, by definition, part-time teachers—even if they taught a full load. These teachers had little identity, few rights, and no respect. Some of these teachers taught part-time for almost twenty years. Few administrators or tenured faculty knew who they were or cared whether they performed their duties effectively. Indeed, several years ago, a senior administrator drafted a memo in which he referred to the English Department's part-time faculty as "terminal housewives." The administrator, whose writing clearly needed dusting, apologized in another memo. It was all a family misunderstanding; he merely meant that these part-timers (mostly women) held master's degrees and would probably not pursue further graduate study.

The days of administrative indifference came to an abrupt halt with the inauguration of affirmative action legislation. Like other universities, Ball State had to review and revise the hiring, evaluation, and dismissal policies stated in its faculty handbook. During this same period, two other factors contributed to the growing complexity (and acrimony) of the part-time problem: (1) the national job market for English faculty closed, creating long lines of talented but unemployed Ph.D.'s queuing up for *any* teaching position—tenure-track or part-time; (2) the "terminal housewives" at our university enrolled in graduate schools and earned doctorates, thus adding professional credentials to their years of professional experience.

The English Department now faced the full complexity of the part-time problem. Most of its students were enrolled in the basic writing courses, and most of its salary dollars went to tenured literature faculty. The data below from the academic year 1981–82 indicate the extent of the problem.

University	Full-Time	Part-Time
Undergraduate enrollment	13,339	2,251
Graduate enrollment	465	2,342

English Department	
Freshman writing courses enrollment (3 courses)	8,722
All other undergraduate and graduate enrollment (48 courses)	4,141
Sections of freshman writing courses taught by part-time faculty	364
Sections of freshman writing courses taught by regular faculty	60
Percentage of departmental salaries for part-time faculty	24%
Percentage of departmental salaries for regular faculty	76%
Part-time faculty (1/3, 2/3, and full-time appointments)	41
Graduate teaching assistants (two classes a year)	19
Doctoral teaching fellows (two classes a year)	19
Regular faculty	38

To complicate the situation further, all the English Department part-timers held or were in the process of earning credentials equal to those of the regular faculty. With the job market closed and new Ph.D.'s graduating each year, this experienced group of temporary professionals would certainly demand a more permanent form of job security.

Or so thought the senior administrators who designed a new policy to protect the university from the potential legal action of part-timers:

> No temporary instructor or temporary assistant professor may serve more than three consecutive academic years or eleven quarters in total on full load. Beyond that point he or she may be employed on a quarter-by-quarter or annual-contract basis as a part-time temporary instructor or temporary assistant professor, *teaching not more than a two-thirds load.*

The intent of this policy, especially the last phrase, was to keep part-timers from accumulating the number of consecutive years of full employment necessary to qualify for tenure. After three years of full-time or part-time teaching, instructors and assistant professors were automatically cut back to "reduced timers"—in other words, given two-thirds or one-third appointments. New temporary instructors and assistant professors were given full loads (and even overloads) in order to staff the writing courses.

Economically, this policy allowed the university to hire cheaper labor and avoid costly litigation. Educationally, this policy produced faculty bitterness and—at the department level—administrative confusion. Experienced instructors, who despite their anonymity had served the department faithfully, wanted to teach full-time. Indeed, they had come to depend on their temporary paychecks. Inexperienced instructors, usually insecure about their professional skills, often preferred to begin with reduced loads until they felt more confident. Ironically, some of our experienced instructors were assigned to help these inexperienced instructors acquire confidence by assisting them in developing, organizing, and teaching the courses *they* had asked to teach. Although they complained privately, many part-timers accepted these policies. To do otherwise was to invite replacement by one of the hundreds of new Ph.D.'s who were bombarding the department with résumés each spring.

When senior administrators were confronted with these inequities, they seemed annoyed by the persistence of this personnel problem. They pointed to the many advantages available to Ball State's part-time faculty. All teachers were eligible for social security, workers' compensation, unemployment compensation, and other special privileges such as bookstore discounts and library carrels. Even part-timers on reduced loads were eligible for group health and major medical insurance, group life insurance, salary continuance insurance, and sick leave. Part-timers were also allowed maternity and child-care leaves. Teachers were not paid for such leaves, but neither were they penalized. They could claim their sick leave pay for such periods and resume their positions at the end of their leaves. In addition to receiving these fringe benefits, all teachers in the English Department had an office, a part-time student secretary, and access to standard communications hardware (typewriters, telephones, duplicating equipment). Teachers could even take a tuition-free course in another department (e.g., word processing) if it related in some way to their teaching.

From the senior administrator's point of view, Ball State was a part-timers' paradise. After all, these faculty members had what many teachers in the nation did not—a steady "temporary" job and a bagful of benefits. What could possibly be wrong? From the part-timers' point of view, Ball State was still limbo—they had jobs that led nowhere and benefits in the personnel office but not in the department meetings. Several courageous part-timers challenged the enforced load reduction policy and other matters relating to salary and contracts. Although Ball State is not unionized—nor is it likely to be in the near future—these challenges helped the part-timers form both a sense of community and a common list of grievances: (1) last-minute contracts, (2) irregular teaching hours, (3) assignment to department committees but no vote in department meetings, and (4) recognition as a tennis partner but rejection as a professional colleague. The list continues, but the items are surely familiar to everyone.

In the last two years, four elements have changed Ball State's part-time problem from conflict to cooperation. First, the chair, mistakenly identified as the initiator of inconsistent hiring policies, had actually been fighting on many fronts to bring order and coherence to the part-time problem. When he lost these battles, he was not able to fulfill the promises he wanted to keep. In the last several months, however, he has been winning more battles, thus enabling part-timers to see him as an ally rather than an enemy.

Second, the directors of the writing program (there have been four during the period under discussion) have always acted as the part-timers' friend in court—airing their complaints, arguing their rights, and applauding their efforts. (These directors have also been accused of causing trouble and building empires.) In recent years, the directors have linked Ball State's writing program to a network of writing programs throughout the country, thus overcoming the sense of professional isolation that haunts so many part-timers.

Third, the part-time faculty themselves must be given credit for changing university attitudes. Although they were trained as linguists and literary scholars, they began to discover the intellectual excitement, research opportunities, and professional activities available in the "new" discipline of composition and rhetoric. They attended conferences, read papers, submitted grant applications, and published articles. Indeed, they became the most professionally active "members" of the English Department, and their new credentials soon began to establish the writing faculty as one of the university's most talented resources.

These first three elements provided the proper mixture for change; the fourth proved the catalyst. In the fall of 1981, at the invitation of the chair, a Writing Program Administration (WPA) consulting team visited the Ball State campus to assess its program. Although the consultants examined a wide range of issues, they focused much of their attention on the status of part-timers. The care with which they conducted their research established their credibility with our faculty and administrators. Hence, their lengthy report received considerable attention. By placing Ball State's part-time problem in a national context, they dramatized both the liabilities and possibilities of our situation. And by looking at our situation as consultants (rather than as evaluators), they presented several reasonable plans for working out our difficulties.

The WPA report is long and complex, but it provides an agenda that part-timers and tenured faculty have agreed to discuss as professionals. Like our embattled chair, part-timers will not win on every item on this agenda. Indeed, we lost our first major battle, the enfranchisement of part-timers, a few weeks after all parties had agreed to negotiate in good faith. But the tenured literature faculty and the senior administrators now know that our part-timers are professionals, worthy of their new designation— "the writing faculty." They are also learning—somewhat more slowly— that the writing faculty will be the eventual salvation of a shrinking department. Under the chair's leadership, the department now offers a Ph.D. with a cognate in composition and rhetoric; is hiring tenure-track faculty members to develop that program; is inaugurating a flexible (merit) salary schedule for part-timers; has given more than half the appointments on the writing program policy committee to part-timers; is financing orientation programs, in-service training seminars, and travel expenses for part-timers who wish to attend professional meetings. With such encouragement, the writing faculty members are taking charge of their own professional and financial destinies by developing correspondence courses, publishing research, reviewing and writing textbooks, and participating in externally funded projects. The writing faculty's morale has been boosted by these successes. And the literature faculty is beginning to believe that it may have a lot to learn from its younger colleagues.

In sum, the part-time profile at Ball State University is up several points. We are not bulls, charging ahead in the blind expectation of unearned profits. We are not bears, retreating to our dens to complain about previous failures or predict future disasters. We are chameleons, adapting our skills and strategies to meet an environment that, we know all too well, is always temporary.

7. Private Colleges

Course by Course, Year by Year: Surviving Seventeen Years as Part-Time Faculty with Professional Image Intact

Janet Powers Gemmill

Gettysburg College

With great diligence, I have quested through much of the literature on my shelves and more in my memory in search of a literary character who would serve as a symbol for the part-time college professor. Although Kamala Markandaya's *The Nowhere Man* (1972) sprang instantly to mind, it was apparent that her story of an aging Indian merchant caught in a wave of anti-Asiatic demonstrations in London had little usefulness except for its handsomely applicable title. So I turned next to Milton's anguished hero Samson Agonistes, who, in a state of angry humiliation, pulled down the temple upon the heads of his enemies as well as upon his own. Recognizing that such an uncompassionate gesture might be unpolitic, even as a symbol, I have settled instead on Saul Bellow's *Dangling Man*. That novel purports to be the journal of a young man, living in Chicago, who gives up his job, expecting to be inducted into the army. Red tape keeps Joseph dangling for almost a year (not a very long time for a part-timer). His journal reveals his psychological reactions to idleness, how he passes his time, his growing unrest, and finally a sense of relief when his call finally comes.

The image of the dangling man came to me in mid-June while I was awaiting the arrival of my contract for the 1982–83 academic year. Even though the budget is drawn up months before and registration figures for fall courses are established by mid-May, the contract never arrives until early July, by which time my fingernails are usually bitten to the quick.

Like Joseph, I always experience a great relief when my contract arrives. But in a larger sense, I am still dangling, for after seventeen years as a part-timer at the same institution, teaching more than half time for over ten years, I am still awaiting my call to a full-time teaching position. Although other part-timers have been brought in to teach literature and composition courses that I could easily teach, my teaching load during the past twelve years has consisted of five courses per year (seven is full load at Gettysburg): two courses in the fall term, two in the spring, and one in January. My India courses, Civilization of India and Literature of India, are two-semester courses taught in alternate years. I have been teaching Literary Foundations of Western Culture, a survey course, regularly since 1963. My January courses have included black literature, children's literature, the Renaissance, and Gandhi. It is not an intolerable situation. A five-sevenths load gives me time to read, write, and do research. In the past seventeen years, I have published three short story translations (from Urdu), sixteen articles, and sixteen book reviews; and I have presented thirteen papers before national and regional professional meetings. In addition, I serve on the editorial board of two respected journals: *Journal of South Asian Literature* and *South Asian Review*.

Yet hovering on the horizon are darker clouds. Word comes from Oakland University in Michigan that, to ease the financial crunch, all part-timers have been let go. The president of my own institution is making noises about shrinking the size of the student body in anticipation of an enrollment crunch in the late 1980s. In the event of an "unsanforized" student population, what will happen to the part-timers? At present, there are thirty-three of us on the payroll of Gettysburg College, distributed through nine departments. Will it make any difference that I am teaching unique courses, which I designed myself, which hold a distinct position in the curriculum, and which are not mere clones of some hugely enrolled required course? Will it matter that my courses in Indian literature and civilization satisfy a newly instituted, non-Western requirement and fill a large gap in our rather meager offerings of international studies? Will it be significant that I teach "interdisciplinary courses," which are always described as "hard to staff" and "unappealing to young scholars who are trying to publish" because such courses require too much preparation? Does it matter that I have sacrificed a good bit of my career preparing for such courses yet have managed to publish extensively as well?

Lest we spend too much time gazing into an uncertain future, let me begin at the beginning and describe some of the irregularities that got me into this dangling situation. In the great American pastime, there are two ways of striking out: one is to keep the bat on one's shoulder; the other is to swing and miss. Looking back over my career, I notice a number of situations in which the bat never left my shoulder. When I came to Gettysburg as a full-time instructor in 1963, I filled a slot in the English department normally thought of as a "folding-chair" position: three courses in English comp each semester and one survey in literary foundations. Those who taught these courses usually stayed two or three years before moving on to graduate school to work on their doctorates. After two years, I resigned to do the same. When I returned to Gettysburg in 1966, I had in the interim become a faculty wife (strike number one); the English department was not interested in hiring me full-time, either in a folding-chair position or in positions vacant in my areas of specialization—English literature of the seventeenth and twentieth centuries. More suspect was my newly initiated work in Indian literature (strike number two). Surely I could not be seriously interested in English literature if I dabbled in matters Oriental (shades of Macaulay), despite the fact that I soon passed all of my prelims in periods of English literature and eventually wrote a dissertation based entirely on Western critical ideas of narrative technique (1972). At the same time, in 1966, Gettysburg College was a joint recipient of a six-college Ford Foundation grant in Asian studies, which involved library acquisitions, faculty enrichment, and syllabi on the civilizations of China and India, respectively. It was a sizable grant that only committed the college to staff a few courses dealing with Asia. Given the dearth of "cheap" India scholars, the college hired me as a part-timer to teach the two-semester Indian civilization course and the two-semester literary foundations course that was "hard to staff."

I taught four courses each year until 1969–70, when I worked for one year as the director of the newly initiated January term. The experience was successful and the job was offered to me again, but I turned it down in order to raise my children (strike number three), born in 1970 and 1972. Although by this time I was out of the game, I didn't know it and continued to teach five courses a year during those childbearing years. The struggle to meet the needs of two infants and to get all my papers graded hardly left me time to worry about losing out in the academic arena. Thanks to a supportive husband and the concept of joint parenting, those frantic years produced not only a dissertation but continuing research and another book-length manuscript as well.

I have no doubt that a period of part-time teaching is ideal for the individual who seriously chooses to bear children without totally giving up her career. As the children become older, however, a crisis may set in, as it did with me. If one has always held the ideal of college teaching as a career goal, it becomes increasingly difficult to sit back and watch first one's peers and then the younger scholars advancing through the ranks while one remains a lecturer. Despite my Ph.D., I continued to earn the same salary as other lecturers holding only a B.A. degree.

In recent years, significant measures have been taken to better the lot of the part-timer. Gettysburg relieved some of my frustration in 1979 by establishing two part-time ranks with a salary differential of $100 per course unit. At that time, I was designated an adjunct assistant professor as befitted one with more impressive credentials. No matter that by this time most of my peers had at least attained the rank of associate professor. Longevity at Gettysburg had no import for part-timers until 1980 when a salary increment of $50 per course per five years at the college was added to the base salary for those with some seniority as adjunct faculty. Bit by bit, the situation has begun to improve, and certainly conditions are better at Gettysburg than at many colleges, yet after seventeen years these increments seem like "too little, too late."

A perpetual part-timer also has the problem of feeling isolated from colleagues. Such alienation may not bother the individual who moonlights from another job in industry or another educational institution, but it is painful for the individual whose career revolves around a part-time position. Although the dean of the college repeatedly encourages me to come to faculty meetings, I find it exasperating to be unable to vote even on issues that affect my courses. I have settled for staying home and reading the published minutes of the meetings in order to be able to discuss faculty politics with some degree of intelligence. Another difficult time is the academic procession at commencement. Although most of my colleagues would be delighted to escape the costume party, I still long to don my doctoral robes and to avoid that insistent student question, "But why didn't *you* march?"

Another problem plaguing the part-timer is lack of fringe benefits. This issue did not surface for me until the collapse of my marriage, which proved unable to bear the double strain of disillusionment at home and in career as well. After my divorce in 1980, the children were covered by my former husband's medical insurance but I was not. Nor could I afford to take out a thousand-dollar medical insurance policy for myself. For a year, I lived in abject fear of falling sick; I could hardly afford to go to the doctor, let alone bear the cost of a sustained illness. The following year, after much lobbying by myself and a few other part-timers, we won the right to participate in the college group-insurance plan, but only on the condition that we pay the total cost of our own coverage. Such payment, however, was far less than if we were to purchase separate policies outside the group plan. The insurance situation at last seemed satisfactory. Then, out of the blue, last summer, I received a notice that the cost of the medical plan to the college would increase forty-seven percent. Because I must bear the full increase in the cost of my policy, what little yearly salary increment I receive was immediately swallowed up by this improbable increase in rates.

The struggle to survive financially continues. In order to pay for property taxes, music lessons for the children, and payments on car and house loans, I have begun to moonlight: teaching English as a second language for the local school system and Lutheran Theological Seminary. Although such work is perhaps preferable to waitressing, it pays little, is less stimulating than Indian philosophy, and cuts heavily into time when I could be reading or doing research. In short, I resent it. I wonder again and again how someone with my credentials, experience, training, and skills could possibly have landed in such an absurd situation. I graduated from my undergraduate institution magna cum laude, Phi Beta Kappa, with honors in English literature; was editor-in-chief of the college newspaper; and received a coveted award for the senior who best exemplified the aims of a Bucknell education. Like Bellow's dangling man, I walked away from a promising job as feature writer for the *Pittsburgh Press* to go to graduate school. I have published numerous articles and reviews in the name of a college that allows me to teach five courses and pays me by the course. In keeping with its excellent support for faculty development, however, Gettysburg does give me an office of my own and provides sizable summer research grants and unlimited travel funds for conferences.

As long as I can continue to work on meaningful projects and publish the results of my research, I can hold up my head in the community of scholars and act "as if" I am one of them, though you and I both know that I am only "passing," that I do not really belong among them, that like Bellow's dangling man I am perpetually waiting to become the real thing.

Maintaining a persona, however, is the key to keeping intact one's professional image. Indeed, the contacts that one makes in the scholarly world beyond one's own institution can go a long way toward sustaining one's sense of self-respect. I must confess that I look forward to professional meetings where I can consort with colleagues, deliver papers, and partic- ipate in heady discussions with no fear of being reminded of my "place" in the academic pecking order. There are always moments, however, when the embarrassment of being "found out" looms large. While at Columbia during the summer of 1981 in an NEH summer seminar, a colleague eagerly proposed a faculty exchange: I would go to her college in California for a semester, and she would come to Gettysburg. I don't suppose she'll ever know why I greeted her proposal less than enthusiastically, or sense that I would have reveled in such an exchange had I been a full-time tenured faculty member.

Being a part-timer also puts one in an ambiguous position regarding off-campus opportunities for faculty enrichment. Some years ago, the Uni- versity of Chicago offered an NEH institute dealing with India. As is cus- tomary with most NEH opportunities, the recommendation of my dean was to accompany the application. When I requested such a nomination, I was told by the president of the college that because I was appointed yearly, I would not be able to meet the terms of the project: to return to my home college and teach for at least one year a course based on the institute experience. Although I was already teaching a similar course and the college had no plan to deny me another year's appointment, I was not permitted to apply for the NEH institute. My status was plainly that of a second-class citizen even though it was to the disadvantage of the college to keep me in that role. Gettysburg College's administration has changed, however, since this incident, and with Gettysburg's current emphasis on faculty development, it's much less likely that such an opportunity would be so easily tossed aside.

Many students may not be aware that some of their professors are not full-time faculty. When a student comes to me for a letter of recommen- dation, I feel obligated to point out that my letter might not be as valuable to his or her job prospects as a letter from someone with a more solid academic title. If the student replies, "Oh, that doesn't matter," I'm always overjoyed, although I suspect even then that I may be doing the person a disfavor. What I'm trying to suggest is that, although my professional image may be intact, years of second-class citizenship have taken their toll.

Although I care deeply about students and enjoy spending time talking with them, I have grown bitter in the realization that I am not being paid to do that but am expected only to meet them in the classroom. When I spend precious hours with students, it is my research time that suffers. Which is the more important lifeline? Even when asked to advise inde- pendent study projects or supervise special majors, I must do so out of the goodness of my heart, for I am paid on a per-course basis and receive no special remuneration for any responsibilities beyond designated courses. When I pointed this fact out to colleagues, they replied, "Then stop doing it. Just say 'no' when a student asks." To turn down a student who wants to do special work in one's field, however, is to violate the professional commitment one makes as an educator. That I have not been able to do.

For a while I tried another tactic: I sought to avoid generating new projects that seemed to spring naturally from my teaching, on the premise that I was not being paid to enhance the academic atmosphere by arranging for Indian musicians or bringing in lecturers. The result was that India was simply ignored by those responsible for those matters; and worse, my own creative wellsprings began to dry up when deprived of an outlet. So as part of a continuing sanity-saving effort, I'm back at it again. This year, I've organized a series of film classics from the non-Western world as a way of reaching students with cinematic inclinations. All this planning is time-consuming and energy-sapping, but if I am to continue to function as a thinking, committed teacher and scholar, I must behave "as if" I were a full-fledged member of the academic community. I must pretend to be something that I am not if my teaching and my writing are to mean anything. One must function as a whole person. There is no such thing as a part-time teacher or an adjunct scholar. These are categories in the minds of administrators, categories that acquire reality only in the bursar's office and the bank account.

This attitude, of course, can be self-defeating, for a college gets more than its money's worth out of a part-timer with such a commitment. In fact, a recent job evaluation by my department chairman stated, "What most disturbs one about her situation is the sense that valuable talent is going to waste and that a contribution is being lost. On the other hand, the price attendant on trying to convert my colleagues is more than I am ready to pay. Even where she is, J.G. is a valuable person." That statement, to me, was the kiss of death, an indication that where I am, which is nowhere, is a satisfactory, even useful, arrangement for the college. The one person who might champion me is not willing to do so. Furthermore, conversations with a representative of the AAUP earlier this year indicated that long-time adjunct faculty are seldom taken on as full-time at institutions where they have been part-time. The difficulty seems to be one of image: once a part-timer, always a part-timer.

I do not mean to suggest that Gettysburg College has been utterly oblivious to the role of part-time faculty. In fact, in recent years, Gettysburg has committed itself to decreasing the number of part-time positions and improving salaries for those remaining. In 1970, the administration realized that they could not in all conscience allow adjunct faculty to serve on committees. It was then that I was removed from the Asian studies committee and my husband placed there instead in order to ensure the continued flow of my ideas to the committee.

In a considerably more positive effort this past year, a faculty task force drafted a remarkable part-time policy, similar to those currently in force at Yale, Princeton, Wesleyan, Oberlin, and Carleton, based on the premise that adjunct faculty are valued professionals who should be compensated fairly for their work, recognized officially for their contributions to college governance, allowed access to fringe-benefit plans, given greater job security, and encouraged to continue academic work through financial reward and promotion. The policy distinguishes between (1) full-time faculty on reduced load; (2) regular part-time faculty (those who teach a one-half load or more or have been at Gettysburg for three or more years and whose qualifications meet the standards set for full-time faculty in terms of teaching experience, degrees, and creativity); and (3) adjunct faculty (who do not meet the criteria set for regular part-timers). If this thoroughly humane policy should be accepted by the faculty and administration, there would be a number of changes, not the least of which would be a prorated salary. I would then carry a prorated load of advisees and be eligible for committee work and departmental duties; I would participate fully in the evaluation process and vote in faculty meetings. My medical insurance would be paid in part by the college. I would be assigned a regular faculty rank and be eligible for promotion. Although I would still be hired on a yearly basis, I would no longer be left dangling until midsummer regarding my contract for the fall. Such a policy would not meet my need for a full-time position, but it would offer job security and certainly make life more bearable.

Contemplating such a change carries one into a quixotic world of double realities. Acceptance of the proposed policy is a wild dream, but only if second-class citizenship is the unchanging reality. If, as Bellow suggests, the "dangling man" lives in unreality, such a humane policy is a way out of the nightmare in which part-timers live. The proposed policy implies financial security, a recovered sense of self-worth, and, most important, realization of the career goal set for oneself as an undergraduate. I cannot predict whether Gettysburg College or any other college will adopt such innovative part-time policies. To do so would involve a larger financial outlay for a previously "cheap" commodity. To make such a commitment, however, would surely be in the interest of any school.

Today's part-timers are as creative and able as regular faculty tenured during the fifties and sixties. Adjunct faculty have a great deal to give if institutions will allow them to give it. Such policies might also allow reduced course loads for those raising families, with the potential of transition to a full-time load, thus regularizing procedures for moving from part-time to full-time positions. To adopt such a policy would also be to acknowledge that times have changed: the academic marketplace is such that well-trained teachers are willing to accept part-time positions rather than give up their allegiance to education. To acknowledge the caliber of those caught in the professional glut is to endow them with a sense of dignity and enable them to work joyfully and therefore productively.

Joseph in *The Dangling Man* describes the negative alternative: "There is nothing to do but wait, or dangle, and grow more and more dispirited. It is perfectly clear to me that I am deteriorating, storing bitterness and spite which eat like acids at my endowment of generosity and good will" (Bellow 12). Like Joseph, I find myself no stranger to corrosive emotions, which have begun to destroy my enthusiasm, my ideals, and my very world view.

Colleges and universities today face difficult personnel decisions as inflation cuts down the margins with which budgets can be manipulated. Despite this realization, we must continue to plead that administrators maintain a sense of academic community based on a sensitivity to faculty morale. Surely it is not too much to ask that institutions of higher learning clarify policies for part-timers and clean up the web of inconsistencies that has grown up around part-time positions at most schools. Nor is it too much to ask that administrators work toward implementing those procedures that will reward fairly the loyalty, commitment, and considerable contributions of the long-term part-timer.

The Carleton Alternative

Julie Grover Klassen and Anne Close Ulmer
Carleton College

Carleton College is a private four-year liberal arts college in southern Minnesota. It has a student body of about 1,750, virtually all of whom are full-time resident students. The faculty numbers 150, of whom 8 are regular part-timers. Of these, 5 are women, and 5 are tenured (2 of them women). In addition, there are a number of temporary part-timers, depending on fluctuating course enrollment and leave-replacement provisions. Language teaching and music instruction are the two areas requiring the most temporary part-timers. In the Department of Modern Languages and Literatures, for example, there are 15 full-time faculty, 13 part-timers, of whom 3 are regular part-timers.

Since 1975 the Carleton College handbook has described a regular part-time faculty member as a person who "normally carries at least a half-time teaching load for the school year" and teaches at least two terms. Although subsequent handbook revisions have refined certain aspects of the policy in important ways, the basic thrust has not changed: regular part-timers enjoy in a measure proportionate to their work load the same general salary scale, fringe benefits, academic benefits, and nonteaching responsibilities (advising and committees) as full-time faculty members.

Until recently, however, the criteria that determined initially whether a less than full-time appointment carried regular part-time or temporary part-time status were not clearly defined. When we were hired in the spring of 1978 for the following academic year, neither the dean nor the department chair at that time could clarify our status, although each urged us to seek a pronouncement from the other. This indecisiveness derived in part from the fact that the one tenure-track position and the one half-time position advertised in German had been redefined during the hiring process as one five-sixths position and one two-thirds position. Furthermore, the dean was apparently also pondering the feasibility of a lectureship category between tenurable and temporary part-timers. Nonetheless, the root of the problem lay in the lack of precise policy guidelines. We did establish that we were to receive a prorated salary and the normal fringe benefits, but the prospects for employment beyond our one-year contract were indeterminate.

In the meantime, we enjoyed full integration into the life of the college. We were told that we could officially participate in faculty meetings and apply for travel funds. Our colleagues never treated us as anything less than full participants in the college's pursuits. In the spring of 1979 we received reappointment letters, and our names appeared on the list of regular faculty members eligible for election to major committees. Somehow we had become de facto regular part-timers. This gratified but also mystified us, as we still had no official indication of our long-term prospects.

The arrival of a new dean in 1979–80 set into motion a number of changes that eliminated all ambiguities about our situations. All part-timers now know from the beginning whether they have a regular, tenurable part-time position or a temporary appointment. (Temporary part-timers include those who regularly teach less than half-time and those hired at the last minute to take on overflow courses. They are paid by the course, fringe benefits do not accrue to them unless circumstances bring them up to half-time within the academic year, and they have no nonteaching responsibilities.) As most regular part-time appointments have emerged from special circumstances, the college has not frequently advertised such positions.

Carleton definitely treats the regular part-time faculty better than they do the temporary part-timers. We have regular, generally private offices, whereas the adjunct people are often crowded into shared facilities, or find themselves shifting offices every term. Untenured, regular part-timers, like untenured full-timers, receive renewable two-year contracts and annual salary letters; they undergo a "third year" review after the equivalent number of courses, and, if successful, are evaluated for tenure after the equivalent of six years. As with full-timers, both evaluations focus on teaching quality, evidence of scholarly research (specifically publications), and committee participation. We can attest to the fact that the third-year review was as grueling for us as for any other faculty members. However, one emerges with the feeling that one has come through the same baptism by fire that the other younger faculty members have survived. Now that we have been through the review, we also have a definite sense of the direction that our development in the succeeding three to five years should take. As part-timers, we have access to or may compete for professional-development resources on an equal basis with full-timers. Promotion terms are the same for both groups.

This standardization of procedures has benefited regular part-timers in psychological as well as objective terms. The boost in morale has done much to promote the fulfillment of one condition that the college has long assumed, stated in the faculty handbook: "Regular part-time faculty members share with the regular full-time faculty a commitment to long-range professional aims and improvement." The college's consistent and equitable treatment of regular part-timers is a major factor in the part-timer's desire to make a clear commitment to professional and college goals. By its own actions, then, the college has eliminated one of the classic objections to part-time employment—lack of commitment.

The other typical prejudices against part-timers also do not impress the current dean. Carleton's size and small-town location do not invite the kind of clamor for part-time employment that would cause management problems or swell office-space needs and costs. Carleton has full computer data on all regular faculty members and the ability to simulate various long-range patterns. Hence any other potential problems with part-timers could be anticipated.

Beyond this, the dean views regular part-time employment as a benefit for the college. This confirms our own assessment that the college and the German section of the Modern Languages and Literatures Department derive several advantages from our particular part-time arrangement. First of all, our positions allow for flexibility in adding the extra sections that enrollment may dictate. Our individual specialities and teaching styles increase variety in a small college with limited FTEs. Our presence allows a more felicitous distribution of tasks related to independent studies, major advising, upper-division literature courses, and senior comprehensive exams. For a school such as Carleton, which is heavily tenured, part-time employment provides a means of getting more professors, more ideas, and more areas of interest on campus than would otherwise be possible. The arrangement is certainly financially valuable for the college, since both we and the dean are realistic enough to acknowledge that a part-time person who takes the job seriously will do more work than the fraction for which she or he is paid. Inherent in a part-time appointment is the fact that, once on campus for the day to teach one course, a part-timer tends to spend more time on preparation or with students than is strictly required. Whereas control over this phenomenon lies largely in the hands of the part-timer, the psychology of the situation usually prevents a teach-and-leave mentality. This is especially true at Carleton, where there exists a high level of dedication among all faculty members. Beyond that, certain activities such as faculty and department meetings do not logically allow a fractional proportion of participation. In short, the college gets at least as much as it pays for, if not more.

On the other side of the balance sheet, both of us in German find the arrangement essentially advantageous. As members of two-career families, we appreciate the personal time benefits of part-time teaching. Our division of labor allows each of us a nonteaching term (ten weeks) every other year.

Although the nonteaching duties are often time-consuming, we see them as a link to better knowledge of the students and as access to faculty decision-making structures. Each of us has also directed a German overseas seminar at least once. Of course, such complete integration into all aspects of faculty life means that people sometimes forget that we should only be assigned duties in proportion to our teaching load. We do have recourse to the Faculty Affairs Committee, which makes or oversees all nonelected committee appointments.

Other regular part-timers would undoubtedly raise other pros and cons. Another regular part-timer in our department sees her half-time position in Spanish as the only way to combine a career with raising her children in the manner she considers essential. A couple in the political science department shares a tenured position, in part for the same reason. Such arrangements provide another benefit to the college in that they present women students with a variety of role models.

In spite of the improvement in benefits and conditions for regular part-timers, there are a few areas where explicit guidelines are impossible. One concerns moving from full-time to regular part-time status, or vice versa. Officially, all full-timers now have the right to negotiate for part-time, and part-timers can petition to become full-time. In both cases, change in status must be mutually desirable. A recent request to change to half-time, however, was denied, in part because the person was not able or willing for personal reasons (child rearing) to continue carrying half of her nonteaching duties. The decision raised a number of issues: To what extent should or can a college be flexible in negotiating tailor-made career options? Is it possible to tune policy so finely that complex conflicts between the good of the college and the good of the individual can be settled to mutual satisfaction? How do we prevent such requests from providing grist for the mills of those who find part-time employees a liability, or women ultimately undependable for serious scholarly careers?

As the last question indicates, many concerns of regular part-timers also spill over into facultywide issues. Their resolution will prove valuable to all of us on the faculty at Carleton.

Against the Wind:
Converting Part-Time Positions to Full-Time

Howard S. Erlich
Ithaca College

Ithaca College's experience with part-time faculty teaching writing has caused the college to take an unusual step: while many colleges and universities are increasing their use of part-time faculty, Ithaca College has created seven full-time writing positions to replace part-time positions in its writing program. This essay will detail the evolution of the Applied Writing Program and the reasons for moving to full-time positions, the mechanics of the move, and the problem of attaining and maintaining professional respect for the writing program.

Ithaca College is the largest private residential college in New York State. The primarily undergraduate student body of 4,500 is taught by 275 full-time and 107 part-time faculty (1980–81 figures). Just over 14% of the college's FTE positions are taught by part-time faculty. The ten-year-old Applied Writing Program is separate from the English Department but has just merged with the Reading Program. This new unit serves the entire campus with fourteen FTE positions, of which seven are full-time (four writing and three reading). But by the end of academic year 1982–83 three more full-time positions will be filled (with a commensurate reduction in part-time positions). Thus, after the transitional stage, the new unit will have ten full-time positions and four FTE positions staffed by part-timers. Certainly this decision is incongruent with the trend toward increasing utilization of part-time faculty, especially for the teaching of writing. Let us turn then to the reasons for moving from part- to full-time faculty.

First, establishment of full-time positions would stabilize the faculty and the program. Heretofore, as a program staffed entirely by part-timers, faculty positions were not attractive enough to cause persons to remain in Ithaca just to teach in the program. With few exceptions, the typical Applied Writing faculty member was either a predictable transient (usually a Cornell grad student) or the spouse or partner of a faculty member with few employment options available. No one came to Ithaca College just to teach writing! (This situation was a geographical and financial reality, not intended to reflect on the writing faculty's qualifications. On the contrary, proximity to Cornell and the intense competition for employment in this area provided I.C. with a higher quality writing faculty than one could reasonably expect.) In any event, creating full-time positions would lessen the college's dependence on a captive labor market and might cause faculty to choose Ithaca College.

A second reason for creation of full-time positions was the college's changed legal position: for years the college had been unwilling to sanction full-time nontenure positions, fearing claims of de facto tenure after a faculty member's seventh year. Now, enough precedent has been established for the college's legal counsel to believe that a policy of long-term nontenure positions need not result in claims of de facto tenure. Finally, full-time faculty positions were created in response both to part-timers' repeated requests and to a desire on the part of faculty and administration to correct the inequities of the system. Without suggesting that the motives of the administration were entirely altruistic, it is accurate to say that the simple desire to treat faculty fairly was the primary reason for the move to full-time positions at Ithaca College.

To suggest that the decision to create seven full-time positions, and thereby reduce substantially the number of part-time positions, was embraced uncritically by faculty teaching in the program would be misleading. Many difficult issues arose, but perhaps the most crucial and instructive for the purposes of this essay was the problem of establishing a professionally respectable program without disregarding the experience and commitment of part-time faculty teaching in the program. That is, some of our part-time faculty would be candidates for the full-time positions, but in some instances their formal training left them at a disadvantage since they lacked advanced coursework or degrees. Other faculty would choose not to compete for full-time positions but soon would find themselves in a program staffed largely by full-timers; suddenly their part-time status, heretofore the norm and therefore respectable, might leave them as second-class citizens. So the decision to create full-time positions, a decision demanding substantial commitment by the college and desired by most writing program faculty, was not without its puzzles and ironies.

Although internal candidates for the full-time positions were promised the inside track in the ensuing search, there were no guarantees. Quite the contrary. A national search was undertaken, the positions widely advertised and publicized, and a nonpartisan search committee established. All things being equal, we would hire internal candidates, but internal candidates had to compete and be prepared to be unsuccessful in the competition. Crucial indeed was the position description, for it would establish the parameters of the applicant pool. I quote the required and the preferred qualifications verbatim:

> Required: Masters degree in an appropriate field. Experience in teaching college-level composition and qualifications to teach in two of these areas: advanced expository writing, technical writing, creative writing.

Preferred: Ph.D. in the Teaching of Composition (or a related field with emphasis in composition). Preference will be given to applicants with demonstrated achievements in the field, evidenced by publications, curricular development, and/or outstanding service to a college or university.

These qualifications, while giving clear preference to the terminal degree in composition-related fields, also reward applicants whose service to an institution has been outstanding. Thus, our own internal candidates, most of whom were fine teachers, active in curricular development and other contributions to the college, would be strong candidates for the full-time positions. (Ultimately, of the four full-time positions filled in the first year of the search, three were filled by internal candidates. But offers first were made to two external and two internal candidates; when one external candidate refused our offer, an internal candidate was next in line.)

This exposition of the move from part-time to full-time positions at Ithaca College has focused only tangentially on the issue of maintaining a professionally respectable program while not penalizing those with long and devoted service to it. To join the issue let us consider two ideas: on the one hand, as the teaching of composition comes into its own in terms of research and pedagogy, responsible administrators and faculty wish to hire educators who have participated in this research and pedagogy; on the other, responsible administrators and faculty want to deal fairly with colleagues who have served an institution well but who, as the argument goes, have been so overloaded with paper grading, student conferences, and other paraphernalia of teaching writing that they haven't had time for their own professional development.

Of course, in application the issue is not as clean as that outlined above; compromise can often be achieved. Still, faculty and administration must recognize their responsibility to their institutions, their peers, and their students by hiring the most qualified applicants. (As the qualifications quoted earlier indicate, one should not equate "most qualified" with "highest degree earned" in any absolute way.) To argue that the institution is responsible for the plight of overworked, underpaid composition teachers by preventing them from developing professionally is to place responsibility unreasonably. Some individuals teach while remaining active professionally; some eschew teaching for a time while pursuing advanced study or degrees, but others do not. I do not mean to minimize the difficulties, nor do I wish to dismiss those who teach writing well. But it is not productive to ignore the dictates of the marketplace or the value of personal and professional initiative. If the teaching of writing is to attain respect and recognition within the academic community, its standards must be those of established disciplines. Some fine teachers likely will be hurt in the process.

I do not know if Ithaca College's experience will be instructive to many. After all, most institutions seem content to use more, not fewer, part-time faculty, and certainly the notion of establishing full-time positions from part-time ones is irregular at this time. Yet my comments, which some might call hard-nosed, are consistent with Ithaca College's move to full-time faculty. If we are serious about improving students' literacy and recognize the dimensions of the task, then we shall want the best persons possible doing the job. Those persons will teach better and their students will learn more if the conditions of employment are reasonable and attractive. To defend reliance on part-timers on economic grounds is to take a short-sighted view of the enterprise; missing is the reality of how much psychic and material support teachers of writing need.

A View from the Inside: What Was Wrong with an All Part-Time Program

Miriam Brody
Ithaca College

It is tempting to begin with what was right with our part-time program; we had disdained hierarchies and tried not to reproduce any. No one could claim ownership of upper-level writing courses; they rotated among all interested faculty. No decision was made without free and open discussion. Curriculum and personnel procedures grew through mutual consent, achieved carefully, if protractedly. The outcome was a faculty that did not burn out, even after more than a half-dozen years of uninterrupted composition teaching. Talk about courses and students went on all the time—in hallways, over coffee, on rides home. We had, I think it is called, community.

Why wasn't this bliss? The first problem was our growing perception of a fundamental inequity in our treatment compared to the treatment of other colleagues in the college. Because of an administrative snaggle, which has since been corrected, we were teaching three courses a semester and called three-quarter-time, and some of our colleagues in other departments were teaching three courses and called full-time. (Today, full-time is four courses.) Furthermore, in those days (not terribly long ago, before jobs tightened and credentials proliferated), some of these other colleagues were reaching tenure levels without terminal degrees and publications; we were dead-ended in a no-promotion job. Since we also saw ourselves as hard-working, successful teachers with a healthy and innovative writing program developing around us (20 courses, a writing minor, a writing contest), we felt undeservedly excluded from the normal course of bargaining for promotion and extension of contracts available to other colleagues.

A second problem was that our different and lesser status isolated us and suggested our work was of lesser value. That we were part-time and predominantly female only supported an unfortunate tendency to see as schoolmarmish, and therefore unscholarly, the work of helping students write better. Until the writing faculty could begin to resemble more, at least in matters of status, our colleagues across the campus, pooling the available human resources at the college to encourage the teaching of writing-across-the-disciplines was needlessly postponed. It will be interesting to see if the professionalization of teaching writing facilitates this important work. We hope it does.

Part-Time Faculty at Hood College

Sylvia Guffin Turner
Hood College

Hood College is a four-year, independent liberal arts college for women in Frederick, Maryland, that also provides career preparation. We admit commuting male students to our undergraduate program, while our graduate school is fully coeducational. We also employ seventy part-time faculty.

We employ so many part-time faculty partly because of changes in our curricula since 1973. We have witnessed student demand for courses in management, for instance, grow so rapidly that, unable to locate sufficient numbers of full-time faculty, we have hired part-timers instead. Thus, in addition to 89 full-timers in the fall of 1981, we had 12 regular part-timers and 58 temporary part-timers (half of whom taught only graduate courses) for an undergraduate student population of 1,122 (826, or 73.6%, full-time; 296, or 26.4%, part-time) and a graduate student population of 694 (39, or 6%, full-time; 655, or 94%, part-time). Ours is not a unionized faculty.

In my eighteen years on the faculty, the policy concerning our part-time faculty has changed, but primarily in proportion to the changes in policy concerning full-time faculty. That is, where full-time faculty have strengthened their position and improved their benefits, so too have our regular part-timers, referred to at Hood as FTEs (full-time equivalents). The policy toward temporary part-timers, or course-contract faculty, has changed to a lesser extent.

The changes that have taken place in our policies for part-timers have come about gradually since 1975–76, when a new president, Martha E. Church, took over. Her desire for a new faculty code, coupled with existing faculty discontent with its lack of participation in college governance, led to the development of a new faculty code, ratified by the faculty and the board of trustees in May 1979, and a revised faculty handbook, issued in September 1981. Between 1976 and 1979, however, most of the unratified changes were gradually implemented. As a result of the new code, the faculty now have a much stronger voice on faculty personnel matters, particularly in the areas of appointment, reappointment, nonreappointment, tenure, and promotion. Prior to 1976–77, such issues were decided almost exclusively among the appropriate chairpersons, the dean, and the president. Although these changes were initiated with full-timers in mind, part-timers (particularly FTEs) have benefited.

In addition, changes have also come about in fringe benefits, thanks to the efforts of Hood's AAUP chapter and President Church's commitment to their improvement. As with the policies concerning personnel decisions, the changes in fringe benefits have helped both full-timers and part-timers.

All course-contract faculty have access to certain fringe benefits. Like all Hood faculty, they may use college services and facilities like the swimming pool and health center, for instance, for no charge or for a minimal charge, and they receive tuition remission for themselves and their families in proportion to their teaching loads. In addition, course-contract faculty who teach at least half-time—two courses a semester—may vote at faculty meetings after two semesters. They are also automatically covered by some kinds of insurance and have access to enrollment in the college's basic medical plan; and they may enroll in TIAA-CREF.

No course-contract faculty, however, are eligible for election to faculty committees or for membership in the faculty caucus. They also do not advise students, conduct independent studies, or supervise internships. In other words, since course-contract faculty are paid a flat stipend and are not eligible for tenure or promotion, the college expects their duties to consist entirely—and only—of teaching the course(s) they were hired to teach. Their contracts do not contract for anything more. In fact, course-contract faculty are, by and large, people whose primary employment is in industry or government. A few are also full-time faculty at other institutions.

FTEs at Hood are treated in almost exactly the same way full-timers are—with one major exception: they are not on a tenure-track (nor is any part-timer) and thus never have the job security provided by tenure. Instead, they are issued annual contracts similar to probationary full-timers. FTEs enjoy all the privileges, coverage, and benefits available to temporary part-timers—and they are voting faculty from the beginning of their employment even if they teach only one-quarter time; they are eligible for membership in the faculty caucus if at least half-time; they are eligible for professional-development and fellowship funds from the college; they may be promoted. Their salaries are based on that portion of the full-time load they teach. Their duties include (in addition to teaching) serving on committees, advising interns and student groups; conducting independent studies; and all other duties expected of full-timers, in proportion, of course, to their teaching load. Unlike full-timers, however, they may not participate in the tuition exchange program, nor will Hood make direct payments for their children to other schools.

Although full-time positions are regularly advertised in national professional publications and sometimes also the *Chronicle* and/or the *Washington Post* and *Baltimore Sun*, part-time positions are advertised on a smaller scale. FTE positions, for instance, are advertised usually in the *Post* and *Sun*, as well as in local newspapers, but rarely in the *Chronicle* or professional publications. We also send job announcements for positions to other schools within a hundred-mile radius; we rarely get applications, however, from these schools. Course-contract positions may also be advertised in the same newspapers or only in the Frederick and Hagerstown papers.

As with continuing full-time contracts, the contracts for continuing FTEs are issued on or before 15 March. For course-contract faculty, they are usually not issued until late spring or early summer (or late fall for the spring semester), largely because so many course-contract faculty are hired only after the next semester's course enrollments have been determined. Contracts for all new faculty, full- or part-time, are issued at the time of hiring, which may be anywhere from six months to one week before the semester starts. Contracts for FTEs are for an academic year; contracts for course-contract faculty are usually for one semester at a time, but on occasion they may be for two semesters.

A number of part-timers, both FTE and course-contract, have moved into full-time positions. It's always a matter of whether a full-time position results from the creation of a new position or from someone's departure. Part-timers go through the same application process followed by other applicants. There is no guarantee, although when part-timers have been particularly successful as teachers and colleagues, they have a decided advantage.

When course-contract faculty are not rehired, it is usually because there is no longer anything for them to teach or their teaching has not been satisfactory, a fact that emerges through the course evaluations students write at the end of all courses. Course-contract faculty also do not go through the normal reappointment procedure for full-timers or FTEs. They simply do not receive new contracts.

FTEs, on the other hand, are formally reviewed periodically according to the same process and schedule used for full-timers. They must prepare dossiers of their teaching, college service, and professional-development accomplishments. These dossiers are reviewed by their chairpersons, the academic dean, and faculty representatives elected to the committee advisory to the president. The recommendations for reappointment and non-reappointment, as well as for tenure and promotion, are forwarded to the college president. Any grievances go to the faculty board of review. FTEs who are not reappointed are protected by the same AAUP guidelines that apply to full-timers.

I believe everyone at Hood would agree with me in saying that our part-time faculty are an invaluable asset and resource on which we rely heavily for their experience and expertise. A few of these part-timers would undoubtedly prefer a full-time position, but the academic marketplace being what it is, we cannot offer them greater employment. And most of the course-contract faculty are doing all the teaching they can do, since they generally hold down full-time positions elsewhere and teach only at night.

Our few FTEs are different from the course-contract faculty and from each other. They are not, for instance, employed regularly somewhere else, either full- or part-time, although one of them does have his own consulting business. Another is retired from the federal government, and a third person moved into a full-time teaching position at Hood in 1982–83. Four others have split appointments: they are part-time administrators as well as part-time faculty. This arrangement, in fact, is one that Hood expects to do more frequently because it promises a way of saving jobs for faculty for whom there is not full-time teaching. Of course, full-time faculty who make a permanent move into this joint appointment arrangement lose their tenure-track status (although those who do it for no more than three years return to it when they go back to full-time teaching), but they also still have full-time employment. It may not be an ideal faculty situation, but it is more humane than having only a part-time teaching salary to live on.

And perhaps "humane" is, after all, the best word to describe Hood's policy on part-time faculty.

Part-Time-Faculty Policy at Central College

Harold M. Kolenbrander
Central College

The following remarks reflect my experience with developing and implementing policies to govern the employment of part-time faculty members at Central College. My experience spans the seven years I have served as Central's chief academic officer. Parts of the policy, particularly the tenure eligibility for part-time faculty, were developed during my tenure.

Central College is an independent, four-year college, with approximately 1,500 students, 2% to 3% of whom are part-time. The faculty for 1981–82 numbered 105. Of the total, 31.4% were part-time; 9.5% shared administrative and teaching responsibilities, 6.7% were regular part-timers, and 15.2% were temporary part-timers.

The establishment of the policy governing regular part-timers grew from our concern that these individuals be treated fairly in their employment arrangements with the college. Indeed, that was the specific objective for the policy.

The policy provides for regular part-time faculty to be treated like full-time faculty, except in terms of proportionate teaching load carried and, consequently, proportion of full salary and benefits earned. There are two exceptions. First, the length of the probationary appointment is prorated (e.g., a person with a regular part-time contract of 50% would be reviewed at the end of the thirteenth year rather than at the end of the sixth year). And, second, a faculty member appointed to regular part-time status, "after completing at least three calendar years of service and before accumulating the equivalent of five years of full-time teaching, may elect to be placed on tenure-track status and should so notify the Dean of the College in writing." (The quotation, taken from the bylaws of our faculty constitution, provides tenure opportunity for the regular part-timer without requiring him or her to stand for tenure review.) Those who elect tenure-track status participate in the same review-evaluation process as full-time faculty.

Part-time faculty are hired in the same manner as full-time faculty. We advertise each open position in the national media, always in the *Chronicle of Higher Education* and usually in a leading journal or publication of the discipline involved. Furthermore, people who hold regular part-time positions are evaluated, and continuing contracts are offered following the same procedures as those used for regular full-time faculty members.

If the demands on the regular part-time position increase, the percentage of full-time appointment can also be increased by action of the administration following consultation with the Policies and Personnel Committee. (This committee at Central College is composed of nine faculty members, elected to three "classes" with rotating three-year terms, plus the president and the dean of the college. In addition, three student members, elected by the student government, sit on the committee.)

Dismissal of a person with a regular part-time faculty position occurs after exactly the same procedures as those employed for termination of regular full-time members. The grievance procedures available to both groups are also the same.

Full fringe benefits are provided to the regular part-timer so long as his or her percentage of full time is at least fifty. If the part-time contract requires less than 50% of full-time service, the fringe benefits are prorated. We have experienced no complications with this policy, and special adjustments have been unnecessary.

Faculty benefits include free tuition for spouse and immediate family, medical coverage under Blue Cross–Blue Shield and major medical plans, and coverage for the faculty member's family at the faculty member's expense. Additional fringe benefits include a $15,000 face-value life insurance policy and a standard disability policy, both of which are provided at college expense. Furthermore, all campus events are available on an equal no-cost basis to regular part-time and regular full-time faculty members.

Responsibilities in addition to teaching are assigned to regular part-timers on a prorated basis. The regular part-timer would normally have a group of student advisees, supervise independent study projects or internships, and serve on all-college committees on a pro rata basis reflecting the percentage of full time that his or her contract represents. All regular part-timers are invited to attend and vote at faculty meetings. Evidence of scholarship is also expected, again on a pro rata basis.

Professional-development opportunities for regular part-timers are equivalent to those available to the regular full-time faculty member. No prejudicial position is taken regarding opportunities for promotion and recognition, and grants for research or attendance at professional conferences are equally available to regular part-time and full-time faculty. Clerical support and postage for mailing of manuscripts are also provided on an equal basis. Leaves of absence or sabbaticals are as available, on a pro rata basis, to the regular part-timer as to the full-time faculty member.

In summary, the regular part-timer at Central College enjoys the same opportunities as full-time faculty for promotion, growth, and development; is evaluated following the same procedures (including both student and colleague inputs); and is a full member of the Central College community. No effort is made to exclude; indeed, our pattern is to include and to avoid any distinctions that might tend to separate and divide. Our program has worked very well, and we are pleased that it provides a meaningful and equal opportunity for the regular part-time faculty member at Central. We believe it has strengthened the college and also provided professionally rewarding opportunities for those to whom we are unable to offer full-time positions.

Temporary part-timers teach an occasional course for us, most often in the areas of business and computer science. Nearly all temporary part-timers hold other full-time professional positions. We do not include them in our regular faculty activities, and they do not have access to the fringe-benefit package or to the grievance procedures. Rather, they are appointed on a term-by-term basis as needed, and they usually teach no more than one course per year.

People who hold reduced-time faculty appointments at Central College typically have assignments requiring their time to be shared between administrative and teaching duties. Reduced-timers are evaluated using the same procedures employed for regular part-timers and full-timers and have access to the same fringe-benefit packages, grievance procedures (for those aspects of their work that involve teaching), and opportunities for professional growth and development.

We have sought to build a program that treats everyone equitably and that recognizes the difference in needs and expectations reflected in those who have a full-time position outside the college and those whose livelihood is primarily dependent on their employment at the college. We believe that our plan has been quite successful.

Will It Happen? When? For How Long? Part-Timers in English at George Washington University

Miriam Dow

George Washington University

and

Cara Chell

University of Wisconsin, La Crosse

At George Washington University, our then English Department Chairman John P. Reesing, our Director of Composition, Astere Claeyssens, and Margaret Strom, formerly his assistant, have worked years for higher salaries for part-time faculty. They managed by those efforts to keep us in the middle range of salaries paid by universities in the Washington metropolitan area. Nevertheless, our situation and professional status in general were grim, as they have been at most institutions until recently. Also until recently, this area had what seemed an inexhaustible supply of people willing to teach under undesirable conditions, a fact that was not lost on the financial officers of local universities. In fact, when enrollments began to drop a few years ago, the *Washington Post* ran a feature in which several financial officers of local universities admitted that they saved money for their institutions by hiring more part-time teachers and increasing class size. Given that philosophy and the collusion of its victims, our situation was inevitable and unenviable.

In the 1981 fall semester the George Washington University English Department had nineteen full-time faculty, twenty-eight part-time, and nine teaching assistants. There was no tenure-track for part-time faculty, and only two of the twenty-eight were eligible for medical, retirement, and tuition benefits. All part-time faculty were paid by the course (no prorating for anyone), and all but two were hired by the semester. It was, in short, as wretched a situation as could be.

In January 1982, several part-timers called a meeting of part-time faculty and teaching assistants and invited full-time faculty who teach composition. Many people came and had a great deal to say, and to give the institution credit, people did not have to be afraid to speak. The full-timers present and the director of composition then suggested to the department chairman that part-time faculty (who normally attend only composition meetings) be given a forum at a regular full-time faculty meeting. The chairman agreed and set a date for the earliest possible day by which faculty could elect two representatives and put together a solid presentation.

We bared our wounds at a well-attended faculty meeting. The full-time faculty present were surprised to hear about the conditions of service of their part-time colleagues (consequently recognized as colleagues perhaps for the first time by some). Judging by their evident and spontaneous dismay, it was clear they had been under some outdated illusions: perhaps we chose part-time teaching, or we were putting in our apprenticeships as they had and were ships in the night on our way to literature jobs elsewhere. Indeed, perhaps as many as six of our part-time faculty had chosen part-time teaching, but the majority certainly had not. The last of these illusions was hardest for us to comprehend; some of us had been invisible men and women in our department for seven to ten years.

That meeting exposed our appalling conditions of service and reminded everyone that our labors generated great sums of money for our institution and that our situation was incompatible with anyone's idea of a university.

At the urging of the director of composition, and with the full support of the entire faculty, the chairman then appointed a committee of six (including the two part-time instructors elected to represent part-time faculty) to investigate and report to him on the conditions of part-time employment in our English Department.

Armed with the resulting seventeen-page report. (also distributed to the entire faculty), the chairman and the committee went to the deans of our college, who supported and endorsed the report and its suggestions. In the July preceding the 1982–83 academic year, the chairman worked on improving policies and practices affecting part-time faculty but not connected to the budget (such as one-year instead of one-semester contracts, office conditions, library privileges) and on negotiating salaries and other budget-related recommendations with the provost.

With our grievances alone, however, even with our department's support, we could not have reached this negotiating stage. Other contributing factors converged to strengthen our case. In April 1982, the entire faculty of our College of Arts and Science voted to reduce composition class size from twenty-five to fifteen students (this change has yet to be effected). Throughout the fall of 1981 and winter of 1982 our full-time Appointments Committee had interviewed sixteen of our part-time faculty for one of the two full-time posts in composition (the other being that of the director of composition). Impressed by their credentials and experience and appalled by their situation here, the Appointments Committee recommended more full-time composition posts, better salaries for part-time faculty, and smaller classes.

Finally, the seventeen-page report of the special committee demonstrated the dangers of the false economies practiced in the composition program. Leaving ethics aside, the report concentrated on economic and other effects of current conditions. Our conditions of service and lack of contract security were driving away the best young professionals available locally. We were always obliged to do a good deal of hiring after registration and inevitably, at that late hour, hired enough inadequate teachers to cheat 150 to 200 students of the required course they were paying for, enough to give the program a bad name, and enough to put the university in legal jeopardy. The report further showed how obscenely overworked the director of composition was and how unable he was to assign responsibilities to poorly paid part-time colleagues. Then, too, however inaccurate and unscientific the recently published and controversial Fiske *Selective Guide to Colleges* is, it stung GW administrators with its evaluation of George Washington University as a school of transfer students taught by part-timers; composition was the subject that gave some validity to the Fiske criticism.

The committee's report also showed that the glut of composition teachers was drying up, even though Washington has always had a great many educated, well-qualified wives. Unless the teaching of composition here is made into a genuine profession and career with a decent income and security, our program would undoubtedly deteriorate. We pointed to other universities that were making significant changes, to underline the fact of a national shift in thinking.

We believe that our administration—in charge of a private university that has always attracted students from the entire country and abroad— cannot and will not ignore current realities. Some of the recommendations of the special committee on the conditions of part-time employment in the English Department are:

- a salary range, subject to annual cost-of-living adjustments, of from $2,200 to $3,500 per course (from the current $1,100 to $1,200)
- one-year contracts for regular part-time faculty
- extension of health benefits to part-time faculty
- reduction of class size from twenty-five to fifteen students
- elimination of the current ranking system, which leads to middle and low salaries
- creation of at least three new full-time posts
- eventual prorating of regular part-time salaries
- granting full participation and voting rights to part-timers at departmental meetings and on committees
- better duplicating facilities

From the part-timer's perspective, the actions of the GW full-time faculty have been particularly encouraging. For example, two part-timers were asked to and did participate in the department's colloquium series during the last winter's term, giving their papers to a considerable audience of both part-time and full-time faculty. The department is starting to see its part-time employees as educated, responsible members of the department. The committee's report on part-timers included concerns such as the cost of parking (appalling in the Washington area) and its impact on actual take-home salary. This attention to the real-life detail of being a part-time teacher at GW is encouraging. More encouraging is the fact that the committee's report was capped off by a section on social justice with recommendations for making the part-timers recognized as professional equals. Part-timers took heart that the department not only recognized the need for social justice but wrote it down on paper, with specific suggestions for achieving it.

What have been the results so far of all these efforts? Part-time salaries went from $1,100 and $1,200 to $1,400 and $1,500 per course—a substantial increase that puts us near the top in the Washington area, but still light years away from the committee's recommended minimum of $2,200. We now have a regular part-time category that carries partial health and tuition benefits, and our classes are kept to twenty (fifteen in the basic writing course). Part-time faculty now also serve as course directors for three of our composition courses, relieving the director and his assistant of some of their burden and gaining administrative experience while being paid. We have five additional offices and are all now decently housed.

Our new chairman, Jon Quitslund, is actively engaged in our affairs: he attends our meetings, belongs to a team teaching a humanities-composition course, and, with the support of the entire department, continues to seek authorization for three new full-time composition posts. Our morale is higher than it has ever been.

However, those part-timers who are still working toward full-time teaching posts worry that minor pay increases and pats on the head will never solve the harder problem of ending part-time employment altogether (except for those teachers who want regular part-time positions). Will the administration keep us barefoot and pregnant by making us temporarily happy with new kitchen curtains? Or will we take those curtains graciously and go on to demand whole new categories of equal pay for equal work? Right now, conditions have improved considerably in the English Department at George Washington University. It will require continued and perhaps increased effort to keep them improving.

Half-Time with Honor

Rae Goodell

Massachusetts Institute of Technology

For the past three years, I have been a half-time, tenure-track faculty member in the writing program at the Massachusetts Institute of Technology. My position has been comparable to those of other writing faculty, except reduced by half in salary and teaching responsibilities. The arrangement is unusual enough that I would like to outline its features and encourage its consideration by other departments.

I requested the adjustment to half-time status after two years as a full-time assistant professor of science writing because I wanted to devote more time to raising a family. I found the MIT administration impressively accommodating. We agreed that my teaching duties would be reduced to one course per term instead of the usual two. The other half of my time would be designated personal leave, so that the tenure clock would be slowed, each year counting as a half-year toward the mandatory tenure date. I would receive prorated benefits and full health benefits. A new junior faculty member was hired who would devote half-time to sharing the work in science writing.

Under the arrangement, I have been able to participate fully in the life of the institute. I have remained involved in the science writing program at MIT, which consists of a series of special undergraduate courses and activities in the writing program designed to sensitize the MIT community to the importance of communicating with the public about science and engineering. And I have continued to be in demand to contribute nationally to organizations concerned with improving science journalism and public understanding of science. I have not generally experienced the second-class status that troubles many part-time lecturers and instructors. In 1981, I was promoted from assistant to associate professor without tenure.

Needless to say, in order to retain these advantages, I have had to work longer and harder than a strictly half-time schedule would suggest. Given that the writing program has a small, relatively junior faculty, at times I have contributed essentially full-time except in actual teaching. The problem is of course endemic to part-time careers but should be less serious in larger departments where there are more faculty members among whom to distribute the service work. It could be further ameliorated, where appropriate, by ensuring that the two half-time people sharing a position are of comparable experience and seniority, to avoid any imbalance in their responsibilities.

More difficult to resolve will be the long-range adjustments MIT and I must make to the half-time arrangement. It is far easier to adjust salaries and teaching loads than career expectations. I find that both my administrators and I tend to expect that I will publish at a level more comparable to full- than to half-time work. We seem to share a sense that there is something wrong with people who produce slowly. There may also be an underlying accommodation of human nature in a system that limits faculty to seven years of the peculiar pressures and transience of pretenure life.

In short, there has evolved a well-established academic career trajectory, and it is not clear what the effects will be of deviating from it.

To address some of these problems, I have just undertaken a different version of half-time; each year I will spend one semester full-time at MIT, the other semester on personal leave. Such a scheme of course carries its own risks, including lower visibility and less involvement in the ongoing affairs of the program.

MIT and I are experimenting, in other words, with innovative, supportive arrangements to accommodate the needs of women—and men—for more flexible working arrangements. No experiment could be more worthwhile.

Some Reflections on Part-Time Faculty

Alan J. Clayton
Tufts University

I do not come to this paper armed with figures and statistics, or even with convictions, regarding the "problem" or the "situation" of part-time faculty; it is quite difficult to hold convictions about the subtle network of denials, complicities, and indifference on the one hand and of economic factors on the other that combine to form what is certainly a "problem"— but for whom? For part-timers, to be sure, forced by market conditions to accept a radically ambiguous status, at salaries often grossly out of phase with their talents and experience, but also for the rest of us: for tenured faculty, chairpersons, administrators, students, and ultimately for their tuition-paying parents. These parents we press, if we are private institutions bent on survival, for ever-increasing financial commitments, while at the same time we relegate to an amorphous and voiceless lower class a very substantial number of professional teachers whom we call upon to instruct students in skills we claim to consider basic. Strange professionals indeed: esteemed enough to be employed in foundation courses required by the university; not enough so, however, to be integrated into departments and the academic community.

Moreover, in an increasingly consumer-oriented academy, part-timers are preeminently vulnerable to the fluctuations of interest, taste, and judgment. How many negative, indeed tepid, student evaluations can they afford before their continued employment is put into question? That they manage to fare so well in such conditions, and without the security of academic freedom, bears witness, I think, to a remarkable adaptability. But one may wonder what values, what professional exigencies, risk being sacrificed in the long term. Here, as elsewhere, the situation of the part-timer mirrors that of the entire academy, where survival and value are bound up in a relationship of reciprocal challenge.

Despite incontestable demands for their services, part-timers are often asked to perform on the perimeter of a department's central concerns. It is this marginality that I consider especially pernicious for programs and departments heavily dependent on part-time faculty. For if, as tenured faculty, we drive part-timers away from our central educational concerns, allowing them only minimal contact with the aims and contents of our "major" programs, ignoring the fact that it is from their courses that our concentrators often emerge and that the effectiveness of our teaching depends to a large extent on the quality of theirs, then it is quite unreasonable to expect them to be aware of the kind of instruction required by those upper-level courses we claim to be defending.

At the center of my remarks, I therefore place the twin notions of solidarity and interdependency. Clearly, it is in our interest as professionals to support part-timers and to defend them against exploitation as well as ambiguities of role and status; to encourage them to work at the highest level of idealism rather than to adopt a merely self-protective attitude, an attitude they inevitably must adopt unless we show real interest in protecting them. No faculty member, however narcissistic, can justifiably complain about the situation of the humanities these days if he or she assumes the posture of the ostrich with regard to the role of part-time faculty. I maintain, therefore, that as professionals we cannot afford to disregard their presence or their plight.

Their plight refers me back to the harsh economic reality that lies at the source of our current status as teachers of language and letters. The scenario is well known: inadequate resources force schools to cut back, thus inhibiting the growth of graduate departments and of "major" programs, inasmuch as the latter nourish the former. Recent Ph.D.'s remain unemployed in large numbers despite often superior qualifications, while the corps of graduate assistants (the proletariat of bygone days) dwindles visibly. Simultaneously, lower-level division classes in English and foreign languages experience mounting enrollments, reflecting the bankruptcy of the "rap session" ideology of the sixties that eroded much high school and college teaching by undermining the notion of skill or mastery. Reluctant to open tenure-track positions in the numbers required to staff these (often remedial) classes adequately, administrations have increasing recourse to part-timers; once employed on a limited scale, they now dominate the foundation course rosters of numerous departments. Tenured faculty recoil in horror at the prospect of providing the services implied by the teaching of such courses. They defend their interests, and rightly so; for it is quite clear that they cannot abandon their courses on Joyce or Proust or Racine without the gravest consequences for the future of the humanities and of literacy in this country. Moreover, even if they were inclined to do so, their numbers would still not suffice to staff the sections that need to be taught.

Part-timers thus emerge, if my view has any merit, as allies in the very defense of that international literary culture we rightly prize. Why then do we not protect them more vigorously against institutional neglect?

At my university, an AAUP committee has been formed to study and report on the status of part-time faculty. It is not yet possible to predict what precise form our recommendations will take. There are, nonetheless, some positive signs. The simple fact that our committee is at work has already produced administrative movement: files are being put in order, statistics gathered, consultations between faculty and administration are beginning, and colleagues from several disciplines are being sensitized to the complexities of the issue. When I gave an interim report at a meeting of the Tufts AAUP chapter, many of my colleagues were amazed to learn that the various departments in our School of Arts and Science currently employ 184 part-time faculty members (men and women in almost equal numbers, a statistic that may surprise). Making the facts known is the start of a remedy, especially when they are stated in behalf of part-timers by tenured colleagues or colleagues who happen to be involved in administration. In short, the sympathetic support of tenured faculty seems particularly vital to the part-timers' cause. It is clear, however, that the portentous issue of cost will hover over any administrative consideration of our report. Our recommendations cover three basic areas:

1. We seek to improve the financial status of part-timers, probably by recommending a pro rata approach to the determination of salary, as well as regular increments. We shall also recommend wider dissemination of information on existing health and retirement benefits. (Currently, health insurance is available for part-timers whose work represents an FTE of one half or more. Those holding the rank of lecturer or instructor are eligible for retirement benefits after a three-year wait, immediate access being available to part-time faculty at the higher ranks.)

2. In addition, we shall urge the granting of three-year renewable contracts to regular part-time faculty and possibly the institution of a system of job security according to seniority. Years of accumulated service must count for something tangible if the notion of commitment is to have any meaning. Those having served the longest, presumably because they will have emerged as the most qualified, would be better protected in the event of future cutbacks. Currently, no such mechanism exists, nor does any mechanism for periodic review of performance. Thus, strong part-timers of long standing with excellent records of performance are officially no more secure in their status than less talented peers on whom systematic inertia could ironically confer unwarranted longevity. In short, job security has to be linked to quality.

3. Furthermore, in an attempt to minimize the proliferation of part-time positions, our committee is considering advocating the consolidation of a certain number of such positions into full-time lectureships and is currently debating the feasibility of placing this rank on an alternative tenure track that would be open to particularly qualified teachers in areas not always requiring the doctorate (while clearly not precluding it), such as the performing arts, foreign languages, or freshman writing. The principal obligation of the lecturer would be teaching. During the sixth year of service, a systematic review of qualifications and performance would take place, and candidates would be considered for promotion to the rank of senior lecturer.

This proposal is under vigorous discussion within our committee and would eventually be subject to the further scrutiny of the entire arts and sciences faculty and the administration. Its major merit is that it recognizes the value to the university of successful teachers who may not necessarily be involved in research and publication. It remains to be seen, however, whether the idea of an alternative career line, divorced from the scholarly criteria traditionally associated with university tenure, will find sufficient support to be explored further.

Addendum

Much has taken place within our committee and at the university since I submitted this article a year ago. The alternative career line survived our deliberations, but the full-time lectureships did not. Since we were dealing with some fifty full-time equivalents in the departments of Romance languages and English, it seemed highly unlikely that such an idea would flourish at a time when the administration is actively striving to limit, indeed to reduce, the size of the full-time faculty. What our committee has finally proposed is a new appointment structure for part-time faculty that would remain shy by one course per year of a full-time teaching load but would not require all the various duties and activities (such as research, publication, committee work) that are associated with tenure-track positions. In all other respects, the new plan—embodied in a five-page document, copies of which are available—is structurally modeled on the professorial track.

Our proposal calls for the creation of a new career line of regular part-time lectureships with progressive advancement through three gradations of rank: lecturer, faculty lecturer, and senior lecturer. During the sixth year of part-time service, the lecturer's achievements are reviewed by a departmental committee joined by at least one faculty member from outside the department. This review committee makes a recommendation to the administration regarding promotion to the rank of faculty lecturer. If promotion is not recommended, no further contracts will be awarded. Once promoted to the rank of faculty lecturer, however, part-timers would be assured of continued employment on a long-term basis, "barring program limitation or serious demonstrable cause." This six-year stint as lecturer is in every respect a probationary period in which the lecturer demonstrates his or her value to the department. Successful teaching would therefore be progressively translated into that sense of security and of place which often eludes the part-time teacher and which is inseparable from real loyalty to an institution—a far cry indeed from the system currently operating in many programs, where the reward for sterling performance and accumulated experience in the classroom is prompt dismissal after x number of years, for reasons that still baffle (something about "burn-out" and "new blood"). Moreover, these dismissals take place despite the losses they admittedly inflict on departments and programs, not to mention the harm they bring to talented individuals.

Six years later, under our proposed plan, faculty lecturers would be eligible for promotion to the rank of senior lecturer by means of the same review procedures, except that individuals not promoted would remain as faculty lecturers and would be eligible for promotion at a later time.

Remuneration for regular part-time faculty would no longer be on a per-course basis. Instead, each of the three ranks would have its own salary scale, with clearly stated benefits and annual increments based on merit.

After receiving approval from the membership of the Tufts AAUP chapter, our proposal was placed on the agenda of the arts and sciences faculty for discussion. I am pleased to report, in conclusion, that it received unanimous support at the faculty's meeting of 2 December 1983. It now awaits implementation at the administrative level.

Part-Time Employment in English at the University of Notre Dame

Thomas Werge
University of Notre Dame

In my capacities as head of the English Department (1978–82), professor, and faculty member at Notre Dame (since 1967), I have dealt firsthand with the considerable problems and considerably fewer joys of part-time faculty. Although I have played no direct part in developing current university policy, my experiences in implementing, refining, and reflecting on it have been substantial.

Notre Dame is a private university with a nonunionized faculty and approximately 7,200 undergraduate and 2,000 graduate students. Very few students are part-time. Our department has thirty-one full-time faculty and three who are part-timers. Although we have appointed from one to three temporary part-timers each year for the past three years, we appointed none this year. Of our thirty-one full-time faculty nominally teaching a regular course load—defined as three courses each semester—nineteen teach a reduced load. Our adjunct part-time faculty teach two courses per semester and our temporary part-timers one, while our regular part-time faculty teach a full complement of three courses. The contracts of regular and adjunct part-timers run for one full year, and those of temporary part-timers ordinarily are issued for one semester.

The university's *Academic Manual* makes provisions with respect to part-time appointments to the regular faculty. I include here the most important among them:

1. The individual's service must be "at least half-time and no more than three-quarters-time and . . . the individual [cannot be] employed outside the University."
2. No more than "one-fourth of the Regular Faculty members in any department . . . shall have part-time appointments."

3. Tenure will be granted to part-time members of the Regular Faculty "on the same basis as for members holding full-time appointments. The prorated portion of each year of part-time service shall be counted toward the maximal probationary period for tenure."
4. The criteria for "appointment and reappointment to the Regular Faculty for part-time service shall be the same as for full-time service as also shall be the duration of contractual periods."
5. A Regular Faculty member with a part-time appointment "has the same voting privileges as a member with a full-time appointment. In general, the responsibilities and privileges of a member of the Regular Faculty with a part-time appointment are the same in nature as, but on a proportionate scale to, those of a member with a full-time appointment."
6. The salary and fringe benefits of a member of the Regular Faculty on a part-time appointment "shall be the proportionate share of the appropriate salary . . . [and] fringe benefits were the appointment to be full-time."
7. Other members of the faculty "include visiting, adjunct, concurrent, guest, retired emeritus faculty, and lecturer. Time spent on the faculty in any nonregular category is not counted for purposes of tenure. Members of the nonregular faculty have a voice in meetings of the faculty, but do not vote."

Such a difficult academic marketplace as this one exacerbates the situation of part-time faculty. Frustrations abound, and even heightened administrative awareness and small improvements may not alleviate the larger structural problems—the light at the end of the tunnel, as the old saw has it, may be an onrushing train. Our department has no part-time tenure-track faculty at present, though our regular part-timers do have access to standard fringe benefits and prorated salaries. But their prospects for continued employment at Notre Dame are problematic. They contribute a great deal to us, yet an understandable anxiety is their common lot. Whether they teach one, two, or three courses each semester, their one-year contracts carry no assurances for the future. Knowing how complex and tense these conditions can make the dynamics of the relationship among administrators, regular faculty, and part-timers, administrators and faculty appointments and promotions committees often tend to favor hiring from the kinds of faculty categories listed in number 7 above and, by so doing, to avoid the complexities associated with tenure-track and/or potentially renewable part-time appointments.

The department tries to affirm and support as strongly and consistently as possible the presence and work of part-time faculty through partial or full assistance for travel to conferences (the amount contingent on travel funds available), secretarial services for all correspondence and manuscript preparation, xeroxing and mailing privileges, and inclusion in all departmental academic and social occasions. In my experience, there have been few exceptions to the general rule that our regular faculty recognize and respect the contributions—pedagogical and scholarly—our part-time faculty make to the tone and substance of departmental life. Yet the special pressures on part-time faculty, including the constant specter of an uncertain "next year" looming immediately ahead whatever the month of the academic year, are never far away. If a part-time faculty member wishes to be considered for a full-time opening the following year, of course, we give him or her every consideration through the same appointments procedures and criteria applied to all candidates. But since the specific fields and even the existence of potential full-time openings are uncertain as the academic year begins, since it is often clear that we will not hire in a specific field (which may be the part-timer's specific field), and since the part-timer invariably has only a one-year contract, the pressures—pressures that are structural and indigenous to the part-time category—are apparent.

From an administrative point of view, the pressures inherent in the hiring of part-time faculty are equally vexing. If we know we will need a visiting professor for a year or semester, we invite a specific person or advertise nationally (in the *Chronicle of Higher Education* and/or MLA *Job Information Lists*). But we appoint part-time faculty to meet needs that often become clear only late in the spring semester, as when we must replace a full-time faculty member who receives a grant or decides fairly late to go on leave. Any replacement we appoint must have the Ph.D. Yet time's winged chariot—or digital clock—ordinarily precludes large-scale advertising. The pool of candidates our appointments committee considers is usually small, while the two or three courses the person will teach each semester are vital parts of our program and include advanced as well as introductory offerings. Our decisions, then, are extremely important, yet the constraints of time and circumstance are keen. Over the years, our part-time faculty have come through in fine form indeed. Yet this speaks better for their abilities than it does for the obvious flaws, not only of part-time academic employment, but of parts of the tenure system itself.

Two observations and a parting reflection: (1) Notre Dame clearly attempts to support part-time faculty members and largely succeeds in doing so, but (2) the underlying and structural problems of such faculty remain pressing and might only be solved by formulating a policy that would allow for renewable contracts, somehow apart from the present tenure system, that would provide sustained benefits for good work, equally sustained security—at least for three years at a time—and safeguards against exploitation. One could not formulate such a structure separate from the standard tenure system without challenging the current nature of tenure and several of the AAUP guidelines. Yet it seems to me impossible to consider the problems of part-time faculty and the conditions of their work without raising questions about the larger and more encompassing forms of work and justice in academe. The need for some change is apparent. If prudence is in order, so is imagination.

Teaching is a solitary vocation in certain very deep respects. Like the phrase "community of nations," the notion of a "community of scholars" or "community of teachers" has its severe limitations (as well as a basic validity). Quite apart from large structural and political considerations, the problems of part-time faculty can often be alleviated, though obviously not resolved, by an administrator's willingness to be forthright and courteous from the outset, to keep the faculty member informed of the possibilities for the coming year, and, in short, to be genuinely attentive to the part-time faculty member's needs and person—and contributions. Orwell was at first impatient with Dickens for his refusal to provide specific political reforms for the vast abuses he condemned. Finally, however, Orwell said he recognized that what Dickens really despised was a certain "expression on the human face" and that Dickens' admonition to act decently was not so shallow as it sounded. Part-time faculty deserve as much recognition, support, and attentiveness as their faculty and administrative colleagues can give them—and more. Collective solutions may not be imminent, but demonstrations of consideration and concern for individual part-time faculty—demonstrations that can break ground for larger reforms—can make a real difference, just as they can and do for job applicants. Kierkegaard's vision remains more compellingly real than Hegel's.

The Expository Writing Program at Harvard

Richard Marius

Harvard University

The Expository Writing Program at Harvard numbers thirty-five part-time instructors out of a total staff of forty-five people.

When I assumed leadership of the program in 1978, I found many problems that are endemic to part-time staffs. Like many universities, Harvard assumed that anybody with an advanced degree could teach writing. Teachers were chosen without regard to their own writing and, once chosen, were flung into the classroom and left pretty much on their own. No real effort was made to supervise them or to evaluate their performance.

The consequences were predictable. Some teachers with warm personalities, high intelligence, and great dedication did well. Others did abominably. Still others floundered about, discovering by trial and error what it was to be a writing teacher. Some asked others for help, and others believed that to ask for aid was to confess inability to do the job. There was little feeling of belonging, either to a program or to the university at large. Harvard loomed there beyond the boundaries of the program, an impersonal monument to some forgotten aspiration. Most staff members hurried away from the university as quickly as their immediate obligations were fulfilled.

Assignments within the program were widely divergent, and little effort was made to coordinate what teachers were doing in class. One teacher required her students to write seventy-five pages during the term; one made his write only twenty. One teacher had her students read several Victorian novels, including *Middlemarch*; many teachers required little or no reading from their students. One teacher year after year had given fourteen grades of A in a class of sixteen or seventeen. One teacher seldom gave an A to anyone. Many teachers required students to write autobiographical essays, and a few used the essays as gateways to counseling sessions in which dime-store psychology pushed writing out the window.

Purposes were chaotic. Some teachers were dedicated to making students think honestly and write clearly. Some were resolved to make them write correctly. One member of the staff told me she would never give a grade lower than a B to any of her students "because I will not injure a student's self-esteem." Her view seemed a thousand miles away from the world of rejection slips, bad reviews, and anonymity that most writers consider normal. One teacher told me that her chief goal was to love students. Another spent an hour of a class I attended telling students how terrible Harvard was and how pure our program was in comparison with those courses where professors only cared what students knew.

From the first I conceived our purpose as the traditional one of rhetoric—to make students observe, know, think, and write in ways that made them respected members of a community of the intellect. Also from the first it seemed clear to me that those most likely to share that view were writers who had been paid to publish their work. I began phasing out people who were not writing and replacing them with people who loved to write and wrote continually—young academics, novelists, journalists, reviewers, and even a few poets.

I had some great advantages in making these shifts. Harvard gave me nearly absolute control over the program. Teachers were hired on one-year contracts, and I could cut out the deadwood quickly and easily. Harvard pays part-timers fairly well. In 1983–84 we paid $3,700 for each section taught by a part-timer; a teacher can teach as many as four sections a year. We average 15.1 students a section, and Harvard has always understood the value of fairly small sections if students are to be taught anything substantial in a writing course. The money and the section size have allowed me to recruit writers who can find time to do their own writing while they teach for me. Part-time people are eligible for many benefits, including Harvard's generous medical care.

We have never demanded advanced degrees for either our part-time or our full-time people. I have nothing against the M.A. or the Ph.D., but I have not noted any correlation between good writing and graduate study. What we do demand is a commitment to writing and some success in the craft. I think it a scandal for writing programs to be filled with people who never write themselves.

We have developed some careful ways of helping our teachers. In 1979 I put together a short essay on teaching that I call the "Informal Notes." This year I revised the work for the third time, and it has now grown to the size of a small book. It covers everything I know about what we are doing, and it prepares teachers to do the job.

I visit all the classes of new teachers during the first term that they teach for us. Two of my assistants now help me conduct visits. We write reports on what we observe and share them with the teachers and with each other. We talk informally with the teachers about what they are doing; we tell them what other teachers are doing; we praise people publicly who have new ideas. Every new teacher puts at least one class on videotape in Harvard's video center where classes are conducted under the view of hidden cameras. (Students and teachers know the cameras are there, but they quickly seem to forget them.) The taping gives me an opportunity to sit with the teacher later on and to make comments on the class. Every student in every section writes an anonymous evaluation of the course when it is done. After the grades are turned in, I read these evaluations and then pass them on to the teachers.

Our program offers courses in various kinds of writing—literature, history, natural sciences, social sciences, fiction, and a general interdisciplinary course called "theory and practice." Each of these groups has monthly meetings where teachers talk with each other about what they are doing.

We have a monthly general staff meeting with a buffet that always includes wine, cheese, beer, and juices. The university gives me a budget for these meetings, and they have proved invaluable in building a sense of community among our teachers. People eat and drink and talk with each other. They form friendships, and they help each other. We do no great business at these meetings beyond a few announcements. They are given over rather to readings by members of the staff from works in progress. I want our staff members to think of themselves as a community of professionals engaged not only in the common enterprise of teaching but also in the exercise of the art that we are supposed to be teaching others.

I like my people to feel proud of being associated with one another and to believe that they share in a small society within the larger community of Harvard itself and that others care what they do and what happens to them.

Part-Time Faculty at Wesleyan University

William Kerr
Wesleyan University

Wesleyan University's policy in regard to part-time members of its faculty, approved in 1974 after three years of discussion, owes its impetus and chief features to Sheila Tobias, associate provost at the time, with a special concern for affirmative action as it pertains to women.

The policy distinguishes three kinds of part-time faculty and allows for movement among them. The kinds bear the catchy names of "moonlighters," "twilighters," and "sunlighters." What this terminology lacks in sedateness, it makes up for in suggestiveness and convenience.

Moonlighters—the most familiar name and the largest category—are those whose primary employment lies elsewhere. Customarily they are hired to meet emergencies, such as sudden sicknesses, leaves of absence in vital fields, or delays in hiring faculty members for regular and longer appointments. Moonlighters ordinarily teach no more than one course in a given semester. They are paid for that and nothing else, for nothing else is expected of them. They do not participate in departmental or university affairs. They receive no fringe benefits. Their titles, duplicating those they enjoy at their home institutions, if any, are modified by the rubric "visiting." They come and go.

Twilighters are those, serving at least half-time, whose primary, or possibly exclusive, employment is at Wesleyan but who are deemed ineligible by their departments for regular faculty status. This may be owing to the lack of an appropriate degree or a scholarly commitment or a continuing position. As a result, they do not become voting members of their respective departments, although they are eligible for longer contracts and larger assignments than are moonlighters. Since Wesleyan is their primary employer, they receive some fringe benefits (but in no case sabbaticals) on a prorated basis.

Sunlighters have regular faculty appointments, alike in every way to full-time appointments save in the amount of time worked. Wesleyan ordinarily is their primary or exclusive employer; their positions are continuing ones; and their qualifications for employment meet all the prevailing academic standards. They participate with vote in all kinds of departmental and facultywide business. Their fringe benefits are prorated. Moreover, at their option, with the concurrence of their departments and the academic administration, they may move on to the tenure track, with a probationary period of not more than seventeen semesters of half-time teaching. In such an instance, the tenure decision would be made not later than the fifteenth semester. Sunlighters opting for, and admitted to, the tenure track would thereby become eligible for sabbaticals, again on a prorated basis. A sunlighter receiving tenure could retain his or her part-time status or, with the concurrence of the department and academic administration, move to full-time status, and, for that matter, back again.

In addition to the foregoing categories of part-time employment, Wesleyan makes provision for full-time employees to take occasional part-time leaves of absence for personal reasons, with salary and most fringe benefits accruing on a prorated basis. The recipient of such a leave, if on the tenure track, will receive a proportionate extension of the probationary period leading up to a tenure decision. Although this option is in no way restricted to faculty members with small children, they are the ones who were most in mind when the policy was framed.

A faculty member, whether employed part-time or full-time, may have six weeks of maternity leave without loss of salary, fringe benefits, or other advantages. In consultation with the academic administration, a substitute instructor would be engaged for the period where required.

Finally, any full-time member of the tenured faculty with ten or more years of full-time service at Wesleyan may elect partial retirement at the age of sixty or thereafter. One so electing will receive a proration of salary equivalent to the portion of active service, a continuing contribution to TIAA-CREF based upon that salary (until the normal retirement age of sixty-eight), a supplemental Wesleyan stipend keyed to the portion of retirement and the length of service, and continued coverage by group insurance based on an assumed full-time salary. Moreover, a participant in the program of partial retirement will continue to be eligible for annual salary increases and to accumulate credit toward sabbaticals, though on a prorated basis. He or she may reduce further the portion of time spent on active service but may not increase it or return to full-time status. This program was instituted in 1972 and expanded in 1974.

In the current academic year (1982–83), there are 311 members of the Wesleyan faculty, of whom 38 (27 men and 11 women) work part-time. Of these, 27 (20 men and 7 women) are moonlighters; 5 (5 men and no women) are twilighters; and 7 (3 men and 4 women) are sunlighters. There is one full-time member of the faculty who is on part-time leave for personal reasons and another who expects to take a maternity leave in the near future. In addition, two full-time members of the tenured faculty are partially retired.

The program is various and flexible: it responds to diverse circumstances and occasions. The option of early retirement (full or partial) has been particularly popular, with approximately one half of those eligible since its inception twelve years ago taking it up in one form or another. Interestingly enough, the sunlighter's option of requesting transfer to the tenure track, available since 1974, has never been taken up. It remains popular in principle but has not met the particular needs and aspirations of anyone in the relatively small group affected. It carries with it, of course, a peril as well as an opportunity, since the faculty member failing in the bid for tenure would, after a brief coda, be obliged to leave.

Summing up, I would say that the congeries of policies just recounted has given satisfaction, since no one in any quarter has suggested any change in them in recent years. Few programs of any sort have been so exempt.

Legal Issues in the Employment
of Part-Time and Term-Contract Faculty

David J. Figuli

Wickens, Herzer & Panza

The relations between part-time faculty and institutions of higher education have been the subject of extensive and significant study and commentary in the last decade. As a result, perceptions concerning the economic and academic status of this segment of the economic work force have generally changed. Once considered a relatively homogeneous, unqualified group of erstwhile scholars with minimal commitment to the traditional academic life, part-time faculty are now understood differently; an enlightened view can no longer countenance such categorical descriptions.

Part-time faculty are a diverse group with a variety of motivations for seeking an academic association. Nevertheless, some reliable generalizations concerning the academic and economic status of part-time faculty within the academic community have been defined. From the academic side, part-timers are found to have little voice in academic governance and limited identity with the goals and objectives of the institution and pertinent subunits. Compared to full-time faculty, they have less access to institutional resources and less institutional support; they are not as well credentialed and not as current in their knowledge of their subject area; they provide fewer services, contribute less to the reputation of the institution, and engage in fewer "scholarly activities." From an economic standpoint, when compared with their full-time counterparts, part-time faculty have lower wages, fewer fringe benefits, fewer perquisites, shorter contract periods, and substantially less job security.[1] These findings have led commentators to describe the relationship between part-time faculty and institutions of higher education as "marginal," "second-class," and "exploited."[2]

In understanding the legal rights of the part-timer, this factual back-drop is a prime consideration. The principles that govern the legal rights of part-timers are to a substantial degree controlled by the existent factual circumstances. Much to the chagrin of many part-time faculty members, there is no definitive independent and external fountainhead of rights to which a part-time faculty member can resort to strengthen the academic or economic aspects of his or her employment relationship. There are, of course, certain limited resources such as the statutory and constitutional guarantees against unlawful discrimination or unconstitutional depriva-tion. These laws, however, do not establish but merely constrain the es-sentials of the employment relationship.

The discussions and litigation of part-time-faculty rights to date have focused primarily on the issues of job security and compensation. These issues have been considered within the framework of the rights established by contract, constitutional, and collective-bargaining laws. It is the purpose of this article to provide an overview of the application of the principles of these areas of the law to the current state of affairs of part-time faculty, to assess the efficacy of faculty resort to these laws to accrue greater rights, and to provide limited recommendations as to how part-time faculty can enhance their legal rights.

Contract Law

The legal relationship between a faculty member and an institution of higher education is one of contract. It is interpreted and enforced in light of principles of contract law. The law, however, does not dictate the es-sentials of the contract. It simply operates upon the agreement of the parties, so long as that agreement is not unlawful or contrary to public policy.

Specifically with regard to part-time faculty, the same rule applies. The law does not create the contract or establish its terms; it merely enforces the agreement of the contracting parties.

Employment contracts for part-timers may be oral or written. They may be integrated, that is, contain all of the terms and conditions of the subject contractual relationship, or merely provide a memorandum of the agreement, which is fleshed out by express reference to external docu-ments, by implication of other documents or practices, or by custom and usage. It is the function of the courts, when confronted with a contractual issue presented by a contracting party and in default of a clear and definitive expression, to determine what the contracting parties intended the sub-stance of their agreement to be as it pertains to the subject matter of any dispute. In fulfilling such responsibility, the courts have frequently looked to institutional policy statements and personnel regulations, such as those frequently found in the faculty handbook; to past practices of the institu-tion; and to externally originated and widely accepted statements of good practice in higher education, such as those promulgated by the AAUP, to determine the governing terms and conditions of faculty employment contracts.

The primary contractual issue that has been considered by the courts revolves around the attempt by part-time faculty to make claim to tenure or similar continuing contractual rights. The cases usually have not involved the interpretation of an express extension of tenure status to part-time faculty but rather have involved the construction of tenure policies that are not expressly limited in application to full-time faculty. The cases have arisen in different contexts. A number of the decisions have come from an elementary-secondary background, some from the community college setting, and a scant few out of higher education. Although in the elementary-secondary cases the courts were required to construe statutory tenure policies, the principles and the analyses employed by those courts are analogous.

The principal analytical issue addressed by the courts in all the cases has required a threshold determination of the intent and purpose that the tenure policies or statutes were designed to achieve. Citing the traditional objectives of providing the scholar with job security and a concomitant freedom from arbitrary dismissal, the courts have held that a part-time teacher who was employed on an occasional or intermittent basis is not entitled to the benefits of tenure.[3] On the other hand, regular part-timers (that is, those who teach part-time on a consistent and substantial basis) have, at least at the elementary-secondary level, been extended tenure coverage.[4]

Claims have also been made by part-time faculty to tenure rights even where the tenure policy is explicitly limited to full-time faculty. The cases have involved claims by part-timers who held what they felt were "full-time equivalent" positions, equivalent teaching loads to those of full-time faculty. The courts, however, have been unwilling to categorically equate part-time teaching service with full-time service, one court finding "that an instructor's contractual obligations under a full-time contract are distinctly different from and greater than an instructor's obligations under a part-time contract."[5]

Where there is a clear expression and limitation of tenure coverage to full-time faculty, and that term is well defined, the courts have been unwilling to extend tenure to part-time faculty.[6] They have been unwilling to expand the agreement of the parties or create independently existing contractual rights. This is consistent with established principles of contract law.

The same principles would militate against any court requiring the payment of equivalent compensation to part-time and full-time faculty based solely on contractual principles. This, of course, does not take into account constitutional or statutory requirements that may impose equal pay standards for reasons unrelated to strictly contractual considerations. From a strictly contractual standpoint, part-time faculty have no right to pro rata compensation without a specific commitment to that effect on the part of the institution.

Constitutional Law

The *equal-protection* clause of the Fourteenth Amendment of the United States Constitution and the parallel provisions of state constitutions require public agencies and private agencies involved in state action to extend equal treatment to all persons unless there exists a legally sufficient basis for discrimination. The focus of the prohibition of the equal-protection clause is on the government's unequal treatment of persons based upon improper classifications of those individuals. It must be noted that the prohibition applies exclusively to states and therefore controls the activities only of public institutions. Private institutions are excluded unless they are determined to be engaged in "state action," a determination that involves analyses and issues beyond the scope of this article.

With regard to part-time faculty, the obvious focus of the equal-protection rubric is upon the relative equality of treatment by public institutions between those classifications of academic employees denominated "part-time" and "full-time." Since the part-time faculty generally are not treated as favorably as full-time faculty, the equal-protection issue placed before the courts requires a determination of whether or not there exists a rational basis for the unfavorable treatment of part-timers. The analysis of the issue requires the court first to determine whether the differential treatment is rationally based upon some legitimate ground. Even if a rational basis is found, the court may pursue a corollary inquiry as to whether the treatment is unduly burdensome upon the affected individuals.

This analysis has been applied by several California courts to cases presented by part-time faculty arguing that since they in all material respects perform the same functions as full-time faculty then they should, under the equal-protection clause, be entitled to equivalent pay and tenure status. The courts, however, have uniformly found that a rational basis for disparate treatment of part-time faculty in salary and tenure status can be founded upon such factual distinctions as part-timers having less experience, performing fewer functions, and having more limited credentials than full-time faculty. On these grounds the courts have found that disparities in salary and tenure status are constitutionally permissible.[7]

Based upon the abstract operation of the principles of equal-protection analysis, it would appear that a case could be presented to a court that would lead to a finding of equal-protection denial by the institution where part-timers are paid at a lower rate or otherwise not treated as favorably (in employment rights and benefits) as full-timers. Such a case would have to be factually founded upon an identity between part-time and full-time faculty in all material respects, including job qualifications and responsibilities. At least the decisions to date would appear to support the probability of success in such a case. Query, however, whether or not disparate treatment could be founded upon such less objective bases as a distinction in market availability between part-timers and full-timers or a perceived distinction in the reputational value of part-timers when compared with full-timers? Although the equal-protection rubric appears theoretically to provide a strong force for assertion of part-time-faculty rights, it could in practice turn out to be too slender a reed.

The *due-process* clause of the Fourteenth Amendment of the United States Constitution and parallel provisions in state constitutions protects, among other things, "property" interests of individuals against divestiture by state action without due process first being accorded. It is firmly established that an employee's contractual right to continued employment is such a property interest that is secured by due process. The focus of the determination as to whether or not an employee has a continuing right to employment is upon the contractual relationship between the employee and the public employer. A contractual right to continued employment may arise by express provision or by implication.

Studies have shown that only one out of every eight part-time faculty have any sort of express tenure guarantees—continuing employment rights.[8] Consequently, few part-time employees have the right to due process prior to termination of their employment. In practical effect, that means that they may be disassociated from employment with any public institution after the conclusion of any contract term without the necessity of the institution showing cause or providing notice and without an opportunity for hearing. During the contract term, of course, a part-time employee, like any other employee, may not be discharged from employment at a public institution without due process.

Nevertheless, in the absence of an express contractual continuing employment right, a part-timer may be found to have acquired an implied right of continuing employment. This doctrine of "de facto tenure" was first enunciated by the United States Supreme Court in the case of *Perry v. Sinderman.*[9] In that case, it was recognized that even though a public institution of higher education specifically disclaims the existence of any tenure rights for faculty, an implied right of continuing employment, and hence a "property" interest, may arise from other statements or practices of the institution. Such an implied property interest in continued employment was found to exist on behalf of part-time faculty by the Supreme Court of California in the circumstances presented in the case of *Balen v. Peralta Junior College District.*[10] In that case, the plaintiff part-time faculty member taught continuously for four and one-half years, having been hired on annual contracts. It was the practice of the junior college district to dismiss its part-time instructors annually and then subsequently rehire them. The court found in this practice the implication of a contractual right to reemployment for Balen and, consequently, a constitutionally protectable property interest. The court, therefore, concluded that Balen was entitled to due process before his employment with the district could be terminated.

The decision in *Perry v. Sinderman* certainly raises the potential for a successful claim by a part-time faculty member to a property interest in continued employment and, consequently, due-process rights. Such a claim would require the showing, at a minimum, of a pattern of continuous and perfunctory reemployment. Written or oral assurances of some degree of continuity of employment or practices raising such an implication of continuity of employment would certainly work to buttress any such claim. It may even be possible to successfully assert a claim to de facto tenure where there exists at the same institution an explicit tenure policy that excludes part-timers from its scope of coverage. Several courts at least have so held, although the reader is cautioned that several courts have held otherwise and the issue therefore remains open.[11]

Even if a part-time faculty member were able to surmount the rather formidable evidentiary obstacles and successfully prove a case of de facto tenure, there yet remain many unanswered questions, not the least of which requires the determination of *what* continuing rights of part-timers are tenured. What contract term is protected? What salary base? What percentage of full-time equivalency? What academic freedom rights are secured? How do the answers to the foregoing questions assimilate with existing rights of full-time faculty? Clearly these are questions best considered in the arena of academic rather than judicial judgment.

Collective Bargaining

The right of employees to negotiate collectively with their employers over the terms and conditions of their employment arises from state (public employers) and federal (private employers) statutory law or by voluntary agreement of the employer. In the latter instance, the requisite substantive and procedural conditions attendant to the exercise of the right are established by the parties. Where the bargaining right is statutorily derived and employer acquiescence is absent, the petitioning employees must usually first demonstrate that their proposed collective is appropriately formulated, appropriateness generally being dependent upon the demonstration of an identity or community of interest as pertains to the subject of bargaining.

Part-time faculty have a rather limited history of collective bargaining. There have been a number of instances where part-timers, by employer agreement, have been integrated with full-time faculty in bargaining units or have received voluntary recognition in units of their own. Where voluntary recognition has not been accorded, part-time faculty have experienced considerable difficulty in demonstrating that they are appropriately integrated into a full-time unit or that they independently constitute an appropriate unit. The future, however, appears to be more promising.

Until very recently it was the apparent position of the National Labor Relations Board that a group of part-time faculty could not exhibit a sufficient community of interest to bargain collectively. In the *Goddard College* case, the board refused to approve such a unit on the basis of its findings that the part-timers had differing wages, hours, responsibilities, locations, and conditions of employment.[12] The board has modified its position, however, holding in its *University of San Francisco* decision that under proper facts a part-time unit is appropriate.[13] The factual findings supporting the changed position in that case established that the part-timers had in common the method by which they were hired and compensated and the terms and conditions of their employment and working hours. It was also evident that the part-timers worked in close geographical proximity and were subject to the same administrative structure. The *University of San Francisco* case, therefore, establishes that part-time faculty may form an appropriate bargaining unit if they meet essentially the same standards of identity of interest required for full-time faculty units.

The National Labor Relations Board has not modified, however, its position concerning the appropriateness of integrating full-time and part-time faculty for purposes of collective bargaining. After first finding that such a unit was proper, *University of New Haven*,[14] the board reversed itself, *New York University*.[15] In the board's estimation a sufficient community of interest does not exist between the two groups of faculty, since they perform different functions, are compensated differently, do not participate similarly in university governance, do not have equivalent rights in regard to tenure, and generally have disparate working conditions.

Whether the board's position on the joinder of part-timers and full-timers into a single unit will again change is, of course, conjectural. If the increasing practice of association of the two groups and the general philosophy regarding such association in higher education are of any influence, then such a change may not be far off. Two of the three major higher education unions have recently promulgated statements calling for the joint representation of both groups in single units.[16] Further, the tenor of the proposals of those statements and of current higher education personnel practices is in support of a greater equivalency in treatment of part-timers and full-timers. Certainly as greater equivalencies are realized, communities of interest will concomitantly be created between part-timers and full-timers, which will establish a factual base for the conclusion that full-time and part-time faculty can properly bargain in a single unit.

Conclusion

If the lot of part-time faculty in higher education is to improve, and certainly improvement is warranted, such improvement will not come from resort to any external processes or forums. The legal rights of part-timers are dependent upon a function of their contractual agreements with their employing institutions. Any broadly based effort to establish greater rights must be focused upon the enhancement of employment terms and conditions.

Whether that enhancement is accomplished through a formal collective organization or informally through casual local or national associations, through formal negotiations or informal persuasion, is a matter of policy that must be determined on an individual basis. What is imperative is that part-timers begin to develop an identity that will facilitate the definition of their professional needs and objectives. Only then can part-timers hope to be recognized as an integral element of the academic work force and escape a second-class existence.

Notes

[1]　Howard P. Tuckman and W. D. Vogler, "The 'Part' in Part-Time Wages," *AAUP Bulletin* (May 1978): 70; Tuckman, "Who Is Part-Time in Academe," *AAUP Bulletin* (Dec. 1978):305. (Both articles appear in Tuckman, Vogler, and Caldwell, *Part-Time Faculty Series*.)

[2]　Tuckman and Vogler, "The 'Part' in Part-Time Wages" 70; Tuckman, "Who Is Part-Time in Academe" 305; David W. Leslie and R. B. Head, "Part-Time Faculty Rights" 46.

[3]　See, e.g., McLachlan v. Tacoma Community College District, 541 P.2d 1010 (Ct. App. Wash. 1975).

⁴ State v. Redman, 491 P.2d 157 (Alaska 1971); Saxtorph v. District Court 275 P.2d 209 (Mont. 1954); Nester v. School Committee of Fall River, 62 N.E.2d 664 (Mass. 1945); Sherrod v. Lawrenceburg School City, 12 N.E.2d 944 (Ind. 1938).

⁵ McLachlan v. Tacoma Community College District, 541 P.2d 1010, 1014 (Ct. App. Wash. 1975).

⁶ See, e.g., Board of Trustees of State Colleges v. Sherman, 373 A.2d 626 (Ct. App. Md. 1977).

⁷ California Teachers Assoc. v. Santa Monica Community College District, 144 Cal. Rptr. 620 (Ct. App. 1978); Peralta Federation of Teachers, Local 1603 v. Peralta Community College District, 27 Cal. Public Employee Relations, 62–63 (1975).

⁸ Tuckman and Vogler, "The 'Part' in Part-Time Wages" 70.

⁹ 408 U.S. 593 (1972).

¹⁰ 114 Cal. Rptr. 589 (1974).

¹¹ Davis v. Oregon State University, 591 F.2d 493 (9th Cir. 1978); Willens v. University of Massachusetts, 570 F.2d 403 (1st Cir. 1978); Soni v. Board of Trustees of University of Tennessee, 513 F.2d 347 (6th Cir. 1975); Tyler v. College of William and Mary, 429 F. Supp. 29 (E.D.Va. 1977); Watts v. Board of Curators, University of Missouri, 363 F. Supp. 883 (W.D.Mo. 1973).

¹² 216 NLRB 457 (1975).

¹³ 265 NLRB 155 (1982).

¹⁴ 190 NLRB 4778 (1971).

¹⁵ 205 NLRB 4 (1973).

¹⁶ "Part-Time Faculty: Roles, Rights and Responsibilities," *Academe* 67 (1981): 29; American Federation of Teachers Advisory Commission on Higher Education, *Statement on Part-Time Faculty Employment*.

Works Cited

"Agreement by and between the Board of Trustees of Whatcom Community College, District No. 21, and Whatcom Community College Federation of Teachers, September 14, 1981–August 31, 1983," Bellingham, Wash.

Albert, Louis. "Part-Time Faculty Policies, Practices, and Incentives in Maryland's Community Colleges." Diss. Univ. of Maryland 1982.

American Federation of Teachers Advisory Commission on Higher Education. *Statement on Part-Time Faculty Employment.* Washington: American Federation of Teachers, 1980.

Andersen, Charles J., and Frank J. Atelsek. *Sabbaticals and Research Leaves in Colleges and Universities.* Higher Education Panel Report, 53. Washington: American Council on Education, 1982.

Andes, John. "The Legal Position of Part-Time Faculty." In *Part-Time Faculty in Colleges and Universities* 8–12.

Association of Part-Time Professionals. "ABC of Part-Time Employment." *APTP National Newsletter* 2.3 (Fall 1982): 1.

Association of Part-Time Professionals. "Competition Stiffens for Part-Timers." *APTP National Newsletter* 2.4 (Winter 1983): 1.

Atelsek, Frank J., and Charles J. Andersen. *Undergraduate Student Credit Hours in Science, Engineering, and the Humanities, Fall 1980.* Higher Education Panel Report, 54. Washington: American Council on Education, 1982.

Bagwell, Richard, and Ione Elioff. "Faculty Development for Part-Timers." In *Part-Time Faculty in Colleges and Universities* 13–17.

Blank, Susan, and Beth Greenberg. "Living at the Bottom." *WPA: Journal of the Council of Writing Program Administrators* 5.1 (Fall 1981): 9–12.

Booth, Wayne C. "A Cheap, Efficient, Challenging, Sure-Fire and Obvious Device for Combatting the Major Scandal in Higher Education Today." *WPA: Journal of the Council of Writing Program Administrators* 5.1 (Fall 1981): 35–39.

Chell, Cara. "Memoirs and Confessions of a Part-Time Lecturer," *College English* 44 (1982): 35–44.

Claxton, Evelyn. "Survey of Part-Time Pay Scales for Illinois Community Colleges." Unpublished ms., 1981. Available from E. Claxton, Chair, Arts and Communications Dept., Rend Lake Coll., Ina, Ill.

Coffinberger, Richard L., and Frank L. Matthews. "Promoting Affirmative Action through Part-Time Faculty: The Need for a Rational Policy." *Labor Law Journal* 31 (1980): 772–78.

Community College of Denver. *Policy Manual.* Denver: Community Coll. of Denver, 1982.

Cook, Barbara, and Diane Rothberg. *A Part-Timer's Guide to Federal Part-Time Employment.* Alexandria, Va.: Assn. of Part-Time Professionals, 1981.

Council of Writing Program Administrators. "A Statement about the Use of Part-Time and Temporary Faculty in College and University English Departments." Unpublished ms., 1983.

DeSole, Gloria, and Leonore Hoffmann, eds. *Rocking the Boat: Academic Women and Academic Processes*. New York: MLA, 1981.

Dykstra, Timothy E. "So What Can I Actually *Do* about It?" *Proceedings of Maryland Composition Conference 16 April 1982*. College Park: Univ. of Maryland, 1982, 53–61.

Emmet, Thomas A. "Overview." In *Part-Time Faculty in Colleges and Universities* 1–3.

Eymonerie, Maryse. *The Availability of Fringe Benefits in Colleges and Universities*. Washington: American Assn. of University Professors, 1980.

Hairston, Maxine. "The Professional Status of Temporary Faculty: What English Departments Can Do for Them and about Them." Paper presented at a forum workshop, "Short-Term Faculty Appointments: Strategies for Change," MLA Convention, Los Angeles. 30 Dec. 1982.

Hechinger, Fred M. "A Lost Generation of Young 'Gypsy Scholars,' " *New York Times* 2 May 1982: E22.

Hoffmann, Leonore, and Gloria DeSole, eds. *Careers and Couples: An Academic Question*. New York: MLA, 1976.

Howe, Ray A. "Program Reduction and Reorganization: Part-Time Faculty Usage and Concerns." Leadership Seminars, American Council on Education, Washington, n.d.

Juhasz, Suzanne, and Joseph Juhasz. "The Great Role Change: Or, Trying to Remain an Academic Couple." In Hoffmann and DeSole, *Careers and Couples* 17–21.

Kantrowitz, Joanne Spencer. "Paying Your Dues, Part-Time." In DeSole and Hoffmann, *Rocking the Boat* 15–36.

Leslie, David W., and R. B. Head. "Part-Time Faculty Rights." *Educational Record* 60.1 (Winter 1979): 46–67.

Leslie, David W., Samuel E. Kellams, and G. Manny Gunne. *Part-Time Faculty in American Higher Education*. New York: Praeger, 1982. (References to Leslie in the text are to this more recent work.)

Levin, Amy Evans. *Part-Time Work: A Bibliography*. Alexandria, Va.: Assn. of Part-Time Professionals, 1982.

Lloyd-Jones, Richard. "Drafting Policy Statements on Part-Time and Short-Term Academic Employment." Paper presented at a forum, "Impermanence and Insecurity: Teaching Careers in the 1980s," MLA Convention, Los Angeles. 28 Dec. 1982.

McClelland, Ben W. "Part-Time Faculty in English Composition: A WPA Survey." *WPA: Journal of the Council of Writing Program Administrators* 5.1 (Fall 1981): 13–20.

McQuade, Donald. "The Case of the Migrant Workers." *WPA: Journal of the Council of Writing Program Administrators* 5.1 (Fall 1981): 29–34.

———. "Integrating Part-Time and Short-Term Faculty into English Departments." Panel presentation, MLA Convention, Los Angeles. 29 Dec. 1982.

Maeroff, Gene I. "Colleges Turn to Part-Time Professors." *New York Times* 26 Feb. 1980: A12.

Maimon, Elaine Plaskow. "English at the Heart of the Curriculum." Panel presentation, ADE Summer Seminar, Rensselaer Polytechnic Inst. July 1982.

Men and Women Learning Together: A Study of College Students in the Late 70's. Rept. of the Brown Project. Providence: Brown Univ., 1980.

Modern Language Association Commission on the Future of the Profession. "Report." PMLA 97 (1982): 940–58.

"Modern Language Association Statement on the Use of Part-Time Faculty." In *Profession 82*. New York: MLA, 1982. 52.

Nollen, Stanley D. *New Work Schedules in Practice: Managing Time in a Changing Society.* New York: Van Nostrand, 1982.

Nollen, Stanley D., B. B. Eddy, and V. H. Martin. *Permanent Part-Time Employment: The Manager's Perspective.* Washington: School of Business Administration, Georgetown Univ., 1977.

Parsons, Michael H., ed. *Using Part-Time Faculty Effectively.* New Directions for Community Colleges, 30. San Francisco: Jossey-Bass, 1980.

Part-Time Employment and Flexible Work Hours. Hearings before the Subcommittee on Employee Ethics and Utilization, Committee on the Post Office and Civil Service. U.S. Cong. House. 95th Cong. Washington: GPO, 1977.

Part-Time Faculty in Colleges and Universities. Current Issues in Higher Education, 4. Washington: American Assn. for Higher Education, 1981.

Robinson, Lora H. *Institutional Analysis of Sex Discrimination: A Review and Annotated Bibliography.* Washington: ERIC Clearinghouse on Higher Education, George Washington Univ., 1973.

Rosow, Jerome M. *New Work Schedules for a Changing Society.* Scarsdale, N.Y.: Work in America Inst., 1981.

Shaughnessy, Mina. *Errors and Expectations.* New York: Oxford Univ. Press, 1977.

Smith College. "Part-Time Teaching at Smith College." Unpublished policy paper, n.d.

Spiegel, Claire. "Feud among Professors May Not Be Just Academic." *Los Angeles Times* 24 May 1982, sec. 2: 1, 6.

"The Status of Part-Time Faculty." *Academe* 67 (1981): 29-39.

Swofford, Joyce C. "Identifying the Part-Time English Faculty Who Share Community of Interest with Full-Time English Faculty." Paper presented at a forum workshop, "Legal and Union Issues in Part-Time and Short-Term Faculty Employment," MLA Convention, Los Angeles. 28 Dec. 1982.

Szilak, Dennis. "Teachers of English Composition: A Re-Niggering." *College English* 39 (1977): 25-32.

Thomas, William W. "Folding Chair Appointments vs. Workable Alternatives to Tenure." Paper presented at a forum workshop, "Short-Term Faculty Appointments: Strategies for Change," MLA Convention, Los Angeles. 30 Dec. 1982.

Tobias, Shelia, and Margaret Rumberger. "Full-Status Part-Time Faculty." In *Women in Higher Education*. Ed. W. Todd Furniss and Patricia A. Graham. Washington: American Council on Education, 1974. 16-21.

Tuckman, Barbara H., and Howard P. Tuckman. "Part-Timers, Sex Discrimination, and Career Choice at Two-Year Institutions." *Academe* 66 (1980): 71-76.

Tuckman, Howard P. "Part-Time Faculty: Some Suggestions of Policy." *Change* 13.1 (Jan.-Feb. 1981): 8-10.

Tuckman, Howard P., and Barbara H. Tuckman. "Who Are the Part-Timers and What Are Colleges Doing for Them?" In *Part-Time Faculty in Colleges and Universities*. 4–7.

Tuckman, Howard P., William D. Vogler, and Jaime Caldwell. *Part-Time Faculty Series*. Washington: American Assn. of University Professors, 1978. (Several of the essays in this volume were published in *AAUP Bulletin* in 1978.)

"Union College Tenure Plan, June 15, 1973." In *Faculty Manual*. Schenectady, N.Y.: Union Coll., 1982. Sec. 3, 2–8.

Wallace, M. Elizabeth. "Comments on 'Memoirs and Confessions of a Part-Time Lecturer.' " *College English* 44 (1982): 859–61.

———. "New Policies for Part-Time Faculty." *ADE Bulletin* 73 (Winter 1982): 47–52.

———. "Possibilities for Part-Time Faculty." In *Proceedings of Maryland Composition Conference 16 April 1982*. College Park: Univ. of Maryland, 1982. 43–51.

Weinberg, Stewart. "Recent Developments in the Law as It Affects Part-Time Employees in California." Paper presented at a forum workshop, "Legal and Union Issues in Part-Time and Short-Term Faculty Employment," MLA Convention, Los Angeles. 28 Dec. 1982.

Weinman, Geoffrey S. "A Part-Time Freshman Writing Staff: Problems and Solutions." *WPA: Journal of the Council of Writing Program Administrators* 5.1 (Fall 1981): 21–28.

Yang, Shu-O Wu, and Michele Wender Zak. *Part-Time Faculty Employment in Ohio: A Statewide Study*. Kent, Ohio: Kent State Univ., 1981.

Contributors

Anne Scrivener Agee is Professor of English and Coordinator of Adjunct Faculty at Anne Arundel Community College. "Integrating Adjunct Faculty: A Matter of Pragmatism," her presentation at the Maryland Composition Conference, 16 April 1982, has been published in its *Proceedings*.

Walter Borenstein is Professor of Spanish and former Chair of the Department of Foreign Languages at the State University of New York, College at New Paltz.

Miriam Brody, coordinator of the newly combined Writing and Reading Program at Ithaca College, has taught in the Writing Program since its inception.

Cara Chell, formerly a part-time lecturer at George Washington University, is now Director of Women's Studies at the University of Wisconsin, La Crosse. While at George Washington, Chell wrote two pieces on part-time faculty for *College English*: "Memoirs and Confessions of a Part-Time Lecturer" (Jan. 1982) and "Cara Chell Responds" (Dec. 1982).

Alan J. Clayton is Chair of the Department of Romance Languages at Tufts University.

Richard J. Colwell serves on the part-time-instruction committee of the Midwest Conference of Teachers of English in the Two-Year College, an affiliate of NCTE. He is Chair of the English Department at St. Clair County Community College.

Miriam Dow is Assistant Director of Composition at George Washington University.

Howard S. Erlich is Assistant Dean for Academic Support Services at Ithaca College. For the past five years he has administered the Writing and Reading programs; the present policy developed under his administration.

David J. Figuli is an attorney with the law offices of Wickens, Herzer & Panza in Lorain, Ohio. He has previously served as Chief Legal Counsel of the Montana University System and as General Counsel for the South Dakota Board of Regents. He has done extensive research in case law on part-time and short-term academic employment. This essay was first presented as a paper at the MLA convention in Los Angeles, 28 Dec. 1982.

Robert Gabriner has been a "temporary" part-time instructor in the Peralta Community College District for the last thirteen years. He teaches history and political economy. He is also Executive Secretary of the Peralta Federation of Teachers and President of the Community College Council of the California Federation of Teachers.

Janet Powers Gemmill has taught in the Interdisciplinary Studies Program at Gettysburg College for seventeen years. Prior to earning her doctorate, she had taught full-time in the English Department for two years. She teaches five sevenths of a full load and carries the title Adjunct Assistant Professor. This essay was presented as a paper at the MLA convention in Los Angeles, 28 Dec. 1982, in a forum entitled "Impermanence and Insecurity: Teaching Careers in the 1980s."

Rae Goodell is Associate Professor of Science Writing—a half-time, tenure-track position—in the Writing Program at the Massachusetts Institute of Technology.

Wendell V. Harris is Head of the Department of English at Pennsylvania State University, University Park.

G. James Jason until recently taught philosophy at San Diego State University and at Saddleback Community College; he now teaches in the philosophy department at Washburn University of Topeka. He has published articles in his field and also about faculty issues; his essay, "Part-Time Teachers Threaten Higher-Education System," appeared in the *Los Angeles Times*, 19 Aug. 1982 (II,11).

William Kerr is Provost at Wesleyan University.

Julie Grover Klassen is Assistant Professor of German at Carleton College.

Harold M. Kolenbrander is Provost at Central College.

Richard Marius is Director of the Expository Writing Program at Harvard University. His presentation, "Faculty Integration: The Harvard Model," was given at the Maryland Composition Conference, 16 April 1982, and published in its *Proceedings*.

Elizabeth W. Miller, a teacher since 1959, has held two tenured positions in English—one at Allegheny County Community College and the other as Department Head, Wallenpaupack Area Schools, Hawley, Pa.—and left both to move with her husband as his career advanced. She is now English Instructor at Bloomsburg University of Pennsylvania. She presented a paper, "Problems of the Profession—Part-Time Faculty," at the English Association of Pennsylvania State Colleges and University Conference in Millersville, Pa., 23 Sept. 1982.

Virginia F. Mulrooney, Vice-Chancellor of Personnel Services for the Los Angeles Community College District, was President of the American Federation of Teachers, College Guild, Local 1521, CFT, AFT, AFL-CIO. This paper was presented at the MLA convention in Los Angeles, 28 Dec. 1982, in a forum workshop entitled "Legal and Union Issues in Part-Time and Short-Term Faculty Employment."

Kathleen Sherfick is "Temporary" Assistant Professor of English and Departmental Examiner at Ball State University.

Merike Tamm is Lecturer in English in the Division of Fine Arts, Languages, and Literature at the University of South Carolina at Spartanburg. She has published articles on Jane Austen, sexist language, and the teaching of writing.

Joseph F. Trimmer is Professor of English and Director of the Writing Program at Ball State University.

Sylvia Guffin Turner is Dean of Students at Hood College.

Anne Close Ulmer is Assistant Professor of German at Carleton College.

M. Elizabeth Wallace taught part-time for six years (one year simultaneously at four different colleges) before joining the Gettysburg College English Department full-time in 1980. In 1982, she became Educational Associate for Basically Computers, Inc., of Westminster and Columbia,

Md. She continues to teach part-time on the faculties of Catonsville Community College, Carroll County Branch, and Western Maryland College and is Director of the KayPro Writing Project in Baltimore County Public Schools, a two-year experiment using a twenty-computer lab for the teaching of writing. She has published articles on part-time-faculty policy in *College English*, *ADE Bulletin*, and elsewhere and has spoken on the issue at academic conferences in Los Angeles, New York, Cincinnati, and College Park, Md. Her doctorate in English literature is from the University of Kent at Canterbury in England, which she attended as a Marshall Scholar, 1970–73.

Thomas Werge is Professor of English at the University of Notre Dame.

Table 6: Innovative Policies for Regular Part-Time Faculty[a]

PRIVATE COLLEGES AND UNIVERSITIES	General			Responsibilities					Academic Benefits				Fringe Benefits					Job Security			
	1. # of PT fac.	2. # paid PR	3. Teaching load	4. Advisees	5. Comm. work	6. Attend fac. mtgs.	7. Fac. vote	8. Scholarship	9. Leave/Sabbatical	10. Tenure	11. Fac. grants	12. Tuit. cred.	13. Soc. sec.	14. Med. plan	15. Life ins.	16. Retirement	17. Disability	18. Hir./Fir./Eval.	19. Mob. to FT	20a. Contracts: a) Length in yrs.	20b. b) Limit on yrs. w/o tenure
American U, DC	c. 200	c. 25	2/3 avg.	PR	PR	PR	PR	PR	PR	PR	PR	Y	PR	PR	PR	PR	PR	FT	P[b]	INA	7
Bryn Mawr C	49	11	INA	Y	Y	Y	(c)	(d, k)	Y	Y	N	N	(e)	N	Y[f]	N	INA	INA	INA	[1,] 2–4[k]	INA
Carleton C	INA	8	(g)	PR	PR	Y	Y	Y	Y	Y	(h)	Y	Y	Y	Y	Y	Y	FT	P[b]	2	INA
Central C	10	6	(n, t)	PR	PR	Y	Y	Y	Y	Y	Y	Y	Y	Y	Y	Y	Y	FT	P[b]	1	none
Columbia U[i]	INA	1	INA	Y	Y	Y	Y	Y	Y	Y	Y	Y	Y	Y	Y	Y	Y	FT	Y	INA	14
Cornell U	144	most	(g)	PR	Y	Y	(j)	(k)	(k) 12 yrs.	Y	PR	Y	Y	Y	Y	Y	Y	FT	P	3-5 avg.	INA
Dickinson C	19	3	1/2 avg.	PR	PR	Y	Y	Y	Y	Y	Y	Y	N	Y	Y	Y	Y	FT	(o)	1	INA
Franklin & Marshall C	18	2	1/2 max.	N	N	Y	N	N	N	Y	N	N	N	N	Y	N	N	INA	INA	sem.	INA
Grinnell C	11	1	(g)	Y	Y	Y	N	PR	Y	Y	N	Y	PR	N	Y	N	N	FT	N	2	10

Harvard U	INA	INA	INA	PR	Y	Y	Y	Y	Y	Y	Y	Y	Y	Y	Y	Y	FT	Y	INA	INA
Hood C	41	16	1/8 min.[t]	PR	PR	Y	Y	INA	N	Y	PR[p]	Y	PR	Y	Y	INA	FT	P	1	none
Moravian C	c. 50	5[q]	2/3 avg.	N	N	Y	N	N	N	INA	(r)	Y	Y	N	N	N	(q)	P	1	INA
Mount Holyoke C[s]	INA	INA	(n)	Y	Y	Y	Y	Y	12 yrs.	Y	PR	Y	PR	Y	Y	Y	FT	(u)	(tt)	12
U of Notre Dame, IN[v]	INA	12	(n, t)	PR	PR	Y	Y	Y	PR	Y	PR	Y	PR	Y	Y	Y	FT	P	INA	INA
Oberlin C[w]	INA	INA	(g)	PR	PR	Y	Y	Y	Y	Y	PR[g]	Y	PR[g]	Y	Y	Y	FT	P	INA	7
Princeton U	INA	60	(g)	Y	(k)	(k)	Y	(k)	Y	INA	Y	Y	Y	Y	Y	Y	FT[k]	INA	INA	INA
Ripon C	2	2	1/2 min.	Y	Y	Y	Y	N	N	Y	Y	Y	Y	Y	N	N	FT	P	INA	none
St. John's C, MD	6	3	no lim.	PR	PR	Y	Y	(z)	7[m]	Y	Y	Y	PR	Y	Y	Y	FT	P	1	none
Scripps C	33	11	(g)	Y	Y	Y	Y	INA	Y	Y	PR[z]	Y	Y	Y	Y	Y	FT	INA	2–3	INA
Smith C	INA	INA	INA	PR	PR	Y	Y	Y	PR	Y	Y	Y	Y	Y	Y	Y	FT	P	1–3	ten.
Stanford U	51	51	1/3 min.[g]	Y	Y	Y	Y	PR	PR	Y	N	Y	Y	Y	Y	Y	FT	P	INA	10
Wellesley C[aa]	82	7/20	1/2 avg.[t]	Y	Y	Y	Y/ (bb)	Y/N	Y/N	Y	Y/N	Y	Y	Y/P[cc]	Y/N	Y/N	FT	P	3/1–3	9/none
Wesleyan U	37	17	1/2 avg.	PR	PR	Y	Y	Y	Y	Y	PR	PR	PR	PR	PR	PR	FT	P	4	9
Wheaton C[dd]	31	11	2/3 avg.	PR	PR	Y	Y (gg)	(ee)	N	Y	PR	PR	Y	PR	PR	PR	FT	Y	1y	INA
Yale U	INA	INA	(g, ff)	PR	PR	Y	Y	Y	Y	Y	N	Y	Y	Y	Y	N	FT	P	INA	13

Table 6: (cont.)

STATE COLLEGES AND UNIVERSITIES	General: 1. # of PT fac.	General: 2. # paid PR	General: 3. Teaching load	Responsibilities: 4. Advisees	Responsibilities: 5. Comm. work	Responsibilities: 6. Attend fac. mtgs.	Responsibilities: 7. Fac. vote	Responsibilities: 8. Scholarship	Academic Benefits: 9. Leave/Sabbatical	Academic Benefits: 10. Tenure[l]	Academic Benefits: 11. Fac. grants	Fringe Benefits: 12. Tuit. cred.	Fringe Benefits: 13. Soc. sec.	Fringe Benefits: 14. Med. plan	Fringe Benefits: 15. Life ins.	Fringe Benefits: 16. Retirement	Fringe Benefits: 17. Disability	Job Security: 18. Hir./Fir./Eval.	Job Security: 19. Mob. to FT	Job Security: 20. Contracts: a) Length in yrs.	Job Security: b) Limit on yrs. w/o tenure
Ball SU	26	6	(g)	Y	Y	Y	N	Y	(hh)	N	Y	Y	Y	Y	Y	Y	Y	FT	P	1	none
Bloomsburg SC	16	INA	(rr)	INA	INA	INA	INA	INA	INA	INA	N	N	Y	Y[ii]	PR	(e)	PR	(jj)	rare	1	INA
U of Iowa	INA	some	INA	PR	PR	Y	Y	Y	(x)	PR	INA	N	Y	PR	PR	PR	PR	FT	P	1	ten.
Michigan SU	INA	INA	(g)	INA	INA	INA	INA	INA	(kk, mm)	INA	INA	INA	Y	PR	N	(ll)	INA	INA	INA	INA	INA
U of Tennessee, Knoxville[nn]	INA	INA	INA	INA	INA	INA	Y	Y	INA	N	Y	(g)	INA	INA	INA	INA	INA	FT	P	INA	INA
U of Wisconsin, Madison	INA	14	(n, t)	Y	Y	Y	Y	Y	N	Y	INA	Y	Y	Y	Y	Y	Y	FT	P	3 (tt)	12
COMMUNITY COLLEGES																					
Comm. C of Denver	INA	all	(g)	INA	INA	INA	INA	INA	(x)	N	INA	INA	Y	Y	Y	Y	Y	FT	P	1	none
St. Clair County Comm. C[oo]	INA	all	(ss)	N	Y	Y	Y	N	N	N	N	Y	Y	N	N	N	N	(pp)	P	INA	INA
Solano Comm. C	390	none	3/5 avg.	N	N	Y	(qq)	N	N	N	Y	N	N	N	N	Y	N	FT	P	INA	INA

ADDENDUM

Hamline U (private): "There are several regular positions for part-time people that we have given some of our regular fringe benefits, but this has been a judgment call on my part, not a matter of adopted policy." Dean Kenneth Janzen.

ABBREVIATIONS

eval.	evaluation
fac.	faculty
fir.	firing
FT	(same as) full-time
FTE	full-time equivalency
hir.	hiring
INA	information not available
ins.	insurance
lim.	limit
max.	maximum
med.	medical
min.	minimum
mob.	mobility
N	no
P	possible
PR	prorated
PT	part-time
sem.	semester
soc. sec.	social security
ten.	until tenure decision
tuit. cred.	tuition credit
Y	yes

NOTES

[a] All listed colleges have at least 1 part-timer paid a prorated salary.
[b] By mutual agreement.
[c] Only if on "multi-year" terms of appointment.
[d] Only after 3 yrs.
[e] Have access but pay full cost.
[f] A 1-yr. wait if below assistant professor.
[g] Half-time minimum to receive benefits.
[h] Only if appointed before 1 Sept. 1974.
[i] The policy described applies only to faculty originally hired full-time who are parents of a child under 9 yrs. and are not employed elsewhere.
[j] Only in the school or college in which they teach (not in the university).
[k] Only if assistant professor or above.
[l] A "yes" indicates that tenure is possible, but that the length of wait for a decision is not known; a number indicates the length in yrs. of wait for a decision.

m A 3-yr. wait before on tenure track.

n Half-time minimum.

o For full-timers on reduced load.

p No tuition exchange with other schools.

q These faculty, all in fine arts, have special appointments. They are on annual salary for teaching private lessons and some courses.

r One free course per term.

s "Regular part-time faculty" include all part-timers who have taught at least half-time for 3 consecutive yrs.

t Three-quarters-time maximum.

u Only if regular part-timer because of maternity or paternity leave.

v "Regular part-time faculty" can make up no more than 25% of any department.

w Part-timers must have the rank of instructor or above.

x No sabbaticals, but other leaves prorated.

y Three-yrs. after 7 yrs. probation.

z Only if on tenure track.

aa Two kinds of part-timers: "Regular part-timers" (assistant professor or above, on tenure track) and other part-timers (not on tenure track). Where differences occur, the information to the left of the slash pertains to the former; the information to the right, to the latter.

bb Only after 2 yrs.

cc Only after 3 yrs.

dd No part-time faculty have so far qualified for 3-yr. contracts. Some full-time faculty have kept tenure while moving into part-time.

ee Eligibility based on FTE service.

ff Benefits only with rank of instructor and above.

gg Only on issues involving the part-timer's rank and below.

hh Maternity leave without pay permitted.

ii Only 50% covered by school.

jj Part-timers are visited and evaluated 5 times per yr.

kk Only tenured faculty eligible for sabbaticals.

ll Only after 5 yrs. of continuous service.

mm Short-term leave only, up to 6 mos. medical leave.

nn Data are based on a draft policy. "Regular part-timers" must have served 12 regular academic quarters, not necessarily in succession.

oo Data apply to English department only.

pp By chair and division administration according to a special plan.

qq Only on union issues.

rr 2 classes per sem.

ss 2 classes per sem. avg.; 5 classes per yr. max.

tt 1-yr. contracts for first 3 yrs.; 3-yr. contracts thereafter.